GREEK IS GOOD GRIEF

Laying the Foundation for
Exegesis and Exposition

GREEK IS GOOD GRIEF

Laying the Foundation for
Exegesis and Exposition

By

John D. Harvey

Wipf & Stock
PUBLISHERS
Eugene, Oregon

GREEK IS GOOD GRIEF
Laying the Foundation for Exegesis and Exposition

ISBN 10: 1-59752-963X
ISBN 13: 978-1-59752-963-1

Contents

WHY WRITE *ANOTHER* FIRST YEAR GREEK TEXT?

With so many first year Greek textbooks already in publication, why produce another? Each individual who teaches the biblical languages doubtless has his or her own approach to the task. The result is often a desire to find a text which conforms as closely as possible to that approach and requires the least modification to use. Since I began teaching first year Greek in 1991, I personally have used four different texts, and the seminary where I teach has, to my knowledge, used at least four others since I took my first Greek course there in 1984. (One of them carried the title *Greek Without Grief*.)

The origins of the present text, however, are more philosophical than pragmatic. The impetus for re-thinking how to teach first year Greek began with an article by P. R. Whale, entitled "More Efficient Teaching of New Testament Greek," published in *New Testament Studies* 40 (1994), 596-605. In it he raised the issue of form frequency as a consideration in organizing the material for a course aimed at enabling students to learn to read New Testament Greek. He also argued that courses should respond to the actual text being read.

In many first year Greek courses the text being read is the Gospel of John and/or 1 John. Such an approach works well initially. When, however, a student who has spent an entire year in the Johannine literature first encounters Pauline syntax, culture shock sets in rapidly. Since many Greek exegesis courses focus on Paul's letters, it seems wise — at least to some degree — to introduce students to his style as well. This book, therefore, uses a graded database, beginning with the simpler Greek of John 1 (Chapters 1-10), moving to Mark 8 (Chapters 11-20) as an example of middle level Greek, and concluding with 1 Thessalonians 1–2 (Chapters 21-30) as representative of Paul's style.

Working from this database, then, the material is organized according to form frequency. Third declension nouns, for example, are often delayed until well into a first year text, even though various forms of third declension nouns occur twenty times in John 1:1-18. By comparison, twelve first declension nouns occur in the same passage, and twenty-one second declension nouns (excluding proper names) are present. As a result, third declension nouns are introduced comparatively early in the text (Chapters 8 and 9).

Since the goal of a course in New Testament Greek is to enable the student to read the New Testament, early exposure to the text is a great motivator. Translation of John 1, therefore, can begin as soon as Chapter 5. Since the first five chapters cannot introduce all of the forms present in John 1, translation helps are provided for those words and forms the student has not yet encountered. Practice sentences are also provided for each chapter. To the greatest degree possible, these practice sentences are taken directly from the Greek New Testament. Finally, form identification exercises afford students the opportunity to drill on forms specific to the content of each chapter.

Each new grammatical concept is introduced by a discussion of English grammar. This discussion enables students both to review their English grammar and to work from the "known" of English to the "unknown" of Greek. Greek grammatical concepts are discussed using terms which correlate with those found in Daniel Wallace's *Greek Grammar Beyond the Basics*. The transition from introductory to intermediate grammar should, therefore, be relatively seamless. Finally, each chapter begins with a "Grammar Grabber" which highlights an aspect of the chapter's content by explaining how that aspect of grammar is important for understanding a portion of the Greek text of the New Testament.

The information included in each chapter is more extensive than would be the case if the book were concerned to provide a bare minimum. Although the architect Mies van der Rohe could declare that "less is more," this text tends to err on the side of completeness. The inclusion of a paradigm in a book, however, does not necessarily mean that it must be memorized. All teachers make decisions about what they will require of their students. It seemed wise, therefore, to provide more information rather than less, if for no other reason than as a point of reference for students should they encounter a form such as the indefinite relative pronoun ἅτινα in Phil 3:7.

Special thanks goes to my colleague, Dr. William Larkin, who both suggested the idea of including the "Grammar Grabbers" and wrote each of them.

HOW IS GREEK "*GOOD* GRIEF"?

Robert L. Short begins the fifth chapter in his book, *The Gospel According to Peanuts*, by writing, "'Good grief!' may seem to be a contradiction in terms. But actually there are two distinct types of grief—good and not-so-good grief: 'For godly grief produces a repentance that leads to salvation and brings no regret, but worldly grief produces death' (2 Cor 7:10)."[1]

Many students view the study of New Testament Greek as an especially nefarious source of "grief." It requires an investment of time, energy, and discipline which runs counter to human nature and flies in the face of twenty-first century culture's "instant" mentality. The lure of interlinear New Testaments is strong, and sophisticated computer software makes verb parsings available at a single keystroke. "Surely," they reason, "there is an easier way to get at the meaning the author intended than by spending all of that time and energy when I could be doing other things."

Charlie Brown might respond, "But adversity is what makes you mature. The growing soul is watered best by tears of sadness." Even more to the point, however, are the words of the author of the letter to the Hebrews: "For the moment all discipline seems painful rather than pleasant; later it yields the peaceful fruit of righteousness to those who have been trained by it" (Heb 12:11). Often, the things most worth possessing are those which require the most effort and tears to obtain.

The ultimate goal of learning New Testament Greek is to be able to handle God's word accurately, and the objective of an introductory grammar such as this one is to lay the foundation for doing so. Laying a foundation is work. It requires breaking up hard ground, establishing the proper form for the foundation material, placing that material, and testing the foundation to insure that it is ready to support what will be built on it. Yet, without a firm foundation, the superstructure is in jeopardy.

It is in this respect that Greek is *good* grief. Yes, at times it might seem painful rather than pleasant. Yes, it will require effort and, perhaps, more than a few tears. The end result, however, is worth the price to be paid. Be patient. Be persistent. If, as some would contend, the study of Greek produces grief, you can be confident that for those who wish to understand and communicate the truth of God's word accurately, Greek is Good Grief!

---

[1] R. L. Short, *The Gospel According to Peanuts* (Richmond: John Knox, 1964), 82.

GRAMMAR GRABBER: *Diacritical Marks*

As with English, the basic building blocks of New Testament Greek are more than letters (i.e., vowels and consonants) and punctuation marks (e.g., commas and periods). There are also **diacritical marks**, most notably breathing marks and accent marks (English, for example, uses apostrophes). These diacritical marks can make a significant difference in meaning when used with the same letter or combination of letters to form a word.

In John 1:1-5 (the Greek text is your transliteration exercise, 1.8), the combination of ε (*epsilon*, a vowel with a short "e" sound) and ν (*nu*, a consonant with an "n" sound) occurs five times. Four of the times it means "in" (vv. 1, 2, 4, 5); one time it means "one" (v. 3).

How does the New Testament Greek writer show you that he intends εν to mean "in" (not "one") in the former cases and "one" (not "in") in the latter case? He uses breathing marks and the presence or absence of the accent mark.

When he intends εν to mean "in" he spells it with a smooth breathing mark and no accent mark — ἐν. When he wants to say "one," he marks the ε with a rough breathing mark and an accent mark — ἕν. You will show this difference in transliterating the words. ἐν will be transliterated as *en*, and ἕν will be translated as *hen*. You will also translate the words differently.

Diacritical marks can make all the difference in rightly understanding the meaning the author intended.

Chapter 1

ALPHABET, DIACRITICALS, PUNCTUATION

The first step in learning any language is mastering the alphabet and punctuation used in that language. Greek also has certain "diacritical marks" which affect pronunciation and indicate stress. Each of these areas will be introduced, beginning with the alphabet.

1.1 Alphabet

The Greek alphabet has twenty-four letters, seven vowels and seventeen consonants. In many places the order of the Greek letters is identical to the order of the letters in the English alphabet. In many instances the shape and sound of a Greek letter is also similar to an English letter. The chart below gives the Greek alphabet with its English "transliteration" and the closest equivalent English sound. You should concentrate particularly on the lower case form of each letter since, in the Greek New Testament, the upper case forms occur only in book titles, at the beginning of paragraphs, at the beginning of recorded speech, and at the beginning of proper nouns.

Greek Letter		Greek Name	English Transliteration	English Sound
Lower case	Upper case			
α	A	alpha	a	cat
β	B	beta	b	**B**ible
γ	Γ	gamma	g	**g**o
δ	Δ	delta	d	**d**ay
ε	E	epsilon	e	met
ζ	Z	zeta	z	da**z**e

η	H	eta	ē	obey
θ	Θ	theta	th	**thin**
ι	I	iota	i	police
κ	K	kappa	k	**keep**
λ	Λ	lambda	l	led
μ	M	mu	m	**man**
ν	N	nu	n	**net**
ξ	Ξ	ksi	x	relax
ο	O	omicron	o	**omelet**
π	Π	pi	p	**party**
ρ	P	rho	r	**run**
σ, ς	Σ	sigma	s	sell
τ	T	tau	t	tall
υ	Υ	upsilon	u	cute
φ	Φ	phi	ph	**phone**
χ	X	chi	ch	loch
ψ	Ψ	psi	ps	to**ps**
ω	Ω	omega	ō	note

Notice that the lower case sigma has two forms (σ, ς). The first (σ) occurs at the beginning and in the middle of words; the second (ς) occurs only at the end of words.

1.2 Vowels and Diphthongs

Greek has seven **vowels**: α, ε, η, ι, ο, υ, ω. Sometimes two vowels are combined in one syllable to create a single sound, or **diphthong**. Greek has seven diphthongs. The chart below gives the Greek diphthong with the closest equivalent English sound.

Diphthong	Pronunciation	Example	Pronunciation
αι	aisle	αἰων	ai-ōn
ει	eight	εἰκων	ei-kōn
οι	oil	οἰκος	oi-kos
υι	suite	υἰος	hui-os
αυ	kraut	αὐτος	au-tos
ευ	feud	εὐλογια	eu-lo-gi-a
ου	soup	οὐρανος	ou-ra-nos

An ι is sometimes combined with the vowels α, η, ω to create "improper" diphthongs in which the ι is written *below* the vowel and is called an **iota-subscript**: ᾳ, ῃ, ῳ The iota-subscript has no effect on the *pronunciation* of the vowel, but it can make a significant difference in *meaning* of a word.

1.3 Consonants

The remaining seventeen letters in the Greek alphabet are consonants. Five of them are **double consonants** which combine another consonant with an "h" or an "s" sound:

θ	=	th	ξ	=	ks
φ	=	ph	ψ	=	ps
χ	=	ch			

All consonants may be classified based on the manner and/or place of articulation. Familiarity with these classifications will be helpful when certain concepts are introduced in later chapters.

Labials	Formed with the lips	β, π, φ
Gutterals	Formed in the throat	γ, κ, χ
Dentals	Formed at or just behind the teeth	δ, θ, τ
Liquids	Formed using a rippling sound	λ, ρ
Nasals	Formed by passing air through the nose	μ, ν
Sibilants	Formed by passing air between the teeth	ζ, ξ, σ, ψ

When the consonant γ is placed before another gutteral (γ, κ, χ), it is pronounced as ν. For example, the word ἀγγελος is pronounced "an-ge-los," not "ag-ge-los."

1.4 Dividing and Pronouncing Words

Once you can pronounce the Greek letters and diphthongs, you can pronounce Greek words. The basic rule for dividing and pronouncing words is that **there is one vowel or diphthong per syllable**.

συναγωγη	=	συ-να-γω-γη	=	su-na-gō-gē
δαιμονιον	=	δαι-μο-νι-ον	=	dai-mo-ni-on
εὐαγγελιον	=	εὐ-αγ-γε-λι-ον	=	eu-an-ge-li-on
ἐπιστολη	=	ἐ-πι-στο-λη	=	e-pi-sto-lē
ἀνθρωπος	=	ἀν-θρω-πος	=	an-thrō-pos

Generally, (1) vowels and diphthongs mark the end of syllables, (2) consecutive vowels which do not form a diphthong are divided, (3) double consonants (e.g., γγ) are divided, and (4) consonant clusters which can begin a word (e.g., στ, θρ, χρ) remain together.

1.5 Diacritical Marks

A word which begins with vowel, a diphthong, or the consonant ρ must have a **breathing mark**. If the word begins with a diphthong, the breathing mark is placed over the second vowel of the diphthong. Greek has two breathing marks: the *smooth breathing mark* (᾿) is not pronounced; the *rough breathing mark* (῾) adds an "h" sound to the beginning of the word.

Smooth breathing:	ἀνθρωπος	= an-thrō-pos
Rough breathing:	ἁμαρτια	= ha-mar-ti-a

In some words, two vowels which would normally form a diphthong are pronounced separately. A **diaeresis** (¨) is placed over the second vowel to indicate the separation.

Ἡσαϊας	=	Ἡ-σα-ϊ-ας	=	Ē-sa-i-as
προϊστημι	=	προ-ϊ-στη-μι	=	pro-i-stē-mi

An **apostrophe** (᾿) at the end of a word marks the omission of a final vowel before a subsequent word beginning with a vowel or diphthong.

δια αὐτου   ➔   δι᾿ αὐτου

A **coronis** (᾿) in the middle of a word marks the omission of one or more letters when two words are combined.

και + εγω   ➔   κἀγω

Nearly every Greek word has an **accent mark** which shows the syllable to be stressed in pronunciation. There are three accent marks: *acute* ('), *grave* (`), and *circumflex* (ˆ).

Χριστός	=	Chri-STOS
Χριστὸν	=	Chri-STON
Χριστοῦ	=	Chri-STOU

There is a system of rules for determining the type of accent to be used with a word and the syllable on which it is to be placed. Since, however, you will be reading, not writing, Greek, it is not necessary to learn those rules. It is enough to know (1) that the accent marks the syllable to be stressed in pronunciation and (2) that accents sometimes differentiate between words or forms which are otherwise identical. The words/forms in which accent marks make a difference in the meaning will be highlighted as they arise. Otherwise, accents will not be included on words which appear in this book except in vocabulary lists and in passages taken directly from the Greek New Testament.

1.6 Punctuation

Printed editions of the Greek New Testament use four **punctuation marks**. The Greek *comma* and *period* are identical to the English, but Greek uses a raised dot for the *semi-colon*. The Greek *question mark* is the same as an English semi-colon and must not be confused with it.

comma	ἀμην,
period	ἀμην.
semi-colon	ἀμην·
question mark	ἀμην;

The earliest Greek manuscripts had no punctuation. The punctuation which is present in modern editions of the Greek New Testament has been added by the editors and is sometimes a matter of interpretation. Generally, however, you should accept the punctuation present in the text unless there is a compelling reason to disregard it.

1.7 Vocabulary

The following words have English cognates and should, therefore, be easy to pronounce and memorize. All but # 6 are nouns. Nouns will always be introduced in the vocabulary lists using the following combination:

definite article	nominative singular form	genitive singular ending
ὁ	ἄγγελος	-ου

The definite article identifies the gender of the noun (masculine, feminine, or neuter). The nominative singular is the form under which the noun is listed in dictionaries and lexica. The genitive singular ending identifies the declension of the noun (first, second, or third). Although at this point you are simply getting acquainted with reading the Greek alphabet and pronouncing Greek words, you should learn all three elements in the left hand column as part of your vocabulary building. The significance of each element will become clear as the definite article and the various noun declensions are introduced. The number at the right hand margin is the number of times the word appears in the Greek New Testament.

1.	ὁ ἄγγελος, -ου	angel, messenger	(175)
2.	ὁ ἄνθρωπος, -ου	man (anthropology)	(550)
3.	ὁ ἀπόστολος, -ου	apostle	(132)
4.	τό δαιμόνιον, -ου	demon	(63)
5.	ὁ διάκονος, -ου	servant, minister (deacon)	(29)
6.	ἐγώ	I (ego)	(2666)
7.	ἡ ἐπιστολή, -ης	letter, epistle	(24)
8.	ὁ θεός, -οῦ	God, god (theology)	(1317)
9.	ὁ θρόνος, -ου	throne	(62)
10.	τό μυστήριον, -ου	mystery	(28)
11.	ἡ παραβολή, -ης	parable	(50)
12.	ὁ προφήτης, -ου	prophet	(144)
13.	τό σάββατον, -ου	the Sabbath	(68)
14.	ἡ συναγωγή, -ης	synagogue, assembly	(56)
15.	ὁ φόβος, -ου	fear (phobia)	(47)
16.	ὁ χρόνος, -ου	time (chronology)	(54)
17.	ὁ Ἰησοῦς, -ου	Jesus	(917)
18.	ὁ Μεσσίας, -ου	Messiah, Anointed One	(2)
19.	ὁ Πέτρος, -ου	Peter	(156)
20.	ὁ Χριστός, -ου	Christ	(529)

1.8 Transliteration - Write the English transliteration of the following passage (John 1:1-5). Be certain to pay attention to breathing marks and punctuation. Vowels with iota-subscripts should be written as "proper" diphthongs (e.g., ᾳ = ai). There is no need to reproduce the accent marks.

'εν ἀρχῇ ἦν ὁ λόγος, καὶ ὁ λόγος ἦν πρὸς τὸν θεόν, καὶ θεὸς ἦν ὁ λόγος. οὗτος ἦν ἐν ἀρχῇ πρὸς τὸν θεόν. πάντα δι᾽ αὐτοῦ ἐγένετο, καὶ χωρὶς αὐτοῦ ἐγένετο οὐδὲ ἕν ὃ γέγονεν. ἐν αὐτῷ ζωὴ ἦν, καὶ ἡ ζωὴ ἦν τὸ φῶς τῶν ἀνθρώπων· καὶ τὸ φῶς ἐν τῇ σκοτίᾳ φαίνει, καὶ ἡ σκοτία αὐτὸ οὐ κατέλαβεν.

GRAMMAR GRABBER: Noun Case Inflection

English relies heavily on word order to indicate the relationship among words in a sentence and follows a common pattern: Subject–Verb–Object. The subject doing the action usually precedes the verb, and the object which receives the action normally follows it. Greek, however, depends on both word order and **inflection**—a change in the spelling of a word which indicates a change of relationship.

John 1:29 provides a good example: Ἴδε, ὁ ἀμνὸς τοῦ θεοῦ. The sentence begins with a verb in a command form: "Look at." That verb is followed by two nouns: "the lamb" and "the God." If we were just following word order we could make basic sense of it— "Look at the lamb, the God." From word order alone (disregarding the punctuation) we would probably conclude that "lamb" was the object and "God" was in apposition to it. When we take note of the inflection of the words—here, the case endings of the nouns—however, we can know more accurately the relationship of the words.

The nominative case ending on ἀμνὸς ("lamb"), tells us that it is not the object of the verb. The verb, therefore, functions as an emphatic interjection: "Look! the lamb . . ." The genitive ending on θεοῦ ("God") indicates that it modifies "lamb" descriptively—"divine lamb"—or, more probably, by pointing to its source—"the lamb from God." In keeping with the pattern of His saving purposes, the "lamb of God," comes from, is provided by God (cf. Gen. 22:8, 13, 14).

Case endings and other inflections, when deciphered in context, are important signs for determining the meaning the writer is seeking to communicate.

Chapter 2

SECOND DECLENSION NOUNS

Greek nouns are different from English nouns in that they change form frequently. These changes follow regular patterns which are called "declensions." Three declension patterns have been identified: first, second, and third. Since the pattern of second declension nouns is the simplest, it will be learned first. Before launching into second declension nouns, however, it might be helpful to review some basic information on nouns, especially the ways in which Greek nouns differ from English nouns.

2.1 Introduction to Nouns

Nouns are words that name persons, places, or things. They may be grouped into three general kinds. **Common nouns** name *general* persons, places, or things (e.g., man, artist, love, hate). **Proper nouns** name *particular* persons, places, or things (e.g., Tom, Athens). **Collective nouns** name *groups or classes* of persons or things considered as a whole (e.g., crowd, team).

Nouns may be used in any of six ways:
1.   A **subject** names the person, place, or thing acting or about which a statement is being made.
         (e.g., The <u>boy</u> hit the ball. The <u>house</u> is green.)
2.   A **complement** completes the thought of the sentence.
      a.   A direct object receives the action of the verb.
               (e.g., The boy hit the <u>ball</u>.)
      b.   An indirect object tells to/for whom the action is done.
               (e.g., The boy hit the ball to the <u>girl</u>.)
      c.   A predicate nominative is used with a linking verb (e.g., "to be") and renames or clarifies the subject.
               (e.g., Bill is a <u>boy</u>; Jill is a <u>girl</u>.)
3.   An **object of a preposition** is a noun which is related to the rest of the sentence by a preposition.
         (e.g., The boy hit the ball with a <u>bat</u>.)

4.   An **appositive** is a noun which closely follows another noun and
        renames or further identifies it.
          (e.g., The boy, <u>Bill</u>, hit the ball.)
5.   A noun of **direct address** names the person being spoken to.
          (e.g., <u>Jill</u>, the boy hit the ball to you.)
6.   A noun of **possession** denotes to whom or what another noun
        belongs.
          (e.g., The boy hit the <u>girl's</u> ball.)

2.2 Gender, Case and Number

Both English and Greek nouns have the properties of gender, case, and
number. **Gender** identifies whether a noun is masculine, feminine, or neuter.
Case identifies the relation the noun has to another word in the sentence
(usually the verb; e.g., subject, object). **Number** identifies whether one or
more than one person, place, or thing is involved.

In English nouns, these properties are comparatively muted. Gender can
be distinguished when speaking of persons or animals, but objects are
seldom thought of as being anything other than "it." A noun's case is
indicated by a change in word order (e.g., "Man bites dog." vs. "Dog bites
man."). Number usually is indicated by a change in form (e.g., boy ➔ boys;
man ➔ men).

In Greek nouns, on the other hand, gender, case, and number are much
more prominent. Each noun has a specific *gender* (masculine, feminine, or
neuter). Gender does not necessarily correlate with a noun's lexical meaning
(e.g., "sea" is feminine, but "river" is masculine). Because nouns change
form in patterns related to their gender, the gender of a noun (indicated by
the definite article assigned to it) must be memorized as a part of learning
vocabulary.

Multiple *case* forms exist to specify a noun's relationship to other words
in the sentence. In contrast to English, a change in a noun's function does
not necessarily involve a change in the word order (although the author may
choose to do so). The Greek word order of the following sentences, for
example, is identical, but the meaning of the second is the opposite of the
first. Note the differences in the way four of the five words are spelled.

ὁ ἄνθρωπος δακνει τον κυνα.   =   Man bites dog.

τον ἄνθρωπον δακνει ὁ κυων   =   Dog bites man.

A change in the *number* of a Greek noun nearly always involves a change
in form.

2.3 More on Greek Cases

Every time a Greek noun occurs, it takes one of four possible case forms: nominative, genitive, dative, or accusative. These four case *forms* encompass eight case *functions*. A full discussion of the various case functions belongs to the study of intermediate grammar. At this point it is enough to introduce them.

Case Form	Case Function	
Nominative	Nominative	(Designation)
	Vocative	(Address)
Genitive	Genitive	(Description)
	Ablative	(Separation)
Dative	Pure Dative	(Personal Interest)
	Local Dative	(Position)
	Instrumental Dative	(Means)
Accusative	Accusative	(Limitation/Extension)

Initially, it is helpful to think of the cases in the following ways:

Nominative	=	the subject
Genitive	=	possession (translate with "of . . .")
Dative	=	the indirect object (translate with "to/for . . .")
Accusative	=	the direct object

2.4 Inflection and Declensions

Although English nouns change form very little (e.g., dog → dog's → dogs → dogs'), Greek nouns change form frequently; these changes are called **inflection**. Greek nouns also follow regular patterns of change (inflection); these patterns are called **declensions**. The best way to learn which declension a Greek noun follows is to learn its article, its nominative singular form, and its genitive singular ending (e.g., ὁ λογος, -ου). As the following chart shows, English pronouns exist in declensions and are closest to Greek nouns.

Number	Case	Gender		
		Masculine	Feminine	Neuter
Singular	Nominative	he	she	it
	Genitive	his	hers	its
	Dative	to/for him	to/for her	to/for it
	Accusative	him	her	it
Plural	Nominative	they		
	Genitive	their		
	Dative	to/for them		
	Accusative	them		

2.5 Greek Second Declension Nouns

Greek second declension nouns are nearly all masculine and neuter in gender. There are a few second declension feminine nouns, but they follow the same pattern as the masculine. The vowel ο predominates in the endings which are summarized in the following chart.

		Masculine/Feminine	Neuter
Singular	Nom.	ος	ον
	Gen.	ου	ου
	Dat.	ῳ	ῳ
	Acc.	ον	ον
Plural	Nom.	οι	α
	Gen.	ων	ων
	Dat.	οις	οις
	Acc.	ους	α

These endings are attached to the noun stem, which remains constant in all case forms. The noun stem is found by removing the final two letters from the dictionary form. For example, the stem of the masculine noun λογος is λογ-, and the stem of the neuter noun ἐργον is ἐργ-. The resulting paradigms are:

		λογος (λογ-)	Translation
Singular	Nom.	λογ ος	a word
	Gen.	λογ ου	of a word (a word's)
	Dat.	λογ ῳ	to/for a word
	Acc.	λογ ον	a word
Plural	Nom.	λογ οι	words
	Gen.	λογ ων	of words (words')
	Dat.	λογ οις	to/for words
	Acc.	λογ ους	words

		ἐργον (εργ-)	Translation
Singular	Nom.	ἐργ ον	a work
	Gen.	ἐργ ου	of a work (a work's)
	Dat.	ἐργ ῳ	to/for a work
	Acc.	ἐργ ον	a work
Plural	Nom.	ἐργ α	works
	Gen.	ἐργ ων	of works (works')
	Dat.	ἐργ οις	to/for works
	Acc.	ἐργ α	works

2.6 Vocabulary

Second Declension Masculine Nouns

21. ὁ ἀδελφός, -ου   brother (Philadelphia)   (343)
22. ὁ ἄρτος, -ου   bread   (97)
23. ὁ θάνατος, -ου   death (euthanasia)   (120)
24. ὁ κόσμος,-ου   world (cosmic)   (186)
25. ὁ κύριος, -ου   lord, master   (717)
26. ὁ λίθος, -ου   stone (lithography)   (59)
27. ὁ λόγος, -ου   word, saying, message   (330)
28. ὁ νόμος, -ου   law   (194)
29. ὁ οἶκος, -ου   house, household   (114)
30. ὁ ὄχλος, -ου   crowd   (175)
31. ὁ οὐρανός, -ου   heaven (Uranus, uranium)   (273)

32. ὁ υἱός, -οῦ	son	(377)

Second Declension Neuter Nouns

33. τό δῶρον, -οῦ	gift	(19)
34. τό ἔργον, -ου	work (ergonomic)	(169)
35. τό εὐαγγέλιον, -ου	gospel (evangelism)	(76)
36. τό πλοῖον, -ου	boat	(68)
37. τό σημεῖον, -ου	sign	(77)
38. τό τέκνον, -ου	child	(99)

Second Declension Feminine Nouns

39. ἡ ἔρημος, -ου	wilderness (hermit)	(48)
40. ἡ ὁδός, -ου	road, way (exodus)	(101)

2.7 Form Identification - For each form, give the gender, case, number, dictionary form, and a translation. Gender may be abbreviated as M(asculine), F(eminine), or N(euter); case as N(ominative), G(enitive), D(ative), or A(ccusative); and number as S(ingular) or Pl(ural). One example is given.

ἀνθρώπῳ   MDS   ἄνθρωπος   to/for a man

1. διακονου		14. ἀγγελου
2. δωρον		15. χρονον
3. ἀδελφοι		16. ἀδελφοις
4. οἰκῳ		17. ὁδος
5. πλοια		18. τεκνα
6. σαββατον		19. ἐργων
7. δαιμονιων		20. λιθους
8. ἀρτοι		21. θανατον
9. τεκνοις		22. εὐαγγελιον
10. λιθων		23. υἱῳ
11. δωρα		24. λογοι
12. πλοιον		25. οὐρανους
13. νομον		

2.8 Practice Exercises - Translate the following phrases.

1. λογους Πετρου
   word   Peter

2. εὐαγγελιῳ Χριστου
   angel   christ

3. ἐργα νομου
   work   law

4. διακονος κυριου
   deacon~~ministers~~   lord

5. φοβον ὀχλων
   fear   crowd

6. υἱοι θεου
   son   God

7. μυστηριοις ἀγγελων
   mystery   angel

8. ἀνθρωπῳ κοσμου
   man   world

9. θρονοι λιθου
   throne   stone

10. χρονον θανατου
    time   death

11. σημεια ἀγγελων
    sign

12. κυριος σαββατου
    lord   sabbath

13. μυστηρια δαιμονιων
    mystery   deamon

14. δωροις διακονων
    gift   servant

15. ἀνθρωποι ἐρημου
    man   wilderness

16. ὁδος θανατου
    road   death

17. ἀρτον οὐρανου
    bread   heaven

18. τεκνα ἀποστολων
    child   apostle

19. οἰκος ἀποστολου
    house   apostle

20. λιθοι οὐρανου
    stone   heaven

GRAMMAR GRABBER: Verb Tense Inflection

Ἦν τὸ φῶς τὸ ἀληθινόν, ὃ φωτίζει πάντα ἄνθρωπον, ἐρχόμενον εἰς τὸν κόσμον. (John 1:9)

The true light, who is shining on every man, was coming into the world. (literal English translation)

Through **verb tense inflection**, a New Testament Greek writer can show us not only the *time* of an action (e.g., past, present, or future) but also the *kind* of action (e.g., progressive, summary, or completed-stative) the verb indicates.

In John 1:1-13, the vast majority of verbs are past tenses. They describe the past events of Jesus' pre-existence, presence at creation, and incarnation. At verse nine, the present tense of the verb φωτίζω sticks out like a "sore thumb." This present progressive tense describes an activity of Jesus, which in John's view, is happening as he writes (80s-90s AD) and continues to happen. Jesus' role as universal Revealer and Judge is "present progressive." He "is shining" on every human being for judgment to reveal what s/he is before God.

Sometimes the differences in kinds of action, often represented by "helping verbs" in English, are "troweled off" in translation (e.g., φωτίζει in NIV and NASB is translated as simple, summary action, "gives light to"; "enlightens"). Close attention to tense in the Greek New Testament text, however, will repay dividends in uncovering the richness of meaning the inspired writers set before us.

Chapter 3

PRESENT AND FUTURE ACTIVE INDICATIVE

Like Greek nouns, Greek verbs change form ("inflect") frequently. In this regard, Greek is more nearly similar to French, German, or Spanish than to English. This high degree of inflection encompasses many of the nuances of meaning expressed in English by "helping verbs" (e.g., "shall," or "have been") and seen in compound tenses (e.g., "shall have been prepared"). It will often take several English words to convey the sense of a single Greek verb.

The simplest form of the Greek verb is the Present Active Indicative. Closely related in form is the Future Active Indicative. It will be helpful to review some basic concepts related to verbs in general before beginning work on either of these tenses.

3.1 Introduction to Verbs

Verbs are words which express action or a state of being. Their function is to assert something about a subject. The verb is the core of every sentence. Without a verb, a group of words is only a fragment or a phrase. Even if a sentence contains only one word, that word must be a verb (e.g., "Run!"). Note that Greek sentences sometimes omit the verb "to be."

Verbs may be grouped into three different kinds. **Action verbs** express either physical or mental action (e.g., The boy <u>hit</u> the ball.). **Linking verbs** indicate a link of identity or description between the subject and its complement (e.g., The boy <u>is</u> young.). **Helping verbs** (also called *auxiliary* or *modal* verbs) help express distinctions in the tense, voice, or mood of the main verb (e.g., The boy <u>might</u> hit the ball.).

Both English and Greek verbs have the properties of tense, voice, mood, person, and number. **Tense** expresses the kind (and time) of action. **Voice** expresses the subject's relationship to the action. **Mood** expresses the degree of certainty on the speaker's part. **Person** expresses the speaker's relationship to the actor. **Number** expresses the number of subjects involved in the action.

3.2 English Verbs

The **tense** of a verb communicates kind and time of action. These distinctions are conveyed in English by the use of the helping verbs "to be" and "to have." It is helpful to think of three *kinds* of action (also known as "aspect"). *Progressive* action tenses present the action as in progress without regard to its beginning or end (e.g., I am reading the book.). *Summary* action tenses present the action as viewed as a whole without regard to its continuity or completion (e.g., I read the book.). *Completed-Stative* action tenses present the action as completed, but with continuing results (e.g., I have read the book.).

The **voice** of a verb communicates the relation of the subject to the verb's action. These distinctions are conveyed in English by the use of the helping verbs "to be" and "to have." In *active* voice the subject produces, performs, or experiences the action (e.g., I hit the ball.). In *passive* voice the subject is acted upon by the action described (e.g., I was hit by the ball.).

The charts which follow summarize the helping verbs and suffixes used to form the various tenses and voices of English verbs. Try forming the tenses and voices of the verb "bless." For example, the Progressive Past Active Voice would be "I was blessing," the Progressive Present Passive Voice would be "I am being blessed," and so forth.

	Progressive Action								
	Progressive Past			Progressive Present			Progressive Future		
	T	V	Suff.	T	V	Suff.	T	V	Suff.
A	was were		–ing	am is are		–ing	shall be will be		–ing
P	was were	being	–ed	am is are	being	–ed	shall be will be	being	–ed

Note: Although the progressive tenses are rarely used in English, they occur frequently in Greek, particularly the progressive present (e.g., "I am blessing.") Much more common in English are the summary tenses in the following table.

Summary Action								
Simple Past			Simple Present			Simple Future		
T	V	Suff.	T	V	Suff.	T	V	Suff
A		—ed				shall will		
P	was were	—ed		am is are	—ed	shall will	be	—ed

Completed-Stative Action								
Past Perfect			Present Perfect			Future Perfect		
T	V	Suff.	T	V	Suff.	T	V	Suff.
A had		—ed	have has		—ed	shall have will have		—ed
P had	been	—ed	have has	been	—ed	shall have will have	been	—ed

The **mood** of a verb portrays the speaker's affirmation of the certainty of the action or state. English verbs occur in three moods. A verb in the *indicative* mood makes a statement or asks a question (e.g., Bill is leaving the room.). A verb in the *subjunctive* mood expresses a thought or wish rather than an actual fact. This mood is commonly indicated by the helping verb "might" and most frequently occurs in subordinate clause introduced by "if" or "in order that" (e.g., Bill might leave the room.). A verb in the *imperative* mood gives a command (e.g., Leave the room, Bill!). Note that in the subjunctive and imperative moods the "time" of the action is muted because the action is contingent either upon circumstances outside the speaker's control (subjunctive) or upon the volition of the person addressed (imperative).

The **person** of a verb communicates the speaker's relation to the action (i.e., Who is doing the action?). In the *first person*, the speaker acts (I, we). In the *second person*, the speaker addresses the actor (you, you). In the *third person*, the speaker describes the actor (he, she, it, they)

The **number** of a verb communicates the number of subjects involved in the action (i.e., How many are there?). The *singular* indicates one subject. The *plural* indicates more than one subject.

	Singular	Plural
First (Person speaking)	I	we
Second (Person spoken to)	you	you
Third (Person spoken about)	he, she, it	they

3.3 Greek Verbs

Greek verbs may occur in any of six tenses. These tenses are often grouped under two headings: primary and secondary. **Primary tenses** present action in present or future time in the indicative. The *present tense* generally indicates progressive action. The *future* tense generally indicates summary action. The *perfect* tense indicates completed-stative action. **Secondary tenses** present action in past time in the indicative. The *imperfect* tense indicates progressive action. The *aorist* tense indicates summary action. The *pluperfect* tense indicates completed-stative action.

Primary Tenses		
Present	Progressive Action	"I am reading the book."
Future	Summary Action	"I shall read the book."
Perfect	Completed-stative Action	"I have read the book."
Secondary Tenses		
Imperfect	Progressive Action	"I was reading the book."
Aorist	Summary Action	"I read the book."
Pluperfect	Completed-stative Action	"I had read the book."

To the active and passive voices present in English verbs, Greek adds a third **voice**, the middle. In the *active* voice, the subject performs, produces, or experiences the action. In the *middle* voice, the subject produces or experiences the action in such a way as to participate in the results. In the *passive* voice, the subject is acted upon by the action described.

Voice		
Active	Subject acts.	"I hit the ball."
Middle	Subject participates in the action.	"I hit myself with the ball."
Passive	Subject is acted upon.	"I was hit by the ball."

To the three moods present in English verbs, Greek adds a fourth **mood**, the optative. In the *indicative* mood the speaker presents the action as real or certain. In the *subjunctive* mood the speaker presents the action as potential. In the *optative* mood the speaker presents the action as possible. It is most frequently used to express wishes. In the *imperative* mood the speaker presents the action as intended (but dependent on the volitional response of the person addressed).

Mood		
Indicative	Action is presented as real.	"Tomorrow she is buying the car."
Subjunctive	Action is presented as potential.	"Next week she might buy the car."
Optative	Action is presented as possible.	"I wish she would buy the car."
Imperative	Action is presented as volitional.	"Buy the car!"

It is helpful to think of the **form** of Greek verbs as consisting of three basic components. The *stem* (ST) identifies the word in terms of its lexical meaning. In regular verbs, the stem remains unchanged in all of the tenses. In irregular verbs, the stem may change in some or all of the tenses. *Suffixes* are letters added to the end of the stem to express tense (tense signs, S), voice, mood, person, and number (personal endings, E). *Prefixes* are letters added to the beginning of the stem to express past time in the indicative mood (augments, A) or a completed-stative action tense (reduplication, R).

3.4 The Indicative Mood

The indicative mood is the mood most frequently encountered in Greek, and so, it is introduced first. The indicative mood is the only mood in which *time* of action is made explicit by the tense of a verb. In all other moods, *kind* of action is the factor indicated by tense. Verbs in the indicative mood may occur in any of the six tenses. The chart below shows the way in which those tenses relate to kind and time of action.

		Time of Action		
		Past	Present	Future
Kind of Action	Progressive	Imperfect	**Present**	(Secondary use of future)
	Summary	Aorist	(Secondary use of present)	**Future**
	Completed-Stative	Pluperfect	Perfect	(Future Perfect)

3.5 Primary Active Endings

As noted above, the present, future, and perfect tenses are the "primary" tenses. This designation has nothing to do with frequency of occurrence or with importance. Rather, it groups together those tenses which, in the indicative mood, are oriented to the present or future. The same active endings are used for all three tenses. These primary active endings are set out in the following chart.

		Primary Active Endings
Singular	1st	–
	2nd	ς
	3rd	–
Plural	1st	μεν
	2nd	τε
	3rd	σι

3.6 Present Active Indicative

Although the present tense is sometimes used to connote summary action, the primary significance of the present active indicative is *progressive* action in *present* time. In order to reflect the progressive action of the present tense, we will translate the present active indicative using the progressive present. The first person singular of the verb "to see" would thus be translated as "I am seeing." The form of the present active indicative may be summarized by the following formula:

Stem + Theme Vowel + Primary Active Endings
(ST +   V   +   PAE   )

▸ Stem: The present stem of a verb is found by removing the final ω of the dictionary form. For example, the stem of λυω is λυ-.
▸ Theme Vowel: Most Greek verbs are "thematic"; that is, they have a theme vowel (V) inserted before the personal ending. For the present active indicative the theme vowels follow the pattern *o-e-e-o-e-o*. In other words, the first person singular, first person plural, and third person plural all include some form of the vowel o, and the second person singular, third person singular, and second person plural all include some form of the vowel e.

Singular	1st	ω	long o
	2nd	ει	dipthong of e
	3rd	ει	dipthong of e
Plural	1st	ο	short o
	2nd	ε	short e
	3rd	ου	diphthong of o

▸ Personal Endings: The present active indicative uses the primary active endings discussed above.

The verb λυω (I am loosing, destroying) is regular in all its forms. For this reason it will be used in most paradigms.

		λυω (λυ-)			Translation
Sing.	1st	λυ	ω	-	I am loosing.
	2nd	λυ	ει	ς	You are loosing.
	3rd	λυ	ει	-	He/she/it is loosing.
Pl.	1st	λυ	ο	μεν	We are loosing.
	2nd	λυ	ε	τε	You are loosing.
	3rd	λυ	ου	σι(ν)	They are loosing.

Special Notes:
1. The personal endings indicate the person and number of the verb. It was not strictly necessary, therefore, for a Greek author to supply a personal pronoun to serve as the subject. In fact, as will be discussed later, when

a personal pronoun is present it either clarifies the *gender* of the subject or is used for *emphasis*.

2. An unusual feature of the Greek language is that *neuter plural subjects take singular verbs*. One example occurs in Luke 10:20:

   τα πνευματα ὑμιν ὑποτασσεται

   "The spirits (neuter nominative *plural*) are being subject (third person *singular*) to you."

3.7 Future Active Indicative

Although the future tense is sometimes used to connote progressive action, the primary significance of the future active indicative is *summary* action in *future* time. In order to reflect the summary action of the future tense, we will translate the future active indicative using the simple future. The first person singular of the verb "to see" would thus be translated "I shall see." The form of the future active indicative may be summarized by the following formula:

Stem + Tense Sign + Theme Vowel + Primary Active Endings
(ST +   S   +   V   +   PAE   )

▸ Stem: The future stem of regular verbs is found by removing the final ω of the dictionary form (as was true in the present). The future stem of irregular verbs often has a different form than the present and must be learned separately.
▸ Tense Sign: The future active indicative uses σ as a tense sign throughout its paradigm.
▸ Theme Vowel: For the future active indicative the theme vowels follow the same pattern as the present: *o-e-e-o-e-o*.
▸ Personal Endings: The future active indicative uses the primary active endings above.

		λυω (λυ-)				Translation
Sing.	1st	λυ	σ	ω	-	I shall loose.
	2nd	λυ	σ	ει	ς	You will loose.
	3rd	λυ	σ	ει	-	He/she/it will loose.
Pl.	1st	λυ	σ	ο	μεν	We shall loose.
	2nd	λυ	σ	ε	τε	You will loose.
	3rd	λυ	σ	ου	σι(ν)	They will loose.

Most Greek verbs have stems which end in a consonant (e.g., πεμπω). These consonants may be grouped into the six classes outlined in Chapter 1. When the tense sign of the future is added to the stem of these verbs, **consonant contraction** (or "amalgamation") occurs. At this point only the labials, gutterals, and dentals will be addressed.

Labial	β, π, φ	+	σ	=	ψ
Gutteral	γ, κ, χ	+	σ	=	ξ
Dental	δ, θ, τ	+	σ	=	σ

The results in the first person singular for three representative verbs are

Labial	πεμπω	πεμπ + σ	=	πεμψω
Gutteral	διωκω	διωκ + σ	=	διωξω
Dental	πειθω	πειθ + σ	=	πεισω

It should be noted (a) that when the stem of a verb ends in σσ, it contracts in the same way that a stem ending in gutteral consonant does (σσ + σ = ξ) and (b) that when the stem of a verb ends in ζ, it contracts the same way that a stem ending in a dental consonant does (ζ + σ = σ).

3.8 The Verb εἰμι ("I am")

The verb "to be" is the most frequently used verb in the New Testament (2460 times). Although it is of an entirely different class than the -ω verbs in this section in that it ends in -μι (a form to be studied much later), it is necessary to begin learning it now. As is true of the English verb "to be" (e.g., am, is, are, was, were, shall be), the Greek verb εἰμι is irregular and must, therefore, be memorized. Fortunately, it occurs in only three tenses, two of which are the present and the future. The past tense will be deferred until later.

The paradigm of the present tense follows. Note the circumflex accent on the second singular form which distinguishes this word εἶ ("you are") from another which looks nearly identical: εἰ ("if").

		Present Tense of εἰμι	Translation
Sing.	1st	εἰμι	I am.
	2nd	εἶ	You are.
	3rd	ἐστι(ν)	He/she/it is.
Pl.	1st	ἐσμεν	We are.
	2nd	ἐστε	You are.
	3rd	εἰσι(ν)	They are.

Note that the future endings in the paradigm which follows are different from those learned earlier in this chapter. Since these endings will be covered later, you are actually ahead of the game!

		Future Tense of εἰμι	Translation
Sing.	1st	ἐσομαι	I shall be.
	2nd	ἐση	You will be.
	3rd	ἐσται	He/she/it will be.
Pl.	1st	ἐσομεθα	We shall be.
	2nd	ἐσεσθε	You will be.
	3rd	ἐσονται	They will be.

The verb εἰμι is a linking ("copulative") verb in that it links two parts of the sentence, the subject and its complement. This link may indicate identity by using a noun (e.g., "Jack is a man.") or description by using an adjective (e.g., "Jack is young."). In the former example, "man" is called the predicate nominative; in the latter example, "young" is called the predicate adjective. Because εἰμι *equates* the subject and its complement, the predicate nominative or predicate adjective will be in the nominative case rather than in the accusative (as would be true with other verbs which take direct objects).

3.9 Vocabulary

All but one of the words (#60) in the following list are verbs. Verbs will always be listed in the form found in dictionaries and lexica — Present Active Indicative First Person Singular (PAI1S). Two of the verbs (#58-59) follow a different sent of endings which will be learned in a later chapter. They occur so frequently in the New Testament, however, that they are included now.

Verbs

41.	ἄγω	I am leading	(67)
42.	ἀκούω	I am hearing, listening to (acoustic)	(428)
43.	ἀποστέλλω	I am sending out (apostle)	(132)
44.	βαπτίζω	I am baptizing (baptism)	(77)
45.	βλέπω	I am seeing, looking	(133)
46.	γινώσκω	I am knowing (agnostic)	(222)
47.	γράφω	I am writing (graphic)	(191)

48.	κράζω	I am crying out, shouting	(56)
49.	λαμβάνω	I am taking, receiving	(258)
50.	καταλαμβάνω	I am attaining, laying hold of	(15)
51.	παραλαμβάνω	I am accepting, receiving	(49)
52.	λύω	I am loosing, destroying	(42)
53.	πέμπω	I am sending	(79)
54.	πιστεύω	I am believing, regarding as reliable	(241)
55.	φαίνω	I am shining	(31)
56.	φωτίζω	I am giving light to	(11)
57.	εἰμί	I am	(2460)
58.	γίνομαι	I am, am becoming, am existing	(669)
59.	ἔρχομαι	I am coming, going	(634)

Negative Particle

| 60. | οὐ, οὐκ, οὐχ, οὐχι | not | (1660) |

3.10 Form Identification - For each form, give the tense, voice, mood, person, number, dictionary form, and a translation. Tense may be abbreviate as **P**(resent) or **F**(uture); voice as **A**(ctive); and mood as **I**(ndicative). One example is given.

λαμβανεις   PAI2S   λαμβανω   you are taking/receiving

1. φαινει _shining_
2. ἐσμεν _we are_
3. γραψομεν _writing_
4. κραζετε _crying_
5. ἀκουσω _hearing_
6. γινωσκουσι _Knowing_
7. πιστευσεις _believing_
8. εἰσι _I am_
9. πεμπεις _sending_
10. φωτιζει _shining_
11. πιστευσομεν _believing_
12. πεμψουσιν _sending_
13. φωτισει _giving light to_
14. φαινετε _shining_
15. ἐστε _I am_
16. ἀποστελλομεν _sending out_
17. βλεπουσι _seeing_
18. ἐστιν _I am_
19. ἀξεις _hearing_
20. κραζει _crying_
21. εἰ _I am_
22. ἀγει _leading_

3.11 Practice Exercises - Translate the following sentences. Parse all verbs (TVMPN, Dictionary form). A good basic strategy to use is (a) find and parse all of the verbs in the sentence; (b) look for a noun in the nominative—it will probably be the subject; (c) look for a noun in the accusative—it will probably be the direct object; (d) put the pieces in standard English word order: subject, verb, object. Remember that a noun in the dative ("to/for") is usually the indirect object and a noun in the genitive ("of") usually modifies the noun immediately preceding it.

1. εἰσιν Πετρου, ἀλλ' (but) ἐσμεν Ἰησου.

2. ἡ (the) ὁδος του (the) κοσμου ἀγει θανατῳ.

3. τον (the) λογον θεου δαιμονια οὐ πιστευσει.

4. ἀνθρωπος ἀγει τεκνα Χριστῳ.

5. τί (why) βαπτιζεις, εἰ (if) οὐκ εἶ ὁ (the) Χριστος;

6. βλεπετε και (and) οὐ πιστευετε.

7. ἐγω εἰμι ἡ (the) ὁδος θεῳ.

8. τον (the) λογον ἀκουουσιν ἀλλ' (but) οὐ λαμβανουσιν.

9. δωρα πεμψουσιν ἀνθρωποις.

10. εἶ ὁ (the) Χριστος;

11. γινωσκει Ἰησους ὁτι (that) ἀκουσουσι οἱ (the) Φαρισαιοι (Pharisees).

12. πιστευεις ὁτι (that) εἷς (one) ἐστιν θεος;

13. ἐρχομαι ἱνα (in order that) βλεψουσιν και (and) πιστευσουσιν.

14. τον (the) νομον θεου οὐ λαμβανετε.

15. γινωσκομεν ὁτι (that) Ἰησους ὁ (the) υἱος θεου ἐστιν.

16. λογους γραφει Πετρος τοις (the) υἱοις θεου.

17. εἰ (if) θεου ἀνθρωπος ἐστιν, λόγους θεου ἀκούσει.

18. ὁ (the) κοσμος οὐ γινωσκει ἡμας (us) ὅτι (because) οὐκ γινωσκει αὐτον (him).

19. ἐγω ἐσομαι αὐτῳ (to him) θεος· αὐτος (he) ἐσται μοι (to me) υἱος.

20. ἀποστελλει ὁ (the) υἱος ἀνθρωπου ἀγγελους αὐτου (his) τῳ (the) κοσμῳ.

GRAMMAR GRABBER: Definite Articles

ἐν ἀρχῇ ἦν ὁ λόγος, καὶ ὁ λόγος ἦν πρὸς τὸν θεόν, καὶ θεὸς ἦν ὁ λόγος. (John 1:1)

In the beginning was the Word, and the Word was with God, and the Word was God.

Since there is no indefinite article in Greek, per se, English speakers are often tempted to translate instances of Greek nouns without a *definite* article by an English word with an *indefinite* article. This tendency leads Jehovah Witnesses, with their unitarian monotheistic doctrine, to render the third clause of John 1:1 as "And the Word was a god."

A noun without a definite article, however—especially when it is a predicate noun used with a verb "to be"—emphasizes the *quality* to which its meaning points. In this case, θεος should be rendered "divine" and the whole clause be translated: "and the Word was God (divine)."

In fact, John is making a carefully nuanced statement. First of all, he uses a definite article to identify ὁ λογος as the subject of the verb "to be" (note that word order does not help since the subject occurs after the verb). Then, by not using the definite article with θεος, he not only lets you know that it is the predicate nominative, but that he is pointing to "quality"—Jesus' nature as fully God. Further, by not using a definite article, he leaves room for a trinitarian monotheism—other members of the Trinity. For if he had said, καὶ ὁ θεὸς ἦν ὁ λόγος he would have been claiming no other particular divine being existed except the second person of the Godhead, "the Word."

Definite articles, whether present or absent, speak volumes of good theology.

Chapter 4

FIRST DECLENSION NOUNS

Chapter 2 introduced second declension nouns; the first and third declensions remain. This chapter will focus on *first* declension nouns; third declension nouns will be introduced in Chapters 8 and 9. Since the definite article is closely associated with nouns, this chapter begins with the various forms of the definite article. Then, nouns which follow the first declension pattern are discussed.

4.1 The Definite Article

Articles are words used with nouns to limit, individualize, or give definiteness/indefiniteness to the nouns. **Definite articles** ("the") point out individual identity (e.g., the man, the artist). **Indefinite articles** ("a" or "an") denote any of a class or group of objects (e.g., a man, an artist). English has both definite and indefinite articles. Greek has only the definite article.

4.2 The Greek Definite Article

The basic role of the Greek definite article is to draw attention to a word or an idea. When used with nouns, the article can individualize or distinguish. Its absence can indicate indefiniteness, quality, or essence. Although the Greek definite article functions in a number of ways, a detailed explanation of those uses belongs to the discussion of intermediate grammar.

Like nouns and adjectives, definite articles have gender, case, and number. The definite article *must* agree in gender, case, and number with the noun and/or adjective with which it is used.

The form of the definite article follows the ending pattern of first and second declension nouns. The *masculine* definite article follows the pattern of the second declension masculine noun. (See Chapter 2.) The *feminine* definite article follows the pattern of the first declension feminine noun. (See later in this chapter.) The *neuter* definite article follows the pattern of the second declension neuter noun. The table which follows sets out all twenty-four forms of the definite article.

Number	Case	Gender		
		Masculine	Feminine	Neuter
Singular	Nominative	ὁ	ἡ	το
	Genitive	του	της	του
	Dative	τῳ	τῃ	τῳ
	Accusative	τον	την	το
Plural	Nominative	οἱ	αἱ	τα
	Genitive	των	των	των
	Dative	τοις	ταις	τοις
	Accusative	τους	τας	τα

4.3 First Declension Feminine Nouns

First declension nouns are predominantly feminine in gender. There are a few masculine first declension nouns (see the discussion below), but they may be distinguished in the vocabulary lists by the presence of the masculine definite article (ὁ) and genitive singular ending (-ου). First declension nouns have α or η in most of their endings and fall into three categories: alpha-pure, alpha-impure, and eta.

These three categories relate strictly to the inflection pattern which the noun follows; they have no impact on the noun's meaning. A given noun will only ever follow *one* of the three inflection patterns. The table below gives an overview of the basic ending patterns.

		Alpha-Pure	Alpha-Impure	Eta
Singular	Nom.	α	α	η
	Gen.	ας	ης	ης
	Dat.	ᾳ	ῃ	ῃ
	Acc.	αν	αν	ην
Plural	Nom.		αι	
	Gen.		ων	
	Dat.		αις	
	Acc.		ας	

Note that the plural endings are the same for all three categories. Note also that the genitive singular ending of alpha-pure nouns is the same as the accusative plural ending. The next three charts give the full paradigm for each category of first declension nouns, including the definite article and a basic translation.

Alpha-pure nouns have the vowel α throughout the singular endings, have stems which end in ε, ι, or ρ, and follow the pattern of the noun ἡ ἡμερα, ἡμερας. Excluding proper names, 310 New Testament nouns follow the alpha-pure pattern.

Alpha-Pure		ἡμερα (ἡμερ-)		Translation
Singular	Nom.	ἡ	ἡμερ α	the day
	Gen.	της	ἡμερ ας	of the day (the day's)
	Dat.	τη	ἡμερ ᾳ	to/for the day
	Acc.	την	ἡμερ αν	the day
Plural	Nom.	αἱ	ἡμερ αι	the days
	Gen.	των	ἡμερ ων	of the days (the days')
	Dat.	ταις	ἡμερ αις	to/for the days
	Acc.	τας	ἡμερ ας	the days

Alpha-impure nouns have the vowels α and η in the singular endings, have stems which end in consonants other than ε, ι, or ρ, and follow the pattern of the noun ἡ δοξα, δοξης. This group is smaller with only 22 nouns in it.

Alpha-Impure		δοξα (δοξ-)		Translation
Singular	Nom.	ἡ	δοξ α	the glory
	Gen.	της	δοξ ης	of the glory (the glory's)
	Dat.	τη	δοξ ῃ	to/for the glory
	Acc.	την	δοξ αν	the glory
Plural	Nom.	αἱ	δοξ αι	the glories
	Gen.	των	δοξ ων	of the glories (the glories')
	Dat.	ταις	δοξ αις	to/for the glories
	Acc.	τας	δοξ ας	the glories

Eta nouns have the vowel η throughout the singular endings and follow the pattern of the noun ἡ φωνη, φωνης. There are 191 nouns which follow this pattern.

Eta		ἀρχη (ἀρχ-)		Translation
Singular	Nom.	ἡ	ἀρχ η	the beginning
	Gen.	της	ἀρχ ης	of the beginning
	Dat.	τη	ἀρχ ῃ	to/for the beginning
	Acc.	την	ἀρχ ην	the beginning
Plural	Nom.	αἱ	ἀρχ αι	the beginnings
	Gen.	των	ἀρχ ων	of the beginnings
	Dat.	ταις	ἀρχ αις	to/for the beginnings
	Acc.	τας	ἀρχ ας	the beginnings

4.4 First Declension Masculine Nouns

Although the vast majority of first declension nouns are feminine, there are a few important first declension masculine nouns. One group consists almost entirely of proper names with a dictionary form ending in –ας (e.g., ὁ Μεσσίας, -ου). Except for the nominative and genitive singular, this group follows the *alpha* patterns above. The other, larger, group has a dictionary form ending in –ης (e.g., ὁ προφητης, -ου). Except for the nominative and genitive singular, this group follows the *eta* pattern above. Rather than learning two additional paradigms, it is enough simply to be alert to these nouns when they appear in the vocabulary lists.

4.5 Vocabulary

First Declension Feminine Nouns

61.	ἡ ἀληθεία, -ας	truth	(109)
62.	ἡ ἁμαρτία, -ας	sin (hamartiology)	(173)
63.	ἡ ἀρχή, -ης	beginning (archaeology)	(55)
64.	ἡ γενεά, -ας	generation (genealogy)	(43)
65.	ἡ γῆ, γῆς	earth, land, ground (geology) *	(250)
66.	ἡ δόξα, -ης	glory (doxology)	(166)
67.	ἡ ἐξουσία, -ας	authority ✓	(102)
68.	ἡ ζωή, -ης	life (zoology)	(135)
69.	ἡ ἡμέρα, -ας	day (ephemeral)	(389)
70.	ἡ καρδία, -ας	heart (cardiac)	(156)
71.	ἡ μαρτυρία, -ας	witness, testimony	(37)
72.	ἡ περιστερά, -ας	dove	(10)

73. ἡ σκοτία, -ας	darkness	(16)
74. ἡ φωνή, -ης	voice (phonology)	(139)
75. ἡ ὥρα, -ας	hour (horoscope)	(106)

Verbs

76. γεννάω	I am begetting, giving birth	(96)
77. δίδωμι	I am giving	(415)
78. λέγω	I am saying, speaking	(2354)
79. μαρτυρέω	I am bearing witness	(76)

Negative Particle

| 80. μή | not | (1042) |

[used with moods other than the indicative]

4.6 Form Identification - For each form give the gender, case, number, dictionary form, and a translation. One example is provided.

ἀμαρτιας   FGS   ἀμαρτια   of a sin (sin's)
         or FAPl   or sins

1. ἀρχῃ *beginning*
2. καρδιων *heart*
3. συναγωγην *synagogue*
4. σκοτια *darkness*
5. δοξῃ *Glory*
6. ἐπιστολαι *epistle*
7. φωνην *voice*
8. ἡμερας *Day*
9. ἀληθεια *truth*
10. παραβολαις *Parables*
11. ὡραν *hour*
12. μαρτυριας *~~bearing~~ witness*
13. ἀρχας *beginning*

14. ἐπιστολην *epistle*
15. συναγωγων *synagogue*
16. δοξαν *Glory*
17. παραβολη *parables*
18. ἡμεραι *Day*
19. περιστεραν *dove*
20. φωναι *voice*
21. καρδιας *heart*
22. ζωη *life*
23. γενεων *generation*
24. ἐξουσια *authority*
25. γης *earth*

dative: to, for, by, with, in

4.7 Practice Exercises - Translate the following sentences. Parse all verbs (TVMPN - Dictionary form). Remember that the dative case can sometimes be translated using "in," "by," or "with," as well as "to/for." (Note: The verb ἀκουω sometimes takes a noun in the genitive case as its direct object.)

1. τῃ ἐρημῳ φωνη κραζει.

2. ἐγω εἰμι ὁ ἀρτος της ζωης.

3. σκοτια ἐν (in) θεῳ οὐκ ἐστιν.

4. τῳ θεῳ οὐρανου διδωμι δοξαν.

5. γινωσκει Ἰησους τας καρδιας ἀνθρωπων.

6. ἐστιν ἡ ὡρα και (and) ἡ ἐξουσια της σκοτιας.

7. την ἁμαρτιαν του κοσμου ὁ υἱος του θεου λαμβανει.

8. οὐ πιστευετε ὁτι (that) ἐγω την ἀληθειαν λεγω;

9. αὑτη (this) ἐστιν ἡ ἀρχη του εὐαγγελιου Ἰησου Χριστου υἱου θεου.

10. κυριος οὐρανου και (and) γης ἐστιν ὁ Ἰησους Χριστος.

11. τον λογον του θεου και την μαρτυριαν Ἰησου Χριστου πιστευομεν.

12. ἐγω εἰμι ἡ ὁδος και (and) ἡ ἀληθεια και (and) ἡ ζωη.

13. τῳ νομῳ γινωσκει ἀνθρωπος την ἁμαρτιαν.

14. λεγει ὁ θεος, τῳ υἱῳ ἀνθρωπου ἐξουσιαν διδωμι.

15. ἡ ὡρα ἐστιν ὁτε (when) ἀκουσουσιν της φωνης του υἱου του θεου.

16. τον λογον του θεου ἐν (in) ἀληθειᾳ λεγεις.

17. την μαρτυριαν ἀνθρωπων οὐ λαμβανω.

18. τον νομον γραψει ταις καρδιαις ἀνθρωπων.

19. ὁ ἀνθρωπος της ἀληθειας ἀκουει της φωνης θεου.

20. εἰ (if) την μαρτυριαν των ἀνθρωπων λαμβανομεν, ἡ μαρτυρια του θεου μειζων (greater) ἐστιν.

Parse:
T V M P N lex meaning

1. A voice crying in the wilderness
2. I am the bread of life
3. Darkness is not in God
4. I give glory to the God of Heaven
5. Jesus knows the hearts of man
6. it is the hour of darkness
7. the son of God takes the sin of the world
8. Do you not believe I'm speaking the truth?
9. This is the beginning of the gospel of Jesus Christ the son of God.
10. Jesus Christ is the Lord of Heaven and Earth
11. We are believing the word of God + testimony of Jesus Christ.

15. The hour is when they will hear the voice of the son of God.
16. you are speaking the word of God in truth
17. I do not recieve the testimony of men.
18 He will write the law on the hearts of men
19
20

GRAMMAR GRABBER: Connectors

οὗτος ἦλθεν εἰς μαρτυρίαν, ἵνα μαρτυρήσῃ περὶ τοῦ φωτός, ἵνα πάντες πιστεύσωσιν δι᾽ αὐτοῦ. (John 1:7)

"This one came <u>for</u> a witness, <u>that</u> he might bear witness <u>concerning</u> the light, <u>in order that</u> all might believe <u>through</u> him."

Connectors—conjunctions and prepositions—normally have a limited range of meaning. Yet, as their name indicates, they provide vital links in meaning between words or groups of words. If we remove all the connectors from John 1:7, we will not be able to make very much sense of it:

οὗτος ἦλθεν ___ μαρτυρίαν, ___ μαρτυρήσῃ ___ τοῦ φωτός, ___ πάντες πιστεύσωσιν ___ αὐτοῦ.

A literal translation would read:
"This one came ___ a witness, ___ he might bear witness ___ the light, _____ all might believe _____ him."

Using the descriptions and charts in Chapter 5, can you begin to make sense of the kind of links these connectors provide. Here is some help.

▶   The preposition εἰς probably does not indicate direction ("into") but the *purpose* for which John the Baptist came: "This one came **for** (the purpose of) witnessing . . ."

▶   The conjunction ἵνα occurs twice. Although the first ἵνα could possibly indicate purpose ("in order that"), it probably introduces a noun clause which stands next to the main clause and *explains* it: "This one came for witnessing, **that is**, he bears witness concerning the light . . ."

▶   The second ἵνα probably introduces purpose ("in order that"), but modifies the first ἵνα clause, explaining for what *purpose* John the Baptist bears witness: "This one came for witnessing, that is, he bears witness concerning the light, **in order that** all might believe through him."

A proper analysis of the connectors which an author uses is vital in understanding the flow of thought in his argument.

Chapter 5

CONJUNCTIONS AND PREPOSITIONS

In Greek, as in English, the sentence is the basic unit of thought. Nouns — with or without definite articles — and verbs are important components of a sentence, and a simple sentence may consist entirely of those elements (e.g., The boy hit the ball.). If, however, a speaker wishes to construct a more complex thought, additional elements are needed. Connectors such as **conjunctions** and **prepositions** are useful in this regard. Conjunctions, for example, can join words, phrases, clauses, and even sentences (e.g., The boy hit the ball, but the girl caught it.). Prepositions can be used to clarify the way in which a noun (its object) is related to another word in the sentence (e.g., The boy hit the ball with the bat.). A knowledge of these connectors and the ways in which they function is crucial for a proper understanding of the Greek New Testament.

5.1 Basic Definitions

A **sentence** is a group of words which expresses a complete thought. A **clause** is a group of words which has a subject and a verb and is used as part of a sentence. There are two kinds of clauses. A *main (independent) clause* (MC) expresses a complete thought and could be a sentence by itself (e.g., The boy hit the ball.). A *subordinate (dependent) clause* (SC) does not express a complete thought and is attached to a main clause by a connector (e.g., The boy hit the ball [MC], because he is a good batter [SC].).

A **phrase** is a group of words which functions as a unit within a sentence and does not contain a subject and finite verb. There are three basic kinds of phrases. A *prepositional phrase* is a group of related words introduced by a preposition and usually ending with a noun or a pronoun (e.g., The boy hit the ball, with the bat.). A *participial phrase* is a group of words which contains a participle (e.g., Swinging wildly, the boy missed the ball.). An *infinitival phrase* is a group of words which contains an infinitive (e.g., The boy tried to hit the ball.).

A **conjunction** is a function word which connects words or word groups. There are two kinds of conjunctions. *Coordinate conjunctions* connect words, phrases, clauses, sentences, or paragraphs of equal value (e.g., Jack and Jill went up the hill.). *Subordinate conjunctions* connect subordinate (dependent) clauses to main (independent) clauses (e.g., Jack went up the hill, although Jill stayed at the bottom.) Although there are (a few) exceptions, a Greek conjunction normally functions as *either* a coordinate *or* a subordinate conjunction. The way in which a conjunction functions (as coordinate or as subordinate) must be learned as a part of vocabulary building.

A **preposition** is a connecting word which clarifies how a noun is related to the sentence containing it (e.g., The boy ran to first base.). The noun joined to the sentence by a preposition is its *object* (e.g., The boy ran to first base.). The word group which includes the preposition and its object is a *prepositional phrase* (e.g., The boy ran to first base.).

5.2 Greek Coordinate Conjunctions

Coordinate conjunctions join equal grammatical units. Those units can be words, phrases, clauses, sentences, or paragraphs. Four simple examples follow. Note that "normal" Greek style (unlike English) introduces sentences with coordinate conjunctions in order to show the logical relation between them.

John 1:17 (words)
ἡ χαρις και ἡ αληθεια δια Ἰησου Χριστου ἐγενετο
Grace and truth were realized through Jesus Christ.

John 1:13 (phrases)
. . . οἳ οὐκ ἐξ αἱματων οὐδε ἐκ θεληματος σαρκος οὐδε ἐκ θεληματος ἀνδρος ἀλλ᾽ ἐκ θεου ἐγεννηθσαν
. . . who were born not of blood, nor of the will of flesh, nor of the will of man, but of God.

John 1:1 (clauses)
ἐν ἀρχη ἠν ὁ λογος, και ὁ λογος ἠν προς τον θεον, και θεος ἠν ὁ λογος
In the beginning was the word, and the word was with God, and the word was God.

John 1:24 (sentences)
και ἀπεσταλμενοι ἠσαν ἐκ των Φαρισαιων. και ἠρωτησαν αὐτον . . .
And those who had been sent were of the Pharisees. And they asked him . . .

The logical relation between the grammatical units joined by coordinate conjunctions may be classified in a variety of ways.

1. *Continuative* ("and") - connects parallel items
2. *Adversative* ("but") - contrasts parallel items
3. *Disjunctive* ("or") - distinguishes between items
4. *Inferential* ("therefore") - introduces a conclusion from what precedes
5. *Explanatory* ("that is, for") - introduces an explanation of what precedes
6. *Transitional* ("now, then") - changes the topic of discussion
7. *Emphatic* ("certainly") - adds a parallel thought stressing the truth of what precedes
8. *Ascensive* ("even") - introduces a final addition or point of emphasis

A full discussion of coordinate conjunctions belongs to the study of intermediate grammar. It is sufficient at this point to introduce the most common conjunctions and their primary uses.

▶ καί is the primary *continuative* conjunction. It joins two or more grammatical units at any syntactical level. It is most commonly translated "and," although it can also have ascensive ("even") or adverbial ("also") force.

▶ ἀλλά is the primary *adversative* conjunction. It contrasts two or more grammatical units at any syntactical level. It is most commonly translated "but." When it is used in the construction οὐ . . . ἀλλα, it establishes a strong contrast ("not . . . but").

▶ ἤ is the primary *disjunctive* conjunction. It distinguishes between two or more grammatical units, usually words or phrases. It is most commonly translated "or."

▶ οὖν is the primary *inferential* conjunction. It is used exclusively with clauses, sentences, and paragraphs to draw a conclusion from the grammatical unit which precedes it. It is most commonly translated "therefore," although it can also have transitional force ("then"). It is a postpositive conjunction and cannot stand first in a clause.

▶ δέ is a *weak connector* which joins grammatical units at any syntactical level. It can have continuative ("and"), adversative ("but"), or transitional ("now") force. It is a postpositive conjunction and cannot stand first in a clause.

5.3 Greek Subordinate Conjunctions

Subordinate conjunctions join subordinate (dependent) clauses to main (independent) clauses. The clause introduced by the subordinate conjunction functions either as an adverbial clause or as a noun clause. An *adverbial subordinate clause* is introduced by a subordinate conjunction and modifies the action of the verb in the main clause (e.g., The boy hit the ball <u>because he was a good batter</u>.). A *noun (substantival) clause* is introduced by a subordinate conjunction and functions as a noun (subject, object, complement, appositive) in relation to the main clause (e.g., I know <u>that the boy hit the ball</u>. [direct object]).

The syntactical relation between an adverbial subordinate clause and the main clause to which it is joined may be classified in a variety of ways.

1. *Comparison* ("as") - presents an analogous thought
2. *Time* ("after, while, before") - limits the action by time
3. *Purpose* ("in order that") - states the aim of the action
4. *Result* ("so that") - states the consequences of the action
5. *Cause* ("because") - states the reason for the action
6. *Condition* ("if") - states the condition under which the action will be realized
7. *Concession* ("although") - states the condition in spite of which the action will be realized

A full discussion of subordinate conjunctions belongs to the study of intermediate grammar. It is sufficient at this point to introduce the most common conjunctions and their primary uses.

▸ ὅτε is the most common of several conjunctions used to introduce *temporal* clauses. It is usually translated "when" or "while."

▸ ἵνα is regularly used to introduce subordinate clauses with verbs in the subjunctive mood (to be studied later). It most frequently introduces a *purpose* clause ("in order that"), but it may also be used to introduce a *result* clause ("so that") or a *noun* clause ("that").

▸ γάρ is the most common conjunction used to introduce *causal* clauses. It is usually translated "for." It is a postpositive conjunction and cannot stand first in its clause. γάρ is unusual in that it can also serve to introduce a sentence, in which case it is best understood as *explanatory* ("so that").

▸ ὅτι can introduce both adverbial and noun clauses. When it is most naturally translated "because," it introduces a *causal adverbial* clause. When it is most naturally translated "that," it introduces a *noun* clause.

▸ εἰ is one of two conjunctions commonly used to introduce *conditional* clauses. (The other, ἐάν, is introduced later.) It is usually translated "if."

5.4 Greek Prepositions

Originally, the cases alone were used to specify the relation of nouns to other words in a sentence. Prepositions were originally adverbs and stood alone to modify verbs. They gradually began to be used with nouns in order to clarify the meaning of cases in given contexts. Some "improper" prepositions still retain their adverbial function as primary and only occasionally are used as prepositions. When used as prepositions their object is usually in the genitive and often *precedes* the preposition (e.g., Eph 3:1, 14 → τουτου χαριν).

Certain Greek prepositions change form (inflect) depending on the word which follows them. In every case but one (ἐκ), the change occurs when the preposition ends in a vowel. These changes are consistent, but they tend to catch students by surprise when first encountered.

1. When the word which follows begins with *a vowel or diphthong and a smooth breathing mark*, the final vowel of the preposition is replaced by an apostrophe (e.g., before ἀνθρωπος, ἀπο becomes ἀπ᾽).

2. When the word which follows begins with *a vowel or diphthong and a rough breathing mark*, the final vowel of the preposition is replaced by an apostrophe and the final consonant changes to the corresponding double consonant (e.g., before ἁμαρτωλος, ἀπο become ἀφ᾽).

The following chart summarizes these changes.

Before consonants	Before vowels with smooth breathing marks	Before vowels with rough breathing marks
ἀνα	ἀν᾽	ἀν᾽
ἀντι	ἀντ᾽	ἀνθ᾽
ἀπο	ἀπ᾽	ἀφ᾽
δια	δι᾽	δι᾽
ἐκ	ἐκ	ἐξ
ἐπι	ἐπ᾽	ἐφ᾽
κατα	κατ᾽	καθ᾽
μετα	μετ᾽	μεθ᾽
ὑπο	ὑπ᾽	ὑφ᾽

Prepositions govern nouns in any of three cases forms: genitive, dative, or accusative. Although some prepositions govern a single case form, others govern two or three case forms. Because the meaning of a preposition is related to the case form of its object, *both* the preposition *and* the case form(s) with which it is used must be learned as a part of vocabulary building.

1 Case		
with Genitive only ἀντι ἐκ ἀπο προ	with Dative only ἐν συν	with Accusative only ἀνα εἰς

2 Cases	
with Genitive and Accusative δια κατα μετα περι ὑπερ ὑπο	with Dative and Accusative προς

3 Cases
with Genitive, Dative, and Accusative ἐπι   παρα

Some prepositions denote spatial relationships when used with certain case forms. In this respect, case forms may be thought of as follows.

Genitive   =   movement away from
Dative   =   position or location
Accusative   =   movement toward

The most common spatial relationships are

ἀπο	+	genitive	=	"away from"	
δια	+	genitive	=	"through"	
ἐκ	+	genitive	=	"out of"	
ἐν	+	dative	=	"in"	
ἐπι	+	dative	=	"upon"	
παρα	+	dative	=	"beside"	(position)
εἰς	+	accusative	=	"into"	
παρα	+	accusative	=	"along"	(movement)
περι	+	accusative	=	"around"	(movement)
προς	+	accusative	=	"toward"	
ὑπερ	+	accusative	=	"above"	
ὑπο	+	accusative	=	"below"	

Prepositional phrases may be used in any of three ways: adverbially, adjectivally, and substantivally. Most prepositional phrases function **adverbially** to modify a verb's action.

John 1:5   και το φως ἐν τῃ σκοτιᾳ φαινει

And the light is shining in the darkness.

("In the darkness" clarifies *where* the light is shining.)

Occasionally, a prepositional phrase may be used **adjectivally** to modify a noun. When it does so, it will be preceded by a definite article which agrees with a noun in gender, case, and number.

Phil 3:9   μη ἐχων ἐμην δικαιοσυνην την ἐκ νομου ...

Not having my own righteousness which is out of law ...

("Out of law" clarifies *what kind of* righteousness, a righteousness which has its source in the law.)

Only when a prepositional phrase is preceded by a definite article and no noun is being modified, can it function **substantivally**.

Phil 1:12   τα κατ᾽ ἐμε εἰς προκοπην του εὐαγγελιου ἐληλυθεν

My circumstances have turned out for the progress of the gospel.

("My circumstances" — literally, "the things according to me" — functions as the subject of the clause.)

5.5 Vocabulary

Co-ordinate Conjunctions

81. ἀλλά	but	(638)
82. δέ	and, but, now [postpositive]	(2792)
83. ἤ	or	(343)
84. καί	and, also, even	(9153)
85. οὐδέ, οὐτέ	and not, nor, not even	(230)
86. οὖν	therefore, then [postpositive]	(499)

Sub-ordinate Conjunctions

87. γάρ	for [postpositive]	(1041)
88. εἰ	if	(503)
89. ἵνα	in order that, so that, that	(663)
90. ὅτε	when	(103)
91. ὅτι	because, that	(1296)

Prepositions

92. ἀντί	+ gen.	instead of, in place of, because of	(22)
93. ἀπό	+ gen.	from, away from, by means of, of	(646)
94. διά	+ gen.	through, by means of (diameter)	(667)
	+ acc.	because of, on account of	
95. εἰς	+ acc.	into, in, to	(1768)
96. ἐκ	+ gen.	out of, from, by means of, by reason of	(914)
97. ἐν	+ dat.	in, with, among, by means of	(2752)
98. παρά	+ gen.	from	(194)
	+ dat.	with, in the presence of	
	+ acc.	beside, by (parallel)	
99. περί	+ gen.	about, concerning, with reference to	(333)
	+ acc.	around (perimeter)	
100. πρός	+ dat.	at, on, near	(700)
	+ acc.	to, toward, with, for the purpose of	

5.6 Form Identification - In the passage below (John 1:1-8) circle all conjunctions and label them as coordinate conjunctions (CC) or subordinate conjunctions (SC). Draw a box around each prepositional phrase; label the preposition (PR) which introduces it and the case of its object.

1.1 Ἐν ἀρχῇ ἦν ὁ λόγος, καὶ ὁ λόγος ἦν πρὸς τὸν θεόν, καὶ θεὸς ἦν ὁ λόγος. 1.2 οὗτος ἦν ἐν ἀρχῇ πρὸς τὸν θεόν. 1.3 πάντα δι᾽ αὐτοῦ ἐγένετο, καὶ χωρὶς αὐτοῦ ἐγένετο οὐδὲ ἕν. ὃ γέγονεν 1.4 ἐν αὐτῷ ζωὴ ἦν, καὶ ἡ ζωὴ ἦν τὸ φῶς τῶν ἀνθρώπων· 1.5 καὶ τὸ φῶς ἐν τῇ σκοτίᾳ φαίνει, καὶ ἡ σκοτία αὐτὸ οὐ κατέλαβεν. 1.6 Ἐγένετο ἄνθρωπος ἀπεσταλμένος παρὰ θεοῦ, ὄνομα αὐτῷ Ἰωάννης· 1.7 οὗτος ἦλθεν εἰς μαρτυρίαν, ἵνα μαρτυρήσῃ περὶ τοῦ φωτός, ἵνα πάντες πιστεύσωσιν δι᾽ αὐτοῦ. 1.8 οὐκ ἦν ἐκεῖνος τὸ φῶς,

ἀλλ᾽ ἵνα μαρτυρήσῃ περὶ τοῦ φωτός.

5.7 Practice Exercises - Translate the following sentences. Parse all verbs (TVMPN - Dictionary form).

1. καὶ κραζουσιν ἀπο του φοβου.
AND they are ~ from fear

2. ἐγω γαρ ἐκ του θεου ἐρχομαι.
for out of God I am coming

3. ἐστιν γαρ ἐν ἐξουσιᾳ ὁ λογος αὐτου (his).
for in authority word For his word is with authority

4. τί (why) δια παραβολων λεγεις τοις (ὀχλοις);
through parable crowds

5. οὐδε γαρ οἱ (ἀδελφοι) Ἰησου πιστευουσιν εἰς αὐτον (him).
For not even the brothers of Jesus a believing in him.

6. ἡ ἁμαρτια οὐκ ἐστιν ἐκ θεου ἀλλ᾽ ἐκ του (κοσμου) ἐστιν.
The sin is not out of God but it is of the world.

7. το (σημειον) οὐκ προς θανατον ἐστιν ἀλλ᾽ προς την δοξαν του θεου.
at

8. ἀλλα λεγω ὁτι βλεπετε και οὐ πιστευετε.
but

9. κυριος γαρ ἐστιν του σαββατου ὁ υἱος του ἀνθρωπου.
lord for For the Son of man is Lord of the sabbath

10. ἐστιν ἡ ἐξουσια Ἰωαννου (John) ἐξ (οὐρανου) ἠ ἐξ ἀνθρωπων;
authority heaven

11. ἐγω δε οὐ παρ᾽ ἀνθρωπου την μαρτυριαν λαμβανω, ἀλλα λεγω ἱνα γινωσκετε την ἀληθειαν.

12. ἀλλ᾽ οὐδε ἀκουετε οὐδε πιστευετε, ὁτι οὐκ ἐστε ἐκ θεου.

13. τί (why) οὐν βαπτιζεις, εἰ οὐκ εἰ ὁ χριστος οὐδε Ἡλιας (Elijah) οὐδε ὁ προφητης;

14. λεγει οὐν ὁ Ἰησους προς τον ἀνθρωπον, εἰ σημειον οὐ βλεπεις πιστευσεις;

15. γραφω δε ἱνα πιστευσεις ὁτι Ἰησους ἐστιν ὁ χριστος ὁ υἱος του θεου.

16. ὅτε δε ἀκουει περι των ἐργων του Χριστου, Ἰωαννης ἀποστελλει ἀγγελους προς Ἰησουν.

17. ἡ ὥρα ἐστιν ὅτε ἀνθρωποι ἀκουσουσιν της φωνης του υἱου του θεου και πιστευσουσιν.

18. παρ' ἀνθρωποις ἐστιν ἀδυνατον (impossible) ἀλλ' οὐ παρα θεω, ὅτι οὐδεν (nothing) ἀδυνατον παρα θεω ἐσται.

19. Παυλος ἀποστολος οὐκ ἀπ' ἀνθρωπων οὐδε δι' ἀνθρωπου ἀλλα δια Ἰησου Χριστου και θεου.

20. Ἰησους δε λεγει τω ἀνθρωπω, πιστευσεις εἰς τον υἱον του ἀνθρωπου; και ὁ ἀνθρωπος λεγει, και τίς (who) ἐστιν, ἱνα πιστευσω εἰς αὐτον (him);

5.8 Translation

The best way to learn to translate is to work with sentences in their context. With the forms and vocabulary in this chapter you have met enough basic grammar to begin translation work directly from the Greek New Testament. Of course, you have not yet learned all of the forms which you will encounter in the text. For that reason, translation helps are provided in Appendix F.

Since the simplest Greek in the New Testament occurs in John's Gospel, that book is the logical place to begin. It will not be enough, however, to translate only from John's Gospel. The helps, therefore, are provided using a graded approach. First, John 1:1-34 will give you exposure to simple grammar and syntax. Next, Mark 8:11-9:1, will give you practice in a more complex portion of the New Testament. Finally, 1 Thessalonians 1–2 will help you become familiar with Paul's style.

Be certain to parse every verb which you encounter (Tense, Voice, Mood, Person, Number, Dictionary form). If the verb has already been parsed for you in the helps, it would be wise to include it in your list anyway so that you become accustomed to listing and parsing every verb in a given text.

Remember that Greek uses inflection to indicate such items as the subject and the direct object. It is not always possible simply to translate word for word. You might need to analyze the pieces of a sentence before you can translate it into "normal" English. It is wise to get into the habit of following a regular procedure for translating passages in the New Testament:

1. Use punctuation (period, raised dot, question mark) to identify the extent of the sentence. A sentence is often longer than one verse of Scripture.
2. Identify any subordinate conjunctions; they always mark the beginning of subordinate clauses. Isolate any subordinate clauses within the sentence.
3. Construct a translation of the main clause by (a) identifying, parsing, and translating the main verb(s), (b) identifying any expressed subject (noun in the nominative), (c) identifying any direct object (noun in accusative), (d) arranging these items in "standard" English word order (subject–verb–object).
4. Construct a translation of any subordinate clauses within the sentence by following the same process as in step 3.

Here is a suggested plan for correlating a graded approach to translation with the chapters of this book.

Chapter 5	John 1:1-5
Chapter 6	John 1:6-13
Chapter 7	John 1:14-18
Chapter 8	John 1:19-23
Chapter 9	John 1:24-28
Chapter 10	John 1:29-34
Chapter 11	Mark 8:11-13
Chapter 12	Mark 8:14-17
Chapter 13	Mark 8:18-21
Chapter 14	Mark 8:22-26
Chapter 15	Mark 8:27-30
Chapter 21	Mark 8:31-33
Chapter 22	Mark 8:34-37
Chapter 23	Mark 8:38-9:1
Chapter 24	1 Thessalonians 1:1-5
Chapter 25	1 Thessalonians 1:6-13
Chapter 26	1 Thessalonians 2:1-4
Chapter 27	1 Thessalonians 2:5-8
Chapter 28	1 Thessalonians 2:9-12
Chapter 29	1 Thessalonians 2:13-16
Chapter 30	1 Thessalonians 2:17-20

GRAMMAR GRABBER: *Pronouns*

᾿Εν ἀρχῇ ἦν ὁ λόγος, καὶ ὁ λόγος ἦν πρὸς τὸν θεόν,
καὶ θεὸς ἦν ὁ λόγος. οὗτος ἦν ἐν ἀρχῇ πρὸς τὸν
θεόν. πάντα δι᾿ αὐτοῦ ἐγένετο, καὶ χωρὶς αὐτοῦ
ἐγένετο οὐδὲ ἓν ὃ γέγονεν. ἐν αὐτῷ ζωὴ ἦν, καὶ ἡ
ζωὴ ἦν τὸ φῶς τῶν ἀνθρώπων.

In the beginning was the Word, and the Word was with God, and
the Word was God. <u>This one</u> was in the beginning with God. All
things were made through <u>him,</u> and apart from <u>him</u> not one thing
came into being which came into being. In <u>him</u> was life, and the life
was the light of men. (Taking γέγονεν with the preceding clause)

Pronouns—words which can stand for nouns (their referents and
antecedents)—allow authors to write in a pleasing style which avoids
constant repetition. Listen to the result if these verses did not use pronouns:

In the beginning was the Word, and the Word was with God, and
the Word was God. <u>The Word</u> was in the beginning with God. All
things were made through <u>the Word,</u> and apart from <u>the Word</u> not
one thing came into being which came into being. In <u>the Word</u> was
life, and the life was the light of men.

Without redundancy yet still with a focus back to the "Word" (the
antecedent), John uses pronouns to move his thought along. A near
demonstrative pronoun, οὗτος, ("this one") introduces the thought that
the Word was in the beginning with God. A simple third person personal
pronoun, αὐτος, serves as the object of three prepositions ("through him
. . . apart from him . . . in him"). Pronouns keep pointing us back to the one
who is the Word and is God in a pleasing, yet focused, way which the
constant repetition of the noun itself could never do.

Chapter 6

PERSONAL PRONOUNS

Closely related to nouns are pronouns. Both English and Greek use a wide variety of pronouns. After a basic introduction to the various kinds of pronouns, the most frequently used type of Greek pronoun—the personal pronoun—will be discussed.

6.1 Introduction to Pronouns

Pronouns are words which take the place of nouns (e.g., The <u>boy</u> hit the ball. ➔ <u>He</u> hit the ball.). A pronoun's **antecedent** is the noun which the pronoun replaces and to which it refers (e.g., This is <u>Jill.</u> <u>She</u> is visiting from England.). Pronouns substitute for nouns in order to reduce repetition. They may be used in the same ways nouns are.

1. Subject (e.g., <u>He</u> hit the ball.)
2. Complement
   a. Direct Object (e.g., The boy hit <u>it</u>.)
   b. Indirect Object (e.g., The boy hit the ball to <u>her</u>.)
   c. Predicate Nominative (e.g., It is <u>he</u>.)
3. Object of Preposition (e.g., The boy hit the ball with <u>it</u>.)
4. Direct Address (e.g., <u>You</u> there, hit the ball!)
5. Possession (e.g., The boy hit <u>her</u> ball.)

Pronouns may be grouped under seven classifications:

1. A *personal pronoun* designates one or more particular person or thing.

First person	I, my, me, we, our, us
Second person	You, your
Third person	He, his, him, she, her, it, its, they, their, them

2. An *intensive pronoun* is placed in apposition to its antecedent for emphasis. (e.g., The general <u>himself</u> is to blame.)

   Note: Do not confuse intensive pronouns with reflexive pronouns (see below).

3. A *demonstrative pronoun* points out a particular person or thing.

Near	This, these
Far	That, those

4. An *interrogative pronoun* asks a question.
   Who, whose, whom, which, what . . . ?
5. An *indefinite pronoun* refers to no particular person or thing.
   Anyone, anybody, anything
   Someone, somebody, something
   No one, nobody, nothing
   Everyone, everybody, everything
6. A *relative pronoun* relates the clause in which it occurs (called a relative clause) to a noun or pronoun in another clause. (e.g., He is the one <u>who</u> hit the ball.)

Definite	Who, whose, whom	(personal)
	Which	(impersonal)
Qualitative/Generic	Whoever, whomever	(personal)
	Whichever	(impersonal)

7. A *reflexive pronoun* refers the action back to the subject.

First person	Myself, ourselves
Second person	Yourself, yourselves
Third person	Himself, herself, itself, themselves

8. A *reciprocal pronoun* denotes the interchange of action among more than one subject. (e.g., See how they love <u>one another</u>.)

6. 2 Greek Personal Pronouns

Since Greek pronouns substitute for Greek nouns, it is not surprising that they mirror the characteristics of nouns. Every pronoun has gender, case, and number and inflects accordingly. Most endings—except those of the first and second person personal pronouns, the interrogative pronoun, and the indefinite pronoun—are virtually identical to those of first and second declension nouns (and the various forms of the definite article). The basic pattern of endings is set out below.

		Masculine	Feminine	Neuter
Sing.	Nom.	-ος	-η	-ο
	Gen.	-ου	-ης	-ου
	Dat.	-ῳ	-η	-ῳ
	Acc.	-ον	-ην	-ο
Pl.	Nom.	-οι	-αι	-α
	Gen.	-ων	-ων	-ων
	Dat.	-οις	-αις	-οις
	Acc.	-ους	-ας	-α

Personal pronouns designate one or more particular person, place, or thing. There are distinct forms for first person (speaker), second person (person spoken to), and third person (person, place, or thing spoken about). Although all three forms inflect to indicate case and number, only the third person personal pronoun has distinct forms for the different genders. The charts below give the full paradigm for each person, including a basic translation.

The first person personal pronoun has two forms in the genitive, dative, and accusative singular. The form with ε prefixed is a slightly more emphatic form: the form without the ε is the more common form. Pay close attention to the similarity between the plural forms of the first person and second person pronouns; it sometimes leads to confusion.

First Person "MY"		Pronoun	Translation
Sing.	Nom.	ἐγω	I
	Gen.	ἐμου, μου	my, mine (of me)
	Dat.	ἐμοι, μοι	to/for me
	Acc.	ἐμε, με	me
Pl.	Nom.	ἡμεις	we
	Gen.	ἡμων	our (of us)
	Dat.	ἡμιν	to/for us
	Acc.	ἡμας	us

Second Person "you"		Pronoun	Translation
Sing.	Nom.	συ	you
	Gen.	σου	your (of you)
	Dat.	σοι	to/for you
	Acc.	σε	you
Pl.	Nom.	ὑμεις	you
	Gen.	ὑμων	your (of you)
	Dat.	ὑμιν	to/for you
	Acc.	ὑμας	you

54 GREEK IS GOOD GRIEF

Third Person		Masculine	Feminine	Neuter
Sing.	Nom.	αὐτ ος	αὐτ η	αὐτ ο
	Gen.	αὐτ ου	αὐτ ης	αὐτ ου
	Dat.	αὐτ ῳ	αὐτ η	αὐτ ῳ
	Acc.	αὐτ ον	αὐτ ην	αὐτ ο
Pl.	Nom.	αὐτ οι	αὐτ αι	αὐτ α
	Gen.	αὐτ ων	αὐτ ων	αὐτ ων
	Dat.	αὐτ οις	αὐτ αις	αὐτ οις
	Acc.	αὐτ ους	αὐτ ας	αὐτ α

6.3 Use of the Personal Pronouns

First person personal pronouns are used to refer to the speaker(s). There is no special exegetical significance to the use of the genitive, dative, or accusative cases beyond their normal meaning. Since, however, Greek verbs have a subject implicit within them, the presence of the nominative first person personal pronoun adds emphasis to the identity of the speaker. The most striking example of this use is in Jesus' "I am" statements.

> ἐγώ εἰμι ὁ ἄρτος τῆς ζωῆς
> I [and no other!] am the bread of life.

Second person personal pronouns are used to refer to the person(s) spoken to. There is no special exegetical significance to the use of the genitive, dative, or accusative cases beyond their normal meaning. Since, however, Greek verbs have a subject implicit within them, the presence of the nominative second person personal pronoun adds emphasis to the person(s) addressed.

> ὑμεῖς ἐστε τὸ ἄλας τῆς γῆς
> You [yes, you disciples!] are the salt of the earth.

Third person personal pronouns are used to refer to the person(s), place(s), or thing(s) spoken about. Since they can be used in any of four ways, it will be necessary to discuss each use separately.

1. The **independent** use is the most common. In this particular construction the pronoun *stands alone with no article or noun* and is translated (with appropriate regard to the case form) as "he," "she," or "it."

> αὐτος λεγει
> *He* is speaking.

2. In the **attributive** use, the pronoun functions as an identifying adjective and is translated as "same." In this particular construction the third

person personal pronoun *follows a definite article,* either preceding or following a noun with which it agrees in gender, case, and number.

ὁ αὐτος ἀνθρωπος λεγει

or ὁ ἀνθρωπος ὁ αὐτος λεγει

The *same* man is speaking.

3. In the **intensive** use (sometimes called the "predicate" use), the pronoun functions to give emphasis to a noun and is translated using a compound with "-self" (e.g., himself, herself, itself). In this particular construction the third person personal pronoun precedes or follows a noun with which it agrees in gender, case, and number *but does not, itself follow a definite article.*

αὐτος ὁ ἀνθρωπος λεγει

or ὁ ἀνθρωπος αὐτος λεγει

The man *himself* is speaking.

4. In the **substantival** use, the pronoun functions as a noun and is translated as "the same (one)." In this particular construction the third person personal pronoun *follows a definite article with no noun present.*

ὁ αὐτος λεγει

The *same one* is speaking.

6.4 Vocabulary

Personal Pronouns

101.	αὐτός, -η, -ο	he, she, it, self, same (auto-)	(5595)
102.	σύ	you	(2905)

Verbs

103.	αἴρω	I am taking, taking up, taking away	(101)
104.	ἀναβαίνω	I going up, ascending	(82)
105.	καταβαίνω	I am coming down, descending	(81)
106.	εὑρίσκω	I am finding (eureka!)	(176)
107.	θέλω	I am wishing [followed by infinitive]	(208)
108.	μένω	I am staying, abiding	(118)
109.	οἶδα	I am knowing	(318)
110.	ὁράω	I am seeing	(454)
111.	ἀκολουθέω	I am following [dative direct object]	(90)
112.	ζητέω	I am seeking	(117)
113.	λαλέω	I am speaking	(296)

114.	περιπατέω	I am walking	(95)
115.	σκηνόω	I am living, dwelling (in a tent)	(5)
116.	φανερόω	I am making manifest	(49)
117.	ἀποκρίνομαι	I am answering [dative direct object]	(231)
118.	ἀρνέομαι	I am denying	(33)
119.	δύναμαι	I can, am able [followed by infinitive]	(210)
120.	θεάομαι	I am beholding	(22)

6.5 Form Identification - For each form below give the person (1, 2, or 3), gender (for third person pronouns), case, number, dictionary form, and a translation. One example is given.

ἐγω   1-xNS   ἐγω   I

3 M D Pl for him
1. αὐτοις
1 N P F me
2. ἡμεις
2 G S you
3. σου *your*
2 G P You your's
4. ὑμων
3 N S N it
5. αὐτο
3 M G Pl. for, your
6. αὐτων
1 Ac. S, I, Me,
7. με
1 Ac. Pl. We, us
8. ἡμας
3 F N S she
9. αὐτη
1 D S I, for me
10. μοι
2 Ac. S you
11. σε
3 F P N, she
12. αὐται
2 P D for you
13. ὑμιν

14. αὐτοι
15. αὐτην
16. αὐτα
17. αὐτος
18. αὐταις
19. αὐτη
20. μου
21. σοι
22. ἡμιν
23. σε
24. ἡμων
25. αὐτον

6.6 Practice Exercises - Translate the following sentences. Parse all verbs (TVMPN - Dictionary form).

1. τα αὐτα γραφει ὑμιν.   *it writing to you*

2. αὐτος Δαυιδ λεγει ἡμιν περι αὐτου.   *for us*
he David   about   of him

3. *Im ascending in he him heaven*
ἀναβαινει εἰς αὐτον τον οὐρανον.

4. *it the witness about my*
αὐτα τα ἐργα μαρτυρει περι μου.

5. *r not he of her*
και αὐτος ὁ θεος μετ' (with) αὐτων ἐσται.

6. *he for in to man it is*
αὐτος γαρ γινωσκει τί (what) ἐν τω ἀνθρωπω ἐστιν.

7. *the voice of it heavens*
και αἰρουσιν τας φωνας αὐτων εἰς τους οὐρανους.

8. *you you speak because sin your*
ὑμεις λεγετε ὁτι βλεπομεν· ἡ οὐν ἁμαρτια ὑμων μενει.

9. οἱ οὐν ὀχλοι λεγουσιν, οἱ θεοι καταβαινουσιν προς ἡμας.

10. οἰδα αὐτον ὁτι παρ' αὐτου εἰμι και με ἀποστελλει.

11. και ὁτε εὑρισκουσιν αὐτον λεγουσιν αὐτῳ, οἱ ὀχλοι ζητουσιν σε.

12. και διαιρεσεις (varieties) διακονιων (ministries) εἰσιν, ἀλλ' ὁ αὐτος κυριος.

13. εὑρισκει δε τον ἀδελφον αὐτου και λεγει αὐτῳ, εὑρισκομεν τον Μεσσιαν.

14. οὐκ γραφω ὑμιν ὁτι οὐκ οἰδατε την ἀληθειαν ἀλλ' ὁτι οἰδατε αὐτην.

15. και οὐκετι (no longer) εἰμι ἐν τω κοσμῳ ἀλλ' αὐτοι ἐν κοσμῳ εἰσιν κἀγω προς σε ἐρχομαι.

16. αὐτοι ἐκ του κοσμου εἰσιν, δια τουτο (this) ἐκ του κοσμου λαλουσιν και ὁ κοσμος αὐτων ἀκουει.

17. οὐκετι (no longer) δια τον λογον σου πιστευομεν, αὐτοι γαρ ἀκουομεν και οἰδαμεν ὁτι αὐτος ἐστιν ὁ υἱος του θεου.

18. ἀμην ἀμην λεγω σοι, ὁτι ὃ (what) οἰδαμεν λαλουμεν και ὃ (what) ὁραμεν μαρτυρουμεν και την μαρτυριαν ἡμων οὐ λαμβανετε.

GRAMMAR GRABBER: Imperfect and Aorist Tense

By using various tenses a New Testament writer can indicate not only that an action took place in past time but that it was of a progressive or summary kind. John uses this latter property of Greek verbs (called "aspect") to good effect at the beginning of his Gospel. He consistently employs the imperfect tense (progressive action) to describe Jesus as the eternal Son in eternity:

᾿Εν ἀρχῇ ἦν ὁ λόγος, καὶ ὁ λόγος ἦν πρὸς τὸν θεόν, καὶ θεὸς ἦν ὁ λόγος. οὗτος ἦν ἐν ἀρχῇ πρὸς τὸν θεόν. (John 1:1-2)

In the beginning the Word was existing, and the Word was existing with God, and the Word was being God. This one was existing in the beginning with God.

Yet when John describes certain particular events—such as the incarnation—he uses the aorist tense (summary action) to describe those events:

Καὶ ὁ λόγος σὰρξ ἐγένετο καὶ ἐσκήνωσεν ἐν ἡμῖν, καὶ ἐθεασάμεθα τὴν δόξαν αὐτοῦ. (John 1:14)

And the Word became flesh and dwelt among us, and we beheld His glory.

In this way, John helps us grasp the wonder of the Eternal Son taking to himself, in space and time, human flesh and "tabernacling" among us. John also reminds us that we were able, as a particular event, both to observe Him and to see His divine glory.

Chapter 7

IMPERFECT AND AORIST ACTIVE INDICATIVE

Chapter 3 introduced the Present and Future Active Indicative. After a brief review of the Indicative Mood, this chapter will present two of the "past" tenses—Imperfect Active Indicative and Aorist Active Indicative.

7.1 The Indicative Mood

The indicative mood is the mood most frequently encountered in Greek, and so, it is learned first. The indicative mood is the *only* mood in which *time* of action is made explicit by the tense of a verb. In all other moods, *kind* of action is the factor indicated by tense. Verbs in the indicative mood may occur in any of the six tenses. The chart below shows the way in which those tenses relate to kind and time of action.

		Time of Action		
		✱ Past	Present	Future
Kind of Action	Progressive	**Imperfect** "I was writing"	Present	(Secondary use of future)
	Simple Summary indefinite	**Aorist** "I wrote"	(Secondary use of present)	Future
	Completed-Stative	Pluperfect	Perfect	(Future Perfect)

7.2 Temporal Augment

In the indicative mood each of the past time tenses (imperfect, aorist, and pluperfect) adds the prefix ε to the stem of the verb. When a verb begins with a vowel or a diphthong, the addition of an augment results in "contraction." These vowel/diphthong contractions follow regular patterns.

Augment	Initial Vowel/ Diphthong	Resulting Contraction
ε	α	η
ε	αι	ῃ
ε	ε	η
ε	ει	ῃ
ε	ο	ω
ε	οι	ῳ

7.3 Secondary Active Endings

As noted in Chapter 3, the present, future, and perfect tenses are the "primary" tenses. This designation has nothing to do with frequency of occurrence or with importance. Rather, it groups together those tenses which, in the indicative mood, are oriented to present or future time.

In contrast, the imperfect, aorist, and pluperfect tenses are the "secondary" tenses. This designation groups together those tenses which, in the indicative mood, are oriented to past time. The same active endings are used for all three tenses. These secondary active endings are set out in the following chart.

		Secondary Active Endings
Singular	1st	ν (–)
	2nd	ς
	3rd	–
Plural	1st	μεν
	2nd	τε
	3rd	ν (σαν)

In the first person singular and the third person plural, two different endings appear. The specifics of this phenomenon will become clear as the various paradigms are introduced. At this point it is sufficient to note two rules:

1. The – ending in the first person singular occurs *only in the first/weak aorist tense* (see the discussion below). All other secondary active tenses use the ν ending.
2. The σαν ending in the third person plural—with a few exceptions— occurs *only in the pluperfect tense* (see the discussion below). All other secondary active tenses use the ν ending.

7.4 Imperfect Active Indicative

The imperfect tense is used only to connote *progressive* action in *past* time. In order to reflect the incomplete action of the imperfect tense, we will translate the imperfect active indicative using the progressive past. The first person singular of the verb "to see" would thus be translated as "I was seeing." The form of the imperfect active indicative may be summarized by the following formula:

Augment + Stem + Theme Vowel + Secondary Active Endings
(A   + ST +   V   +   SAE   )

▸   Augment: The vowel ε is attached as a prefix to the verb stem in order to indicate past time.
▸   Stem: The imperfect tense stem of a verb is found by removing the final ω of the dictionary form.
▸   Theme Vowel: For the imperfect active indicative the theme vowels follow the pattern *o-e-e-o-e-o*.

Singular	1st	o	Plural	1st	o
	2nd	ε		2nd	ε
	3rd	ε		3rd	o

▸   Personal Endings: The imperfect active indicative uses the secondary active endings discussed above.

The paradigm of the imperfect active indicative of the verb λυω follows.

✳		λυω (λυ-)				Translation
Sing.	1st	ἐ	λυ	o	ν	I was loosing.
	2nd	ἐ	λυ	ε	ς	You were loosing.
	3rd	ἐ	λυ	ε	– (ν)	He/she/it was loosing.
Pl.	1st	ἐ	λυ	o	μεν	We were loosing.
	2nd	ἐ	λυ	ε	τε	You were loosing.
	3rd	ἐ	λυ	o	ν	They were loosing.

past time indicators

7.5 Imperfect of the Verb εἰμι

The present and future tenses of the verb εἰμι were introduced in Chapter 3. The imperfect tense may now be introduced. Because it was used so frequently, εἰμι resisted standardization as the Greek language developed. The paradigm, therefore, differs slightly from the normal pattern and must be memorized.

		εἰμι	Translation
Sing.	1st	ἤμην	I was
	2nd	ἤς	You were
	3rd	ἤν	He/she/it was
Pl.	1st	ἤμεν	We were
	2nd	ἤτε	You were
	3rd	ἤσαν	They were

7.6 Aorist Active Indicative

The aorist ("air-ist") tense is used to connote *summary* action in *past* time. In contrast to the imperfect, the aorist says nothing about the duration of the action; it simply states that the action happens. In order to reflect the simple action of the aorist tense, we will translate the aorist active indicative using the simple past. The first person singular of the verb "to see" would thus be translated as "I saw."

The form of a verb in the aorist tense will follow one of two patterns. Some verbs follow the "first" or "weak" aorist form. Other verbs follow the "second" or "strong" aorist form. These two forms will be set out in detail below. It is essential to note, however, that a verb follows *either* the first aorist *or* the second aorist pattern. They do *not* change back and forth, nor do they (with a few exceptions to be learned much later) have *both* a first *and* a second aorist form.

7.7 Weak/First Aorist Active Indicative

Certain less frequently used verbs yielded to standardization as the Greek language developed. These verbs are said to follow the "weak" (or "first") aorist pattern. Verbs with a weak/first aorist form may be considered "regular" in that they retain the same stem as is found in the present tense.

The form of the weak/first aorist active indicative may be summarized by the following formula:

Augment + Stem + Tense Sign + Theme Vowel + Secondary Active Endings
(A   + ST +   S   +   V   +   SAE   )

▸ Augment: The vowel ε is attached as a prefix to the verb stem in order to indicate past time.

▸ Stem: The aorist tense stem of a verb with a weak/first aorist form is found by removing the final ω of the dictionary form.

▸ Tense Sign: The weak/first aorist form adds a σ after the stem and before the theme vowel. This fact means that when a verb stem ends in a consonant, the identical consonant contraction occurs as was seen in the future tense.

▸ Theme Vowel: The weak/first aorist active indicative form has α as its theme vowel except in the third person singular, where it uses an ε.

	Singular			Plural	
Singular	1st	α	Plural	1st	α
	2nd	α		2nd	α
	3rd	ε		3rd	α

▸ Personal Endings: The weak/first aorist active indicative uses the secondary active endings discussed above, including the - ending in the first person singular.

The verb λυω has a weak/first aorist form. The complete paradigm follows.

1st/regular

		λυω (λυ-)					Translation
Sing.	1st	ἐ	λυ	σ	α	–	I loosed.
	2nd	ἐ	λυ	σ	α	ς	You loosed.
	3rd	ἐ	λυ	σ	ε	– (v)	He/she/it loosed.
Pl.	1st	ἐ	λυ	σ	α	μεν	We loosed.
	2nd	ἐ	λυ	σ	α	τε	You loosed.
	3rd	ἐ	λυ	σ	α	ν	They loosed.

7.8 Strong/Second Aorist Active Indicative

The most frequently used verbs resisted standardization as the Greek language developed. These verbs are said to follow the "strong" (or "second") aorist pattern. Verbs with a strong/second aorist form may be considered "irregular" in that the stem in the aorist tense differs from that in the present tense. *This strong/second aorist stem must be memorized as a part of vocabulary building,* for there is no way to predict with certainty what form it will take.

The form of the strong/second aorist active indicative may be summarized by the following formula:

Augment + Changed Stem + Theme Vowel + Secondary Active Endings

(A   +   ST*   +   V   +   SAE   )

▸ Augment: The vowel ε is attached as a prefix to the verb stem in order to indicate past time.

▸ Changed Stem: The strong/second aorist tense stem of a verb must be memorized.

▸ Theme Vowel: For the strong/second aorist active indicative the theme vowels follow the pattern *o-e-e-o-e-o*.

	Singular	1st	O		Plural	1st	O
		2nd	ε			2nd	ε
		3rd	ε			3rd	O

▸ Personal Endings: The strong/second aorist active indicative uses the secondary active endings discussed above.

The verb βαλλω has a strong/second aorist form. The complete paradigm follows.

2nd/Irregular *

		βαλλω (βαλ-)				Translation
Sing.	1st	ἐ	βαλ	ο	ν	I threw.
	2nd	ἐ	βαλ	ε	ς	You threw.
	3rd	ἐ	βαλ	ε	– (ν)	He/she/it threw.
Pl.	1st	ἐ	βαλ	ο	μεν	We threw.
	2nd	ἐ	βαλ	ε	τε	You threw.
	3rd	ἐ	βαλ	ο	ν	They threw.

1. Notice that the strong/second aorist has no tense sign comparable to that which appears in the weak/first aorist. It can, therefore, be easy to confuse the strong/second aorist active indicative form of a verb with the imperfect.

2. **The key to identifying the strong/second aorist form is the changed stem.** Compare the imperfect and strong/second aorist active indicative forms of the verb βαλλω:

Imperfect

ἐ	βαλλ	ο	ν
ἐ	βαλλ	ε	ς
ἐ	βαλλ	ε	– (ν)
ἐ	βαλλ	ο	μεν
ἐ	βαλλ	ε	τε
ἐ	βαλλ	ο	ν

Aorist

ἐ	βαλ	ο	ν
ἐ	βαλ	ε	ς
ἐ	βαλ	ε	– (ν)
ἐ	βαλ	ο	μεν
ἐ	βαλ	ε	τε
ἐ	βαλ	ο	ν

Stem change

The *only* difference between the two forms consists in the presence of a double λ (βαλλ-) in the imperfect. This difference reflects the fact that the imperfect tense is built on the present tense stem. The aorist, however, is built on a changed stem.

Although the difference in the forms of βαλλω is minor, the change in the strong/second aorist form of other verbs can be extreme. Here are three examples using the first person singular:

Present	Imperfect	Aorist
ἄγω	ἦγον	ἤγαγον
λέγω	ἔλεγον	εἶπον
εὑρίσκω	εὑρίσκον	εὗρον

Each of these verbs reflects a different phenomenon. ἄγω uses "Attic reduplication" (a phenomenon from Classical Greek) to form its aorist tense. λέγω uses a completely different verb stem to form its aorist. εὑρίσκω uses a shortened stem to form its aorist. **Because the changed stem of a verb with a strong/second aorist form cannot be predicted, the strong/second aorist stem must be memorized as a part of vocabulary building.**

7.9 "Irregular" Verb Forms

The list below gives the present, future, and aorist tenses (active) of "irregular" verbs which you already know. To this point—although you have not met the -ομαι and -όμην endings—you should begin to memorize these basic forms as additional vocabulary.

First   Second   Third

	PAI1S	FAI1S	AAI1S
41.	ἄγω	ἄξω	ἤγαγον
46.	γινώσκω	γνώσομαι	ἔγνων
49.	λαμβάνω	λήμψομαι	ἔλαβον
58.	γίνομαι	γενήσομαι	ἐγενόμην
59.	ἔρχομαι	ἐλεύσομαι	ἦλθον
78.	λέγω	ἐρῶ	εἶπον
104/5.	βαίνω	βήσομαι	ἔβην
106.	εὑρίσκω	εὑρήσω	εὗρον
110.	ὁράω	ὄψομαι	εἶδον

7.10 Vocabulary

For most of the verbs in the list below three forms are provided. They are the Present Active Indicative First Person Singular (PAI1S), the Future Active Indicative First Person Singular (FAI1S), and the Aorist Active Indicative First Person Singular (AAI1S). When a verb is so listed, it is

"irregular," and you should learn all three forms so that you will recognize
them when you encounter them. These three forms are actually the first
three (of six) "principal parts," a concept to which you will be introduced
in Chapter 10.

ῥἈ\   ϜΚΙ *Verbs*   ΑΑΙ

121.	ἁμαρτάνω	I am sinning (hamartiology)	(43)
	ἁμαρτάνω, ἁμαρτήσω, ἥμαρτον		
122.	ἀνοίγω	I am opening	(77)
	ἀνοίγω, ἀνοίξω, ἥνοιξα		
123.	βάλλω	I am throwing (ballistic)	(122)
	βάλλω, βαλῶ, ἔβαλον		
124.	ἐσθίω	I am eating	(158)
	ἐσθίω, φάγομαι, ἔφαγον		
125.	ἔχω	I am having	(708)
	ἔχω, ἔξω, ἔσχον		
126.	λείπω	I am leaving	(6)
	λείπω, λείψω, ἔλιπον		
127.	μανθάνω	I am learning	(25)
	μανθάνω, μαθήσομαι, ἔμαθον		
128.	πάσχω	I am suffering	(42)
	πάσχω, πείσομαι, ἔπαθον		
✳ 129.	φέρω	I am bringing, bearing *carried*	(66)
	φέρω, οἴσω, ἤνεγκα		
130.	φεύγω	I am fleeing (fugitive)	(29)
	φεύγω, φεύξομαι, ἔφυγον		
131.	βοάω	I am shouting, crying out	(12)
132.	ἐρωτάω	I am asking, requesting	(63)
133.	καλέω	I am calling	(148)
	καλέω, καλέσω, ἐκάλεσα		
134.	ὁμολογέω	I am confessing, declaring	(26)
135.	φωνέω	I am calling	(43)

Subordinate Conjunctions

136.	καθώς	as, just as	(182)
137.	ὡς	as, like, about	(504)

Prepositions

138.	ἐπί	+ gen., dat., acc.	upon, on (epidermis)	(890)
139.	ὑπέρ	+ gen.	for	(150)
		+ acc.	above, over (hyper-)	
140.	ὑπό	+ gen.	by	(220)
		+ acc.	below, under (hypo-)	

7.11 Form Identification - For each form give the tense, voice, mood, person, number, dictionary form, and a translation. Abbreviations for Tense include **P**(resent), **F**(uture), **I**(mperfect), and **A**(orist). One example has been provided.

ἔλυσας   AAI2S   λυω   You loosed.

1. ἔλυον *[IAI1S] I was loosing*
2. ἔβαλλε *[IAI3S] it was throwing*
3. ἔβαλε *it threw AAI2S 3rd*
4. ἐπιστεύσαμεν *IA 1 Pl. we believed*
5. ἦλθεν *~~AI 1Pl we were the~~ ~~AI 3S they were~~ came*
6. εὕρετε *2AI 2Pl You found*
7. ἔβλεψα *1A 1S. I saw/I was seeing*
8. ἠκούομεν *IA 1Pl. we were hearing*
9. ἤγαγον *2AAI 3Pl they lead*
10. παρέλαβες *2AAI 2S you received*
11. ἔγνω *2AAI 3S he knew*
12. εἶχον *IAI 1S I had*
13. εἶπεν *2AAI 3S he said λεγω*

14. ἐπέμψαμεν *1A 1Pl me sent πεμπω*
15. εἴδετε *2A 2Pl. you'll saw οραω*
16. ἠκούσατε *1A 2Pl. you heard ακουω*
17. ἤνοιξα *IAI1S I opened*
18. ἤνεγκα *IA 1S - I carried*
19. κατελάβετε *2AI 2Pl you were coming down*
20. εἶδεν *I 3S I he knew/you saw*
21. κατέβαινε *he was coming down IAI 3S*
22. ἔλυε *he was loosing*
23. ἔγραψα *IA 1S I wrote/I was writing*
24. ἦγε *IAI 3S he was leading*
25. ἐλίπετε *2AI 2Pl You left λειπω*

7.12 Practice Exercises - Translate the following sentences. Parse all verbs (TVMPN - Dictionary form).

1. ἄνθρωπός τις (a certain) εἶχεν δυο (two) υἱούς. *A certain man was having two sons*

2. Χριστός ἅπαξ (once) περι ἁμαρτιων ἔπαθεν. *Christ suffered concerning sin once (for all)*

Now he was speaking ~~about the parables~~

3. ἔλεγεν δε παραβολην προς αὐτους. *to them in parable*

And then came a voice from heaven

4. ἦλθεν οὐν φωνη ἐκ του οὐρανου.

And ~~he was carried~~ me not carried them here?

5. εἶπεν δε, ἠνεγκατε μοι ὡδε (here) αὐτους;

And Mary was ~~hearing~~ to the word of the lord

6. και Μαρια (Mary) ἠκουεν τὸν λογον του κυριου.

And he saw two brothers and he called to them

7. και εἰδεν δυο (two) ἀδελφους και ἐκαλεσεν αὐτους.

For he knew what was in the man

8. αὐτος γαρ ἐγινωσκεν τί (what) ἦν ἐν τω ἀνθρωπω.

For John came ~~came~~ to you and you did not believe him

9. ἦλθεν γαρ Ἰωαννης (John) προς ὑμας και οὐκ ἐπιστευσατε αὐτω. *because we were*

we were sinning not under law but under grace?

10. ἡμαρτανομεν ὅτι ἡμεν οὐκ ὑπο νομον ἀλλ᾽ ὑπο χαριν (grace);

11. εἰ μη ἦλθον και ἐλαλησα αὐτοις, ἀμαρτιαν οὐκ εἰχοσαν.

And they believed in the word in which Jesus spoke

12. και ἐπιστευσαν τω λογω ὃν (which) εἶπεν ὁ Ἰησους.

13. ἡμεις ἠκουσαμεν ἐκ του νομου ὅτι ὁ χριστος μενει εἰς τον αἰωνα (age).

Because of this the world wasn't knowing

14. δια τουτο (this) ὁ κοσμος οὐκ ἐγινωσκε ἡμας, ὅτι οὐκ ἐγνω αὐτον. *because ~~they~~ it did not know him*

And when the Pharisees heard his parables

15. και ὁτε οἱ Φαρισαιοι (Pharisees) τας παραβολας αὐτου ἠκουσαν, ἐγνωσαν ὅτι περι αὐτων ἐλεγεν. *they knew he was speaking about them*

16. ἡμεις δε οὐ το πνευμα (spirit) του κοσμου ἐλαβομεν ἀλλα το πνευμα (spirit) του θεου.

17. ἃ (what) και ἐμαθετε και παρελαβετε και ἠκουσατε και εἰδετε ἐν ἐμοι, ἐν τουτων (these things) μενετε.

18. και ἀνθρωπος ἐκ του ὀχλου εἶπεν τω Ἰησου, ἠνεγκα τον υἱον μου προς σε.

19. και ὁ κοσμος σε οὐκ ἐγνω, ἐγω δε σε ἐγνων, και οὑτοι (these) ἐγνωσαν ὅτι συ με ἐπεμψας.

20. δια τουτου (this) του σημειου ὁ Ἰησους ἐφανερωσεν την δοξαν αὐτου και ἐπιστευσαν εἰς αὐτον οἱ μαθηται (disciples) αὐτου.

16. And we ʸ ourselves did not receive the spirit of the world but the spirit of God.

17. what you both learned + heard + received you are abiding in these things

18. And a man out of the crowd said to Jesus i brought my son to you

19. And the world did not know you ~~but~~ ~~and~~ i knew you + they ~~came together~~ knew that you sent me.

20. Through this sign Jesus made manifest ~~the~~ his glory of him and made ~~the~~ disciples believe in him.
HIS

gnosto / ωμεν
ἐγνων / ως / ωτε
      / ω / ωσιν

GRAMMAR GRABBER: *Third Declension Nouns in the Genitive Case*

οἳ οὐκ ἐξ αἱμάτων οὐδὲ ἐκ <u>θελήματος σαρκὸς</u> οὐδὲ ἐκ
<u>θελήματος ἀνδρὸς</u> ἀλλ᾽ ἐκ θεοῦ ἐγεννήθησαν.
(John 1:13)

. . . who were born not from bloods, nor from the flesh's will, nor
from a husband's will, but from God.

There is a whole set of Greek nouns which exhibit a stem change
between the nominative and genitive singular forms. Their case endings are
also different from what we learned so far. They are nouns of the third
declension with stems ending in a consonant. Learning the paradigm for
these nouns helps you make sense of John 1:13.

In this verse there are four phrases involving the preposition ἐκ and a
total of six nouns. At first glance, four of the nouns appear to be masculine
nominative singular (see the words underlined above). The natural question
would be "What are nouns in the nominative doing after a preposition
which normally takes the genitive?" These four nouns are actually genitives,
because the genitive singular ending in third declension nouns is -ος.

The four prepositional phrases, then, all indicate source: "not from blood
. . . nor from will . . . nor from will . . . but from God." In addition, the nouns
σαρκὸς and ἀνδρὸς are both subjective genitives and further specify the
subject of the action contained in the noun they modify. This combination
of nouns in the genitive makes the meaning of the verse crystal clear.

John is teaching us that those who have the right to be called sons of
God (v.12) are not "born" from any human cause. Regeneration, therefore,
is not of human origin. It is not a matter of natural descent ("from bloods"),
nor of sexual desire ("from the flesh's will"), nor of human decision ("from
a husband's will"). Being born to eternal life has no other source than "from
God!"

Chapter 8

THIRD DECLENSION NOUNS:
CONSONANT STEMS

The final category of Greek nouns is that of Third Declension Nouns. They include all three genders and have as their key characteristic the fact that all forms except the nominative singular are built on the genitive singular stem. For this reason, *both the nominative and genitive singular forms must be memorized as a part of vocabulary building*. Third declension nouns may be divided into two groups: (1) those which have a stem ending in a consonant and (2) those which have a stem ending in a vowel. The discussion below will focus on the first group.

8.1 Finding the Stem

The nominative singular form is the form under which every third declension noun will be listed in a dictionary and provides the basic lexical meaning of the word. In all three genders, however, it is the genitive singular form which is the key to understanding the pattern the noun follows. The genitive singular ending is -ος. When that ending is removed from the genitive singular form, what remains is the stem to which other endings are added. Here are three examples:

	Nom. Sing.	Gen. Sing.	Noun Stem
Masculine	ἀρχων	ἀρχοντος	ἀρχοντ-
Feminine	ἐλπις	ἐλπιδος	ἐλπιδ-
Neuter	γραμμα	γραμματος	γραμματ-

8.2 Endings

The basic ending patterns for masculine and feminine nouns are identical. Those for neuter nouns are slightly different. The chart below summarizes the basic ending patterns.

Two points should be noted about these endings: (1) The fact that the dative plural ending is -σι means that contraction will occur when the σ of the ending comes in contact with the final consonant of the stem, and (2) the fact that the form of the neuter accusative singular is identical to the form of the nominative singular, means that the final consonant will be omitted

there also. These points are readily seen when the full paradigms are
presented.

		Masculine/Feminine	Neuter
Sing.	Nom.	Must be memorized	--
	Gen.	ος	ος
	Dat.	ι	ι
	Acc.	α (ν)	--
Pl.	Nom.	ες	α
	Gen.	ων	ων
	Dat.	σι	σι
	Acc.	ας	α

8.3 Representative Paradigms

Masculine ✴		ἀρχων (ἀρχοντ-)	Translation
Sing.	Nom.	ὁ ἀρχων	the ruler
	Gen.	του ἀρχοντ-ος	the ruler's
	Dat.	τῳ ἀρχοντ-ι	to/for the ruler
	Acc.	τον ἀρχοντ-α	the ruler
Pl.	● Nom.	οἱ ἀρχοντ-ες	the rulers
	Gen.	των ἀρχοντ-ων	the rulers'
	₌ Dat.	τοις ἀρχ<u>ουσι</u>	to/for the rulers
	Acc.	τους ἀρχοντ-ας	the rulers

Feminine ✴		ἐλπις (ἐλπιδ-)	Translation
Sing.	Nom.	ἡ ἐλπις	the hope
	Gen.	της ἐλπιδ-ος	the hope's
	Dat.	τῃ ἐλπιδ-ι	to/for the hope
	Acc.	την ἐλπιδ-α	the hope
Pl.	● Nom.	αἱ ἐλπιδ-ες	the hopes
	Gen.	των ἐλπιδ-ων	the hopes'
	₌ Dat.	ταις ἐλπ<u>ισι</u>	to/for the hopes
	Acc.	τας ἐλπιδ-ας	the hopes

Neuter		σωμα (σωματ-)	Translation
Sing.	Nom.	το σωμα	the body
	Gen.	του σωματ-ος	the body's
	Dat.	τῳ σωματ-ι	to/for the body
	Acc.	το σωμα	the body
Pl.	Nom.	τα σωματ-α	the bodies
	Gen.	των σωματ-ων	the bodies'
	Dat.	τοις σωμασι	to/for the bodies
	Acc.	τα σωματ-α	the bodies

8.4 Vocabulary

Third Declension Neuter Nouns

141.	τό αἷμα, -ατος	blood (hematology)	(97)
142.	τό θέλημα, -ατος	will	(62)
143.	τό ὄνομα, -ατος	name (onomatopoeia)	(231)
144.	τό οὖς, ὠτός	ear	(36)
145.	τό πλήρωμα, -ατος	fulness	(17)
146.	τό πνεῦμα, -ατος	Spirit, spirit (pneumatic)	(379)
147.	τό ῥῆμα, -ατος	word, saying (rhetoric)	(68)
148.	τό σῶμα, -ατος	body (somatic)	(142)
149.	τό ὕδωρ, ὕδατος	water (hydro-)	(76)
150.	τό φῶς, φωτός	light (photography)	(73)

Third Declension Feminine Nouns

151.	ἡ γυνή, γυναικός	woman, wife (gynecology)	(215)
152.	ἡ ἐλπίς, -ιδος	hope	(53)
153.	ἡ μήτηρ, μητρός	mother (maternal)	(83)
154.	ἡ νύξ, νυκτός	night (nocturnal)	(61)
155.	ἡ σάρξ, σαρκός	flesh (sarcophagus)	(147)
156.	ἡ χάρις, -ιτος	grace, favor	(155)

Third Declension Masculine Nouns

157.	ὁ αἰών, αἰῶνος	age (aeon)	(122)
158.	ὁ ἀνήρ, ἀνδρός	man, husband	(216)

| 159. | ὁ ἄρχων, -οντος | ruler (monarchy) | (37) |
| 160. | ὁ πατήρ, πατρός | father (paternal) | (413) |

8.5 Form Identification - For each form give the gender, case, number, dictionary form, and a translation. One example is provided.

πνευματος   NGS   πνευμα   of a spirit, spirit's

1. σαρξι   14. γυναιξι
2. ὀνοματων   15. ἀνδρα
3. αἱμασι   16. χαρισι
4. χαριτι   17. σαρκας
5. σαρκι   18. ἐλπιδι
6. σωματα   19. αἱματα
7. ἀρχοντες   20. πατερα
8. θεληματων   21. φωσι
9. ἐλπιδας   22. ἀρχοντας
10. αἰωνες   23. νυκτι
11. πληρωμα   24. φωτων
12. ὑδατι   25. ἀρχουσι
13. ῥηματος

8.6 Practice Exercises - Translate the following sentences. Parse all verbs.

1. ἐγω εἰμι το φως του κοσμου.

2. οὐ γαρ ἐστε ὑπο νομον ἀλλα ὑπο χαριν.
   for   *by*   *but*   *grace*

3. μη τις (any) ἐκ των ἀρχοντων ἐπιστευσεν εἰς αὐτον;
   the rulers'

4. ἡ δε γυνη εἰπεν αὐτω οὐκ ἐχω ἀνδρα.
   woman

5. ἠν ἀνθρωπος παρα θεου, ὀνομα αὐτω Ἰωαννης (John).

6. Ἀβρααμ (Abraham) παρ' ἐλπιδι ἐπ' ἐλπιδι ἐπιστευσεν εἰς τον θεον.

7. εἰ ἀνθρωπος πνευμα Χριστου οὐ ἐχει, οὐκ ἐστιν αὐτου.

8. ἐκ του πληρωματος αὐτου ἡμεις ἐλαβομεν και χαριν ἀντι χαριτος.

9. ὁ θεος φως ἐστιν, και σκοτια ἐν αὐτῳ οὐκ ἐστιν.

10. οὐ γαρ ἐστιν ἀνηρ ἐκ γυναικος, ἀλλα γυνη ἐξ ἀνδρος.

11. τῃ δε γυναικι ἐλεγον ὁτι οὐκετι (no longer) δια τα ῥηματα σου πιστευομεν.

12. ἠν δε ἀνθρωπος ἐκ των Φαρισαιων (Pharisees), Νικοδημος (Nicodemus) ὀνομα, ἀρχων των Ἰουδαιων (Jews).

13. τα ῥηματα ἀ (which) ἐγω εἰπον ὑμιν πνευμα ἐστιν και ζωη ἐστιν.

14. ἐν αὐτῳ ζωη ἠν, και ἡ ζωη ἠν το φως των ἀνθρωπων.

15. ἐγω ἐβαπτισα ὑμας ἐν ὑδατι, αὐτος δε βαπτισει ἐν τῳ πνευματι.

16. ἐγω ἠλθον ἐν τῳ ὀνοματι του πατρος μου, και οὐ λαμβανετε με.

17. εἰ δε χαριτι οὐκετι (no longer) ἐξ ἐργων ἐστιν, ἐπει (otherwise) ἡ χαρις οὐκετι (no longer) ἐστιν χαρις.

18. οὑτος (this one) ἠλθεν προς αὐτον νυκτος και εἰπεν αὐτῳ, οἰδαμεν ὁτι ἀπο θεου ἠλθες.

19. ὁ νομος δια Μωϋσεως (Moses) ἠλθεν· ἡ χαρις και ἡ ἀληθεια δια Ἰησου Χριστου ἠλθεν.

20. Ἰησους Χριστος ἠλθεν οὐκ ἐν τῳ ὑδατι μονον (only) ἀλλ' ἐν τῳ ὑδατι και ἐν τῳ αἱματι.

GRAMMAR GRABBER: Punctuation and Interpretation

ἔφη,
    ἐγὼ φωνὴ βοῶντος ἐν τῇ ἐρήμῳ,
    εὐθύνατε τὴν ὁδὸν κυρίου,
καθὼς εἶπεν Ἡσαΐας ὁ προφήτης. (John 1:23)

He (John) said, "I am a voice crying in the wilderness, 'Make straight the way of the Lord,' just as Isaiah the prophet said."

In answering questions about his identity John the Baptist quotes Isaiah 40:3. The punctuation and arrangement of the text by the Greek New Testament editors clearly identifies the phrase ἐν τῇ ἐρήμῳ with John's description of himself: "I am a voice crying *in the wilderness*." Under this arrangement of the text the command is to "Make straight the way of the Lord."

Interestingly, the Dead Sea Scroll community took the phrase ἐν τῇ ἐρήμῳ with the command: "*In the wilderness* make straight the way of the Lord." They took it as a mandate to abandon their towns and villages of Judea and go out into the wilderness. There, by their communal life of righteousness in the Judean desert near the Dead Sea, they were literally to "make straight" (i.e., prepare) the way for the Lord. The poetical pattern in the Hebrew of the Isaiah passage seems to point in a similar direction.

Remembering that punctuation is the result of later editing for clarity, where would you place the comma and start the "quote within a quote" in John 1:23? What would the difference in meaning between the two ways of punctuating the quote be? How are both true theologically?

Chapter 9

THIRD DECLENSION NOUNS:
VOWEL STEMS

The second category of third declension nouns consists of those nouns which have stems ending in a vowel. This group of nouns is slightly more complex than the third declension nouns with consonant stems. The endings are similar to those used with the first group, but the final form of the nouns is often different as a result of vowel contraction.

9.1 Basic Endings

The basic ending patterns for masculine and feminine nouns are identical except in the accusative singular. Those for neuter nouns are slightly different. The chart below summarizes the basic ending patterns. In the accusative singular form, masculine nouns use the α ending; feminine nouns use the ν ending.

		Masculine/Feminine	Neuter
Sing.	Nom.	ς	—
	Gen.	ως	ος
	Dat.	ι	ι
	Acc.	α/ν	—
Pl.	Nom.	ες	α
	Gen.	ων	ων
	Dat.	σι	σι
	Acc.	ες	α

9.2 Masculine Nouns

Third declension masculine nouns with vowel stems are readily recognized in dictionaries and lexicons because they follow the pattern –ευς, –εως. That is, the nominative singular form ends in –ευς, and the genitive singular form ends in –εως. One example is the noun ὁ βασιλευς, βασιλεως.

		βασιλευς (βασιλε-)		Translation
Sing.	Nom.	ὁ βασιλ-ευς	(ευ-ς)	the king
	Gen.	του βασιλ-εως	(ε-ως)	the king's
	Dat.	τῳ βασιλ-ει	(ε-ι)	to/for the king
	Acc.	τον βασιλ-εα	(ε-α)	the king
Pl.	Nom.	οἱ βασιλ-εις	(ε+ες)	the kings
	Gen.	των βασιλ-εων	(ε-ων)	the kings'
	Dat.	τοις βασιλ-ευσι	(ευ-σι)	to/for the kings
	Acc.	τους βασιλ-εις	(ε+ες)	the kings

The basic stem of this noun is βασιλε-. In the nominative singular and the dative plural, however, an υ also appears, probably for euphonic reasons. Further complicating the paradigm is the fact that vowel contraction takes place in the nominative and accusative plural forms. For these reasons students often find it easier to think of the stem as being βασιλ-, for that portion of the noun remains constant throughout the paradigm. It must be remembered, however, that these nouns actually have *vowel stems* and, consequently, follow a slightly different ending pattern. The paradigm above includes in parentheses the way in which the endings interact with the vowel at the end of the stem.

9.3 Feminine Nouns

Third declension feminine nouns with vowel stems are also readily recognized, for they follow the pattern –ις, –εως. That is, the nominative singular form ends in -ις, and the genitive singular form ends in -εως. One example is the noun ἡ πολις, πολεως.

feminine

		πολις (πολε-)		Translation
Sing.	Nom.	ἡ πολ-ις	(ι-ς)	the city
	Gen.	της πολ-εως	(ε-ως)	the city's
	Dat.	τη πολ-ει	(ε-ι)	to/for the city
	Acc.	την πολ-ιν	(ι-ν)	the city
Pl.	Nom.	αἱ πολ-εις	(ε+ες)	the cities
	Gen.	των πολ-εων (ε-ων)		the cities'
	Dat.	ταις πολ-εσι	(ε-σι)	to/for the cities
	Acc.	τας πολ-εις	(ε+ες)	the cities

The basic stem of this noun is πολε-, but in the nominative and accusative singular an ι appears instead. As was true with masculine nouns, vowel contraction occurs in the nominative and accusative plural forms. For these reasons students often find it easier to think of the stem as being πολ-, for that portion of the noun remains constant throughout the paradigm. It must be remembered, however, that these nouns actually have *vowel stems* and, consequently, follow a slightly different ending pattern. The paradigm above includes in parentheses the way in which the endings interact with the vowel at the end of the stem.

9.4 Neuter Nouns

Third declension neuter nouns with vowel stems are also readily recognized, for they follow the pattern –ος, –ους. One example is the noun το γεν-ος, γεν-ους.

Neuter

			γεν-ος (γενε-)		Translation
Sing.	Nom.	το	γεν-ος		the race
	Gen.	του	γεν-ους	(ε+ος)	the race's
	Dat.	τῳ	γεν-ει	(ε-ι)	to/for the race
	Acc.	το	γεν-ος		the race
Pl.	Nom.	τα	γεν-η	(ε+α)	the races
	Gen.	των	γεν-ων	(ε+ων)	the races'
	Dat.	τοις	γεν-εσι	(ε-σι)	to/for the races
	Acc.	τα	γεν-η	(ε+α)	the races

The basic stem of this noun is γενε-, but the ε seldom appears in the paradigm. For this reason students often find it easier to think of the stem as being γεν-, for that portion of the noun remains constant throughout the paradigm. It must be remembered, however, that these nouns actually have *vowel stems* and, consequently, follow a slightly different ending pattern. The paradigm above includes in parentheses the way in which the endings interact with the vowel at the end of the stem.

9.5 Vocabulary

Third Declension Neuter Nouns

161.	τό γένος, -ους	family, race, kind (genus)	(20)
162.	τό ἔθνος, -ους	nation, Gentile (ethnic)	(162)
163.	τό ἔλεος, -ους	mercy	(27)
164.	τό μέρος, -ους	part, piece, member	(42)

| 165. | τό σκότος, -ους | darkness | (31) |

Third Declension Masculine Nouns

166.	ὁ ἀρχιερεύς, -εως	high priest, chief priest	(122)
167.	ὁ βασιλεύς, -εως	king	(115)
168.	ὁ γραμματεύς, -εως	scribe, teacher of the law	(63)
169.	ὁ ἱερεύς, -εως	priest (hierarchy)	(31)

Third Declension Feminine Nouns

170.	ἡ ἀνάστασις, -εως	resurrection	(122)
171.	ἡ δύναμις, -εως	power (dynamic)	(119)
172.	ἡ γνῶσις, -εως	knowledge (agnostic)	(29)
173.	ἡ κρίσις, -εως	judgment (critic)	(47)
174.	ἡ πίστις, -εως	faith	(67)
175.	ἡ πόλις, -εως	city (metropolis)	(162)

Prepositions

176.	ἀνά	+ acc.	up, again	(13)
177.	κατά	+ gen.	against, down	(473)
		+ acc.	according to	
178.	μετά	+ gen.	with	(469)
		+ acc.	after	
179.	πρό	+ gen.	before (prologue)	(47)
180.	σύν	+ dat.	with (synthesis)	(128)

9.6 Form Identification - For each form below give the gender, case, number, dictionary form, and a translation. One example is provided.

| πολιν | FAS πολις | a city |

1.	γενη	9.	γνωσεως
2	ἀρχιερεα	10.	ἀναστασιν
3.	ἐλεεσι	11.	βασιλευσι
4.	δυναμεως	12.	ἐθνη
5.	πιστει	13.	πολεων
6.	σκοτους	14.	ἱερεα
7.	μερος	15.	σκοτος
8.	γραμματει	16.	ἱερεις

"ε-αy-res"

17. γενων

18. ελεη

19. εθνος

20. αναστασεως

9.7 Practice Exercises - Translate the following sentences. Parse all verbs (TVMPN - Dictionary form).

1. συ εἰ ιερευς εἰς τον αἰωνα.

2. οὐκ οἰδατε την δυναμιν του θεου.

3. εἰπεν αὐτῳ ὁ 'Ιησους, ἐγω εἰμι ἡ ἀναστασις και ἡ ζωη.

4. ὁ θεος ἠνοιξεν τοις ἐθνεσιν θυραν (door) πιστεως.

5. νυν (now) ἡ κρισις ἐστιν του κοσμου τουτου (this).

6. και ὁ 'Ιησους λεγει αὐτοις, ἐχετε πιστιν θεου;

7. ἐχομεν ιερεα μεγαν (great) ἐπι τον οἰκον του θεου.

8. οἱ βασιλεις των ἐθνων ἐχουσιν ἐξουσιαν ἐπι της γης.

9. ἠτε γαρ ποτε (once) σκοτος, νυν (now) δε φως ἐν κυριῳ.

10. συ εἰ ὁ υἱος του θεου, συ βασιλευς εἰ του 'Ισραηλ (Israel).

11. πως (how) λεγουσιν οἱ γραμματεις ὁτι ὁ Χριστος υἱος Δαυιδ (David) ἐστιν;

12. ὑμεις γαρ υἱοι φωτος ἐστε και υἱοι ἡμερας· οὐκ ἐσμεν νυκτος οὐδε σκοτους.

13. και ἠλθεν ὁ 'Ιησους ἐν τη δυναμει του πνευματος εἰς την Γαλιλαιαν (Galilee).

14. και οἱ μαθηται (disciples) ἠλθον εἰς την πολιν και εὑρον καθως εἰπεν αὐτοις.

15. ἐλεγεν ὁ 'Ιησους ὡς ἀνθρωπος μετ' ἐξουσιας και οὐκ ὡς οἱ γραμματεις αὐτων.

GRAMMAR GRABBER: Perfect Tense

God's Word is eternal. Its authority has a validity which spans time and vanquishes all contemporary assertions of historical relativity. When a New Testament writer wants to communicate this quality about God's message he can use a Greek tense which brings out that validity. The **perfect tense** is one of two tenses which indicate completed action with continuing results (completed-stative action). The action so described can be confined to the past by using the pluperfect tense, or it can be brought into the present by using the perfect tense.

As the writer John introduces John the Baptist's testimony he strongly points to the present validity and significance of that testimony by combining a present tense (μαρτυρεῖ) with a perfect tense (κέκραγεν):

ʼΙωάννης μαρτυρεῖ περὶ αὐτοῦ καὶ κέκραγεν.
(John 1:15)

John is bearing witness concerning Him and has cried out.

Later in the chapter, John the Baptist climaxes his testimony with a double use of the perfect tense:

κἀγὼ ἑώρακα, καὶ μεμαρτύρηκα ὅτι οὗτός ἐστιν ὁ
υἱὸς τοῦ θεοῦ. (John 1:34)

And I have seen and have born witness that this one is the Son of God.

In order to bring out the significance of the perfect tense in 1:34, John's testimony could translated as "I have seen, and my eyewitness testimony is still valid; and I have testified, and my witness still stands: This one is the Son of God." What a powerful grammatical tool for communicating the continuing validity and present significance of God's message!

Chapter 10

PERFECT AND PLUPERFECT ACTIVE INDICATIVE

In Chapters 4 and 7, four of the six tenses in the indicative mood were introduced. What remains is a discussion of the completed-stative action tenses, Perfect and Pluperfect. First, however, a brief review of the indicative mood is in order.

10.1 Indicative Mood

The indicative mood is the mood most frequently encountered in Greek, and so, it is learned first. The indicative mood is the only mood in which *time* of action is made explicit by the tense of a verb. In all other moods, *kind* of action is the factor indicated by tense. Verbs in the indicative mood may occur in any of the six tenses. The chart below shows the way in which those tenses relate to kind and time of action.

		Time of Action		
		Past	Present	Future
Kind of Action	Progressive	Imperfect	Present	(Secondary use of Future)
	Summary	Aorist	(Secondary use of Present)	Future
	Completed-Stative	**Pluperfect**	**Perfect**	(Future Perfect.)

10.2 Completed Action Tenses

The Perfect and Pluperfect are considered to be completed-stative action tenses, because they combine a completed act with continuing results. The **Perfect** tense speaks of results existing in the *present* time. Pilate's statement in John 19:22 is a good example: "What I have written I have written." Pilate had already written the inscription which was to be affixed to Jesus' cross;

the action was completed. The Jewish leaders wanted him to change it, but he responded that the act of writing was completed. He would not change his words; they continued to express his evaluation of Jesus.

The **Pluperfect** tense speaks of results existing in the *past* time. For this reason it most frequently occurs in narrative. John 9:22 provides a good example: "His parents said this because they were afraid of the Jews; for the Jews *had already agreed*, that if anyone should confess Him to be Christ, he should be put out of the synagogue." John is narrating events which had taken place in past time (e.g., "His parents *said*—not say—this . . ."), but the Jews' decision had occurred *prior* to the event he is currently describing. Their decision was made and continued to be in effect at the time of Jesus' healing of the man born blind.

10.3 Reduplication

The most prominent characteristic of completed action tenses is the reduplication which occurs at the beginning of verbs in both the perfect and (normally) the pluperfect tenses. Reduplication can take any of several forms.

1. The simplest form of reduplication is the addition of a prefix consisting of the first letter of the verb followed by ε. For example, the verb λυω reduplicates with λε-.

    λυω   =   λυ-   →   λελυ-

2. Verbs beginning with one of the so-called "double consonants" (θ, φ. or χ) reduplicate with the corresponding single consonant followed by the vowel ε.

    θεραπευω   =   θεραπευ-   →   τεθεραπευ-
    φυτευω   =   φυτευ-   →   πεφυτευ-
    χωριζω   =   χωριζ-   →   κεχωριζ-

3. When reduplication is added to verbs beginning with a vowel or diphthong, contraction takes place which often makes reduplication difficult to distinguish from an augment.

    ἁμαρτάνω   =   ἁμαρτάν-   →   ἡμαρτή-

4. Some verbs reduplicate using an augment.

    γινώσκω   =   γινώσκ-   →   ἔγνω-

The latter two examples point out that some verbs also exhibit different stems in the perfect and pluperfect tenses. In most cases, the altered stem must simply be memorized. (See the discussion of principal parts below.)

10.4 Perfect Active Indicative

The perfect tense is used only to connote *completed-stative* action with continuing results in *present* time. In order to reflect the completed action of the perfect tense, we will translate the perfect active indicative using the present perfect. The first person singular of the verb "to see" would thus be translated as "I have seen." The form of the perfect active indicative may be summarized by the following formula:

$$\text{Reduplication} + \text{Stem} + \underset{\text{Sign}}{\text{Tense}} + \underset{\text{Vowel}}{\text{Theme}} + \underset{\text{Endings}}{\text{Primary Active}}$$

$$(\quad R \quad + \quad ST \quad + \quad S \quad + \quad V \quad + \quad PAE \quad)$$

▸ Reduplication: The initial letter/diphthong is added as a prefix to the verb stem in order to completed action.

▸ Stem: The perfect tense stem of a regular verb is found by removing the final ω of the dictionary form.

▸ Tense Sign: The normal tense sign for the perfect active indicative is κ.

▸ Theme Vowel: For the perfect active indicative the theme vowel is α, except for the third person singular, where it is ε.

Singular	1st	α	Plural	1st	α
	2nd	α		2nd	α
	3rd	ε		3rd	α

▸ Personal Endings: The perfect active indicative uses the primary active endings discussed in Chapter 3.

The paradigm of the perfect active indicative of the verb λυω follows.

		λυω (λυ-)					Translation
Sing.	1st	λε	λυ	κ	α	–	I have loosed.
	2nd	λε	λυ	κ	α	ς	You have loosed.
	3rd	λε	λυ	κ	ε	– (ν)	He/she/it has loosed.
Pl.	1st	λε	λυ	κ	α	μεν	We have loosed.
	2nd	λε	λυ	κ	α	τε	You have loosed.
	3rd	λε	λυ	κ	α	σι (ν)	They have loosed.

10.5 Pluperfect Active Indicative

The pluperfect tense is used only to connote *completed-stative* action with continuing results in *past* time. In order to reflect the completed action of the perfect tense, we will translate the perfect active indicative using the past perfect. The first person singular of the verb "to see" would thus be translated as "I had seen." The form of the pluperfect active indicative may be summarized by the following formula:

Augment + Reduplication + Stem + Tense + Theme + Secondary Active

			Sign	Vowel		Endings	
(A	+ R	+ ST	+ S	+ V	+	SAE	)

▶ Augment: The vowel ε is attached as a prefix to the verb stem in order to indicate past time.

▶ Reduplication: The initial letter/diphthong is added as a prefix to the verb stem in order to completed action.

▶ Stem: The pluperfect tense stem of a regular verb is found by removing the final ω of the dictionary form.

▶ Tense Sign: The normal tense sign for the pluperfect active indicative is κ.

▶ Theme Vowel: For the pluperfect active indicative the theme vowel is the diphthong ει.

▶ Personal Endings: The pluperfect active indicative uses the secondary active endings discussed in Chapter 7.

The paradigm of the pluperfect active indicative of the verb λυω follows.

		λυω (λυ-)						Translation
Sing.	1st	ἐ	λε	λυ	κ	ει	ν	I had loosed.
	2nd	ἐ	λε	λυ	κ	ει	ς	You had loosed.
	3rd	ἐ	λε	λυ	κ	ει	–	He had loosed.
Pl.	1st	ἐ	λε	λυ	κ	ει	μεν	We had loosed.
	2nd	ἐ	λε	λυ	κ	ει	τε	You had loosed.
	3rd	ἐ	λε	λυ	κ	ει	σαν	They had loosed.

10.6 "Irregular" Verb Forms

The list below gives the present, future, aorist and perfect tenses of "irregular" verbs which you already know. To this point—although you have not met the –ομαι and –όμην endings—you should begin to memorize these basic forms as additional vocabulary.

	PAI1S	FAI1S	AAI1S	PfAI1S
41	ἄγω	ἄξω	ἤγαγον	ἦχα
42	ἀκούω	ἀκούσω	ἤκουσα	ἀκήκοα
46	γινώσκω	γνώσομαι	ἔγνων	ἔγνωκα
49	λαμβάνω	λήμψομαι	ἔλαβον	εἴληφα
53	πέμπω	πέμψω	ἔπεμψα	πέπομφα
58	γίνομαι	γενήσομαι	ἐγενόμην	γέγονα

59	ἔρχομαι	ἐλεύσομαι	ἦλθον	ἐλήλυθα
78	λέγω	ἐρῶ	εἶπον	εἴρηκα
104/5	βαίνω	βήσομαι	ἔβην	βέβηκα
106	εὑρίσκω	εὑρήσω	εὗρον	εὕρηκα
110	ὁράω	ὄψομαι	εἶδον	ἑώρακα
121	ἁμαρτάνω	ἁμαρτήσω	ἥμαρτον	ἡμάρτηκα
122	ἀνοίγω	ἀνοίξω	ἤνοιξα	ἀνέῳγα
123	βάλλω	βαλῶ	ἔβαλον	βέβληκα
125	ἔχω	ἕξω	ἔσχον	ἔσχηκα
126	λείπω	λείψω	ἔλιπον	λέλοιπα
127	μανθάνω	μαθήσομαι	ἔμαθον	μεμάθηκα
128	πάσχω	πείσομαι	ἔπαθον	πέπονθα
129	φέρω	οἴσω	ἤνεγκα	ἐνήνοχα

10.7 Principal Parts of Greek Verbs

All six of the tenses of the Greek verb have now been introduced. So far, only the active voice has been discussed, but Greek verbs have middle and passive voice forms as well. Six tenses times three voices times six combinations of person and number results in 108 possible forms of any verb in the indicative mood alone. When three other moods, participles, and infinitives are added to the mix, the number of theoretical forms climbs to close to 600!

The good news is that all of those theoretical forms can be related to six basic forms on which they are built, called the **Principal Parts**. These principal parts are numbered (naturally enough) 1 through 6, and consist of the following forms:

First	Present Active Indicative First Person Singular (PAI1S)
Second	Future Active Indicative First Person Singular (FAI1S)
Third	Aorist Active Indicative First Person Singular (AAI1S)
Fourth	Perfect Active Indicative First Person Singular (PfAI1S)
Fifth	Perfect Middle/Passive Indicative First Person Singular (PfM/PI1S)
Sixth	Aorist Passive Indicative First Person Singular (API1S)

A quick look at the preceding list shows that the first four of these forms have already been introduced. The fifth and sixth principal parts will be discussed in detail when the middle and passive forms are introduced.

When a verb is "regular" (e.g., λυω) it is possible to *construct* each of the principal parts using the present tense stem and the formulae given as each tense and voice is introduced. When a verb is "irregular" (e.g., φέρω), the principal parts must be *memorized*. The relationship of the principal parts to the various forms of a verb may be summarized as follows:

Principal Part	1 (PAI1S)		2 (FAI1S)	3 (AAI1S)
Tense	Present	Imper-fect	Future	Aorist
Active	X	X	X	X
Middle	X	X	X	X
Passive	X	X	–	–

Principal Part	4 (PfAI1S)		5 (PfM/PI1S)		6 (API1S)	
Tense	Perfect	Pluper-fect	Perfect	Pluper-fect	Aorist	Future
Active	X	X	–	–	–	–
Middle	–	–	X	X	–	–
Passive	–	–	X	X	X	X

10.8 Vocabulary

First Declension Nouns

181.	ἡ γλῶσσα, -ης	tongue, language (glossalalia)	(50)
182.	ἡ γραφή, -ης	writing, Scripture (graphic)	(50)
183.	ἡ διακονία, -ας	ministry, service (diaconate)	(34)
184.	ἡ εἰρήνη, -ης	peace (irenic)	(92)
185.	ἡ ἐκκλησία, -ας	church (ecclesiology)	(114)
186.	ἡ ἐπιθυμία, -ας	desire, lust	(38)
187.	ἡ θάλασσα, -ης	sea (thallasic)	(91)
188.	ἡ κώμη, -ης	village	(27)
189.	ἡ ψυχή, -ης	life, soul (psychology)	(103)

Second Declension Nouns

190.	ὁ ἁμαρτωλός, -ου	sinner	(47)

191.	ὁ δοῦλος, -ου	slave, servant	(124)
192.	ὁ σταυρός, -ου	cross	(27)
193.	ἡ βίβλος, -ου	book (Bible)	(10)

Third Declension Nouns

194.	ὁ μάρτυς, -υρος	witness (martyr)	(35)
195.	ὁ σωτήρ, σωτῆρος	savior (soteriology)	(24)
196.	ἡ χείρ, χειρός	hand	(177)

Verb

| 197. | στρέφω | I am turning | (21) |

Prepositions

198.	ἔμπροσθεν + gen.	before, in front of	(48)
199.	χωρίς + gen.	without, apart from	(41)
200.	ὀπίσω + gen.	behind, after	(35)

10.9 Form Identification - For each form give the tense, voice, mood, person, number, dictionary form and a translation. Abbreviations for tenses are **P**(resent), **F**(uture), **I**(mperfect), **A**(orist), **Pf** (for perfect), and **Plpf** (for pluperfect). One example is provided.

ἐλελύκειν   PlpfAI1S   λυω   I had loosed

1. λελυκε *loosed*
2. λελυκας *loosed*
3. πεπιστευκε *believing*
4. ἀκηκοα
5. οἰδατε *knowing*
6. εὑρηκα *found*
7. γεγραφατε *written*
8. βεβληκα
9. ἐπεπιστευκεισαν *believing*
10. λελυκασι *loosed*
11. ἡμαρτηκα *witnessed*
12. ἐγνωκασι

making known
γνωριζω

13. ἐληλυθα *set free*
14. γεγραφαμεν *written*
15. λελοιπα *loosed*
16. ἐπεπιστευκεις *believing*
17. γεγονα
18. ἐσχηκαμεν *last*
19. ἐλελυκειτε *loosed*
20. ἐληλυθατε
21. εἰληφα
22. βεβηκασι
23. ἐλελυκεισαν *loosed*
24. πεπιστευκατε *πιστευω*

believing

10.10 Practice Exercises -Translate the following sentences. Parse all verbs (TVMPN - Dictionary form).

1. νυν (now) ἐγνωκαμεν ὅτι δαιμονιον ἔχεις.

2. γεγραφα ὑμιν, ὅτι ἐγνωκατε τον πατερα.

3. ἐγω ὡς φως εἰς τον κοσμον ἐληλυθα.

4. ἐγω πεπιστευκα ὅτι συ εἶ ὁ Χριστος ὁ υἱος του θεου.

5. εἶπεν ὁ Πιλατος (Pilate), ὃ (what) γεγραφα, γεγραφα.

6. ἀλλα το ἀποκριμα (sentence) του θανατου ἐσχηκαμεν.

7. ὃ (what) ἑωρακαμεν και ἀκηκοαμεν, λεγομεν και ὑμιν.

8. και πεπιστευκατε ὅτι ἐγω παρα του θεου ἠλθον.

9. ἀλλ' εἶπον ὑμιν ὅτι και ἑωρακατε με και οὐ πιστευετε.

10. δι' Ἰησου την προσαγωγην (access) ἐσχηκαμεν τῃ πιστει εἰς την χαριν.

11. και σκοτια ἠδη (already) ἐγεγονει και οὐπω (not yet) ἐληλυθει προς αὐτον ὁ Ἰησους.

12. κἀγω ἑωρακα και μεμαρτυρηκα ὅτι οὑτος (this one) ἐστιν ὁ υἱος του θεου.

13. και οὐδεις (no one) ἀναβεβηκεν εἰς τον οὐρανον εἰ μη (except) ὁ υἱος του ἀνθρωπου.

14. αὐτοι γαρ ἀκηκοαμεν και οἰδαμεν ὅτι οὑτος (this one) ὁ σωτηρ του κοσμου ἐστιν.

15. και ἡμεις πεπιστευκαμεν και ἐγνωκαμεν ὅτι συ εἶ ὁ υἱος του θεου.

16. αὑτη (this) ἐστιν ἡ κρισις, ὅτι το φως ἐληλυθεν εἰς τον κοσμον.

17. καὶ ᾿Ιησοῦς εἶπεν, οὐ διὰ με ἡ φωνὴ αὕτη (this) γέγονεν ἀλλὰ δι᾿ ὑμᾶς.

18. καὶ οὐδεὶς (no one) ἔβαλεν ἐπ᾿ αὐτὸν τὴν χεῖρα (hand) ὅτι οὔπω (not yet) ἐληλύθει ἡ ὥρα αὐτοῦ.

19. εἰ ἐγνώκατε με, τὸν πατερα μου γινωσκετε· καὶ γινωσκετε αὐτὸν καὶ ἑωράκατε αὐτόν.

20. καὶ ἔλεγον, οὐχ οὗτος (this one) ἐστιν ᾿Ιησοῦς ὁ υἱὸς ᾿Ιωσηφ (Joseph) οὗ (whose) ἡμεῖς οἴδαμεν τὸν πατερα καὶ τὴν μητερα; πῶς (how) νυν (now) λεγει ὅτι ἐκ τοῦ οὐρανοῦ καταβέβηκα;

GRAMMAR GRABBER: Relative Clauses

New Testament Greek allows a writer to link thoughts in a variety of ways. One elegant option is the use of relative pronouns ("who, whom, whose, which"). Relative pronouns and the clauses they introduce serve to describe an idea in more detail.

In Eph 1:3-14, Paul masterfully employs three relative clauses introduced by the prepositional phrase "in whom" (ἐν ᾧ). In each instance the person described in more detail (the "antecedent") is Jesus Christ. These relative clauses structure the entire passage and portray God's blessings toward us — in Christ — from three perspectives: past, future, and present.

▸ In verse 7, He is the source of the past blessing of our redemption:
   ἐν ᾧ ἔχομεν τὴν ἀπολύτρωσιν
   in whom we are having the redemption

▸ In verse 11, He is the source of the future blessing of our inheritance:
   ἐν ᾧ καὶ ἐκληρώθημεν
   in whom we were also assigned an inheritance

▸ In verse 13, He is the source of the present blessing of the Spirit's indwelling:
   ἐν ᾧ καὶ ἐσφραγίσθητε τῷ πνεύματι τῆς ἐπαγγελίας τῷ ἁγίῳ
   in whom we were also sealed with the Holy Spirit of promise

The relative pronoun with its clause, then, can both center our attention on its antecedent (here, Jesus Christ) and usher us into a deeper understanding of all that a spiritual reality (here, salvation) has to offer.

Chapter 11

RELATIVE PRONOUNS

Chapter 5 presented the concept of subordinate (dependent) clauses which are introduced by subordinate conjunctions. Most subordinate conjunctions introduce clauses which function adverbially. Two subordinate conjunctions (ὅτι and ἵνα) can also introduce clauses which function substantivally. A third type of subordinate clause functions *adjectivally* to describe, clarify, or restrict a noun. This latter type of clause is most frequently introduced by a **relative pronoun**. It is necessary, therefore, to discuss relative pronouns before considering the clauses which they introduce.

11.1 Relative Pronouns

Relative pronouns relate the clause in which they occur (the relative clause) to a noun or a pronoun (the antecedent) in another clause. There are two forms of the relative pronoun: **definite** relative pronouns and **indefinite** relative pronouns. Since the indefinite form is comparatively rare, it will be deferred until Chapter 23. The discussion which follows will focus on the more frequently used definite form.

A **definite relative pronoun** refers to a specific antecedent—whether a person, place, or thing. In English the difference between an antecedent which is a person and one which is a place or thing is reflected by the use of "who, whose, whom" when the antecedent is a person and by the use of "which" when the antecedent is a person or thing. This distinction is seen in the following sentences:

Personal: Here is the boy, <u>who</u> hit the ball.
Impersonal: Here is the ball, <u>which</u> the boy hit.

Since all Greek nouns (and pronouns) have gender, it will be necessary to determine from the context whether a given Greek relative pronoun should be translated personally or impersonally.

The full paradigm of the definite relative pronoun follows. Note that both a rough breathing mark and an accent appear on each form.

		Masc.	Fem.	Neut.	Translation
Sing.	Nom.	ὅς	ἥ	ὅ	who, which
	Gen.	οὗ	ἧς	οὗ	whose, of which
	Dat.	ᾧ	ᾗ	ᾧ	to/for whom/which
	Acc.	ὅν	ἥν	ὅ	whom, which
Pl.	Nom.	οἵ	αἵ	ἅ	who, which
	Gen.	ὧν	ὧν	ὧν	whose, of which
	Dat.	οἷς	αἷς	οἷς	to/for whom/which
	Acc.	οὕς	ἅς	ἅ	whom, which

11.2 Use of Relative Pronouns

The use of the relative pronoun is comparatively easy to master. It helps to remember three rules.

1. A relative pronoun always introduces (i.e., stands first or second in) its clause but is not always the subject of the clause.

    ... ὅς ἐστιν εἰκὼν του θεου του ἀορατου

    ... who (subject) is the image of the invisible God

    ... ἐν ᾧ ἐχομεν την ἀπολυτρωσιν

    ... in whom (object of preposition) we are having the redemption

2. A relative pronoun always agrees with its antecedent in gender and number.

    εἰς την βασιλειαν του υἱου ... ὅς ἐστιν εἰκὼν του θεου του ἀορατου

    into the kingdom of the son (masc. sing.) ... who (masc. sing.) is the image of the invisible God

3. The *case* of a relative pronoun is determined by its use in its clause.

    εἰς την βασιλειαν του υἱου ... ἐν ᾧ ἐχομεν την ἀπολυτρωσιν

    into the kingdom of the son (masc. *gen.* sing.) ... in whom (masc. *dat.* sing.) we are having the redemption

11.3 Review of Subordinate Clauses

In order to set relative clauses in their proper grammatical context, it will be helpful to review briefly the concept of clauses, in particular, subordinate clauses.

A **clause** is a group of words which has a subject and a verb and is used as part of a sentence. There are two kinds of clauses. A *main (independent)*

clause [MC] expresses a complete thought and could be a sentence by itself
(e.g., The boy hit the ball.). A *subordinate (dependent) clause* [SC] does not
express a complete thought and is attached to a main clause by a connector
(e.g., The boy hit the ball [MC], <u>because he is a good batter</u> [SC].)

Clauses introduced by **subordinate conjunctions** function either as
adverbial clauses or as noun clauses. An *adverbial subordinate clause* is
introduced by a subordinate conjunction and modifies the action of the verb
in the main clause (e.g., The boy hit the ball <u>because he was a good batter</u>.).
A *noun (substantival) clause* is introduced by a subordinate conjunction and
functions as a noun (subject, object, complement, appositive) in relation to
the main clause (e.g., I know <u>that the boy hit the ball</u>. [direct object]).

Most subordinate conjunctions introduce adverbial clauses. The
subordinate conjunctions ἱνα and ὅτι, however, can also introduce noun
(substantival) clauses. The following rules of thumb are helpful in
determining the kind of clause these conjunctions introduce.

1. When ὅτι is translated "because," it introduces an adverbial clause
    showing cause.

    1 John 4:19   ἡμεις ἀγαπῶμεν, <u>ὅτι</u> αὐτος πρωτος
    ἠγαπησεν ἡμας.

    We love, <u>because</u> (cause) He first loved us.

2. When ὅτι is translated "that," it introduces a noun clause.

    1 Cor 15:3   παρεδωκα γαρ ὑμιν... <u>ὅτι</u> Χριστος
    ἀπεθανεν ὑπερ των ἁμαρτιαν ἡμων.

    For I delivered to you . . . <u>that</u> (object) Christ died
    for our sins.

3. When ἱνα is translated "in order that" or "so that" it introduces an
    adverbial clause showing either purpose ("in order that") or—less
    commonly—result ("so that"). This use is the most frequent.

    John 10:10   ἐγω ἠλθον <u>ἱνα</u> ζωην ἐχωσιν

    I came <u>in order that</u> (purpose) they might have life.

4. When ἱνα is translated "that," it introduces a noun clause. This use is
    less frequent (although comparatively common in John's writings).

    John 13:35   ἐντολην καινην διδωμι ὑμιν, <u>ἱνα</u>
    ἀγαπᾱτε ἀλληλους

    I am giving a new commandment to you, <u>that</u>
    (apposition) you love one another.

11.4 Relative Clauses

Because most relative clauses describe, explain, or restrict a noun in some way, their primary syntactical function is that of an **adjectival subordinate clause**. These clauses may be grouped into two categories.

A *definite relative clause* refers to a specific antecedent and contains a verb in the indicative mood. The pronoun agrees with its antecedent in gender and number, but its case is determined by its function in its own clause.

Mark 10:29 οὐδεις ἐστιν ὅς ἀφηκεν οἰκιαν . . .

There is no one who has left home . . .

An *indefinite relative clause* refers to an unspecified individual, group, event, or action (i.e., it has no antecedent) and contains a verb in the subjunctive mood (to be introduced later) plus the particle ἄν or ἐάν.

Matt 20:27 ὅς ἄν θελῃ ἐν ὑμιν εἰναι πρωτος . . .

Whoever wishes to be first among you . . .

In some instances the referent of the relative pronoun is sufficiently clear from the context, that an explicit antecedent is omitted. The relative clause which results stands alone and functions as a **noun (substantival) subordinate clause** (subject, object, complement, appositive) in relation to the main clause. In such instances it might be necessary to add the helping words "the one" or "the thing(s)" in the English translation.

John 4:18 πεντε ἀνδρας ἐσχες και νυν ὃν ἐχεις οὐκ ἐστιν σου ἀνηρ.

You have had five husbands and {the one} whom you now are having is not your husband.

11.5 Vocabulary

Relative Pronouns

201.	ὅς, ἥ, ὅ	who, which, that	(1365)

Nouns

202.	ἡ ἀγαπή, -ης	love	(116)
203.	ἡ ἐντολή, -ης	commandment	(67)
204.	ἡ ζύμη, -ης	leaven	(13)
205.	ὁ μαθητής, -ου	disciple	(261)
206.	ὁ τελώνης, -ου	tax collector	(21)
207.	ὁ διδάσκαλος, -ου	teacher (didactic)	(59)

Verbs

208.	ἀπολύω	I am releasing, setting free	(66)
209.	διαλογίζομαι	I am discussing, reasoning (dialog)	(16)
210.	διδάσκω	I am teaching (didactic)	(97)

211.	πειράζω	I am testing, tempting	(38)
212.	συνίημι	I am understanding, comprehending	(26)
213.	σώζω	I am saving (soteriology)	(106)
214.	ὑπάγω	I am departing, going away	(79)
215.	χορτάζω	am feeding, satisfying	(16)

Adjectives

216.	ἀδύνατος, -ον	impossible	(10)
217.	αἰώνιος, -ον	eternal	(71)
218.	ἀκάθαρτος, -ον	unclean	(32)
219.	ἄπιστος, -ον	unbelieving, faithless	(23)
220.	πονηρός, -α, -ον	evil	(78)

11.6 Form Identification - In the paragraph which follows (Eph 1:3-14) circle all subordinate conjunctions (1) and relative pronouns (8). For each conjunction, state whether it introduces an adverbial clause or a noun clause. For each relative pronoun, state (a) its gender, case, and number, (b) its most likely antecedent, and (c) its most likely use in its clause. Do not attempt to translate the passage; use the case form to make your decisions.

εὐλογητὸς ὁ θεὸς καὶ πατὴρ τοῦ κυρίου ἡμῶν Ἰησοῦ Χριστοῦ, ὁ εὐλογήσας ἡμᾶς ἐν πάσῃ εὐλογίᾳ πνευματικῇ ἐν τοῖς ἐπουρανίοις ἐν Χριστῷ, καθὼς ἐξελέξατο ἡμᾶς ἐν αὐτῷ πρὸ καταβολῆς κόσμου εἶναι ἡμᾶς ἁγίους καὶ ἀμώμους κατενώπιον αὐτοῦ ἐν ἀγάπῃ, προορίσας ἡμᾶς εἰς υἱοθεσίαν διὰ Ἰησοῦ Χριστοῦ εἰς αὐτόν, κατὰ τὴν εὐδοκίαν τοῦ θελήματος αὐτοῦ, εἰς ἔπαινον δόξης τῆς χάριτος αὐτοῦ ἧς ἐχαρίτωσεν ἡμᾶς ἐν τῷ ἠγαπημένῳ. ἐν ᾧ ἔχομεν τὴν ἀπολύτρωσιν διὰ τοῦ αἵματος αὐτοῦ, τὴν ἄφεσιν τῶν παραπτωμάτων, κατὰ τὸ πλοῦτος τῆς χάριτος αὐτοῦ ἧς ἐπερίσσευσεν εἰς ἡμᾶς, ἐν πάσῃ σοφίᾳ καὶ φρονήσει, γνωρίσας ἡμῖν τὸ μυστήριον τοῦ θελήματος αὐτοῦ, κατὰ τὴν εὐδοκίαν αὐτοῦ ἣν προέθετο ἐν αὐτῷ εἰς οἰκονομίαν τοῦ πληρώματος τῶν καιρῶν, ἀνακεφαλαιώ-σασθαι τὰ πάντα ἐν τῷ Χριστῷ, τὰ ἐπὶ τοῖς οὐρανοῖς καὶ τὰ ἐπὶ τῆς γῆς ἐν αὐτῷ. ἐν ᾧ καὶ ἐκληρώθημεν προ-ορισθέντες κατὰ πρόθεσιν τοῦ τὰ πάντα ἐνεργοῦντος κατὰ τὴν βουλὴν τοῦ θελήματος αὐτοῦ εἰς τὸ εἶναι ἡμᾶς εἰς ἔπαινον δόξης αὐτοῦ τοὺς προηλπικότας ἐν τῷ Χριστῷ. ἐν ᾧ καὶ ὑμεῖς ἀκούσαντες τὸν λόγον τῆς ἀληθείας, τὸ εὐαγγέλιον τῆς σωτηρίας ὑμῶν, ἐν ᾧ καὶ πιστεύσαντες ἐσφραγίσθητε τῷ πνεύματι τῆς ἐπαγγελίας τῷ ἁγίῳ, ὅ ἐστιν ἀρραβὼν τῆς κληρονομίας ἡμῶν, εἰς ἀπολύτρωσιν τῆς περιποιήσεως, εἰς ἔπαινον τῆς δόξης αὐτοῦ.

11.7 Practice Exercises - Translate the following sentences. Parse all verbs (TVMPN - Dictionary form).

1. ὃ δε οὐκ ἐκ πιστεως ἐστιν, ἁμαρτια ἐστιν.

2. ὃ λεγω ὑμιν ἐν τη σκοτια λεγετε ἐν τω φωτι.

3. ἦν το φως ὃ φωτιζει παντα (every) ἀνθρωπον.

4. και ὁ λογος ὃν ἀκουετε οὐκ ἐστιν ἐμος (mine) ἀλλα του πατρος.

5. ὁ δε ἀρτος, ὃν διδωμι ὑπερ του κοσμου, ἡ σαρξ μου ἐστιν.

6. οἰδα ὅτι ἀληθης (true) ἐστιν ἡ μαρτυρια ἣν λεγει περι ἐμου.

7. ἐστιν ὁ πατηρ μου, ὃν ὑμεις λεγετε ὅτι θεος ὑμων ἐστιν.

8. και ἡμεις ἐγνωκαμεν και πεπιστευκαμεν την ἀγαπην ἣν ἐχει ὁ θεος ἐν ἡμιν.

9. γραφω ὑμιν ἐντολην ἣν εἰχετε ἀπ' ἀρχης· ἡ ἐντολη ἐστιν ὁ λογος ὃν ἠκουσατε.

10. ὁ ἀνθρωπος γαρ ὃν ἀπεστειλεν ὁ θεος/τα ῥηματα του θεου λαλεῖ.

11. και ἡ φωνη ἣν ἠκουσα ἐκ του οὐρανου παλιν (again) ἐλαλεῖ μετ' ἐμου.

12. οὐ πεπιστευκασιν εἰς την μαρτυριαν ἣν εἰρηκε ὁ θεος περι του υἱου αὐτου.

13. το πνευμα, ὃ πεμψει ὁ πατηρ ἐν τῳ ὀνοματι μου, ὑμας διδαξει.

14. ἡμεις ἐκ του θεου ἐσμεν· ὃς γινωσκει τον θεον ἀκουει ἡμων, ὃς οὐκ ἐστιν ἐκ του θεου οὐκ ἀκουει ἡμων.

15. αὐτος ἐστιν ὑπερ οὗ ἐγω εἰπον, ὀπισω μου ἐστιν ἀνηρ ὃς ἐμπροσθεν μου ἠν.

16. και ἐπιστευσαν τῃ γραφῃ και τῳ λογῳ ὃν εἰπεν ὁ Ἰησους.

17. και ὃς οὐ λαμβανει τον σταυρον οὐκ ἐστιν μου ἀξιος (worthy).

18. ὃ ἑωρακεν και ἠκουσεν/τουτῳ (to this) μαρτυρει και την μαρτυριαν αὐτου οὐ λαμβανετε.

19. εὑρισκει Φιλιππος (Philip) τον Ναθαναηλ (Nathanael) και λεγει αὐτῳ, αὐτον περι οὗ ἐγραψεν Μωϋσης (Moses) ἐν τῳ νομῳ εὑρηκαμεν, Ἰησουν τον υἱον του Ἰωσηφ (Joseph).

20. γινωσκετε το πνευμα του θεου, το γαρ πνευμα ὃ διδασκει ὁτι Ἰησους Χριστος ἐν σαρκι ἐληλυθεν ἐκ του θεου ἐστιν.

GRAMMAR GRABBER: Liquid and Contract Verbs

καὶ διεστέλλετο αὐτοῖς λέγων, Ὁρᾶτε, βλέπετε ἀπὸ
τῆς ζύμης τῶν Φαρισαίων καὶ τῆς ζύμης Ἡρῴδου.
(Mark 8:15)

And He began commanding them saying, "Keep on watching out, keep on being on guard against the leaven of the Pharisees and the leaven of Herod."

Just as third declension nouns with consonantal and vowel stems introduced us to a different type of word formation, so verb stems which end in certain consonants or vowels manifest a different word formation. As you look at the verbs in Mark 8:15, do you notice anything odd about those which are underlined?

The first, διεστέλλετο, is the imperfect deponent indicative third person singular form of διαστέλλομαι ("I am commanding"). At first glance it seems normal enough, but you will learn in Chapter 12 that it is a nasal verb. As such, its aorist form — διεστειλα — has a lengthened stem (στελ to στειλ), a single lambda, and no tense sign.

The second, ὁρᾶτε, looks a bit odd. Does the -ᾶτε ending indicate an aorist or a perfect tense? It is actually the present active imperative second person plural (command) form of the alpha contract verb ὁράω ("I am seeing"). The circumflex accent (ˆ) reflects the contraction of two vowels. The final vowel of the verb stem (ὁρα-) has "swallowed up" the theme vowel (ε) which normally precedes the personal ending.

Getting these forms right will guide us to the correct understanding of the action Mark intended to convey. Jesus had an important lesson to teach the disciples. He "began commanding them" (imperfect indicative of διαστέλλομαι) "Keep on watching out" (present imperative of ὁράω), "keep on being on guard" (present imperative of βλέπω) "against the leaven of the Pharisees and the leaven of Herod."

Chapter 12

LIQUID, NASAL, AND CONTRACT VERBS

"Regular" verbs such as λύω or πιστεύω create few problems when they occur in a tense other than the present, because their principal parts can be constructed using consistent rules. On the other hand, "irregular" verbs often change form so radically from tense to tense that their principal parts must be memorized. Between these two poles are verbs which are not truly irregular but which, because of the letter with which their stem ends, change form slightly under certain circumstances. Such verbs may be grouped under three types: (1) labial, gutteral, and dental verbs, (2) liquid and nasal verbs, and (3) contract verbs. Each type will be examined in turn, beginning with a brief review of labial, gutteral, and dental verbs.

12.1 Labial, Gutteral, and Dental Verbs

The consonant contraction which results when the tense sign σ is added to a verb stem ending in a labial, gutteral, or dental consonant was discussed in Chapter 3. A similar phenomenon occurs with the tense sign κ is added to those verb stems. Before introducing liquid and nasal verbs, it will be helpful to review the contractions which occur when the tense signs of the future (σ), first aorist (σ), perfect (κ), and pluperfect (κ) tenses come in contact with the consonants at the end of verbs discussed to this point. The resulting contractions are set out in the following chart.

	Stem consonant	σ	κ
Labial — lips	β, π, φ	ψ	φ
Gutteral throat	γ, κ, χ	ξ	χ
Dental teeth	δ, θ, τ	σ	θ/κ

12.2 Liquid and Nasal Verbs

Two special groups of verbs have stems ending in "liquid" consonants (formed using a rippling sound: λ and ρ) or "nasal" consonants (formed by passing air through the nose: μ and ν). Rather than contracting with tense signs, these verbs tend to absorb the tense signs and adjust their stems slightly. This phenomenon is particularly evident when the tense sign is σ.

Liquid Verbs (ἐγείρω, stem = ἐγερ-)
    Present stem is often lengthened   (ἐγείρω)
    Future has diphthong/long theme vowel   (ἐγερῶ)
    Aorist stem is often lengthened   (ἤγειρα)

Nasal Verbs (κτείνω, stem = κτεν-)
    Present stem is sometimes lengthened   (κτείνω)
    Future has diphthong/long theme vowel   (κτενῶ)
    Aorist stem is sometimes lengthened   (ἔκτεινα)

The adjustment which takes place reflects the difficulty created by trying to pronounce the combination of certain consonants, and the process involved is rather complicated. It is sufficient to remember that liquid and nasal verbs do not like the tense sign σ. Liquid verbs "drown" it out, and nasal verbs "inhale" it. The end result in both instances is that the σ is missing in those tenses where it normally appears. These adjustments can be seen in the listing of principle parts of important liquid and nasal verbs which follows.

PAI1S	FAI1S	AAI1S	PfAI1S	PfM/PI1S	API1S
-στέλλω	-στελῶ	-εστειλα	-εσταλκα	-εσταλμαι	-εστάλην
αἴρω	ἀρῶ	ἦρα	ἦρκα	ἦρμαι	ἤρθην
μένω	μενῶ	ἔμεινα	μεμένηκα	—	—
-κτείνω	-κτενῶ	-εκτεινα	—	—	-εκτάνθην
ἐγείρω	ἐγερῶ	ἤγειρα	ἐγήγερκα	ἐγήγερμαι	ἠγέρθην
κρίνω	κρινῶ	ἔκρινα	κέκρικα	κέκριμαι	ἐκρίθην
-ἀγγέλλω	-ἀγγελῶ	-ηγγειλα	-ηγγελκα	-ηγγελμαι	-ηγγέλθην
σπείρω	σπερῶ	ἔσπειρα	ἔσπαρκα	ἔσπαρμαι	ἐσπάρην

12.3 Contract Verbs

A number of Greek verbs have stems which end in a "short" vowel. These verbs may be grouped into three classes:

Alpha contract	(-αω)	→	ἀγαπ<u>αω</u>	(ἀγαπα-)
Epsilon contract	(-εω)	→	φιλ<u>εω</u>	(φιλε-)
Omicron contract	(-Oω)	→	σταυρ<u>οω</u>	(σταυρο-)

When theme vowels are added directly to these stems, vowel contraction takes place. This group of verbs is called "contract" verbs.

One piece of good news is that contract verbs are *always* regular (no second aorists or stem changes!). Another piece of good news is that they are perfectly consistent. The less good news is that they are consistent within their own set of rules—rules which differ slightly from those for "normal" verbs. These rules may be summarized as follows:

1. In the present and imperfect tenses, the vowel of the stem always *contracts* with the theme vowels which precede the personal endings. The resulting contraction can be identified by the presence of a circumflex accent (ˆ) over the resulting vowel or diphthong.

2. In all other tenses, the vowel of the stem always *lengthens* prior to the tense sign. That is, α and ε become η, and O becomes ω. For instance,

The future of	ἀγαπ<u>αω</u>	is	ἀγαπ<u>ησω</u>
The future of	φιλ<u>εω</u>	is	φιλ<u>ησω</u>
The future of	σταυρ<u>οω</u>	is	σταυρ<u>ωσω</u>

That lengthening can be seen in the list below of the principal parts of three representative contract verbs.

PAI1S	FAI1S	AAI1S	PfAI1S	PfM/PI1S	API1S
ἀγαπάω	ἀγαπήσω	ἠγάπησα	ἠγάπηκα	ἠγάπημαι	ἠγαπήθην
ποιέω	ποιήσω	ἐποίησα	πεποίηκα	πεποίημαι	ἐποιήθην
δηλόω	δηλώσω	ἐδήλωσα	δεδήλωκα	δεδήλωμαι	ἐδηλώθην

It also needs to be noted that contract verbs will *always* be spelled in the *uncontracted* form in dictionaries and lexicons (e.g., ἀγαπάω), but they will *never* appear in that form in the text of the NT (e.g., ἀγαπῶ).

As explained above, vowel contraction occurs only in forms built on the first principal part of contract verbs (i.e., the present and imperfect tenses). For this reason the paradigms of those forms will be set out in full. First, however, it will be helpful to have an overview of the contractions which occur.

		Verb Stem Ending		
		α-	ε-	ο-
Theme Vowel/ Diphthong	ω	ω	ω	ω
	ει	ᾳ	ει	οι
	ο	ω	ου	ου
	ε	α	ει	ου
	ου	ω	ου	ου

The present active indicative of **alpha contract verbs** (stems ending in α) follows the paradigm below. It is particularly important to note (a) the *circumflex accent* over the vowels in the contracted form and (b) the *iota subscripts* in the second and third person singular contracted forms.

		ST	+ V	+ PAE	Contracted Form
Sing.	1st	ἀγαπα	ω	-	ἀγαπῶ
	2nd	ἀγαπα	ει	ς	ἀγαπᾷς
	3rd	ἀγαπα	ει	-	ἀγαπᾷ
Pl.	1st	ἀγαπα	ο	μεν	ἀγαπῶμεν
	2nd	ἀγαπα	ε	τε	ἀγαπᾶτε
	3rd	ἀγαπα	ου	σι (ν)	ἀγαπῶσι(ν

The imperfect active indicative of alpha contract verbs follows the paradigm below.

		A +	ST	+ V	+ SAE	Contracted Form
Sing.	1st	ἐ	ἀγαπα	ο	ν	ἠγαπων
	2nd	ἐ	ἀγαπα	ε	ς	ἠγαπας
	3rd	ἐ	ἀγαπα	ε	-	ἠγαπα
Pl.	1st	ἐ	ἀγαπα	ο	μεν	ἠγαπῶμεν
	2nd	ἐ	ἀγαπα	ε	τε	ἠγαπᾶτε
	3rd	ἐ	ἀγαπα	ο	ν	ἠγαπων

The present active indicative of **epsilon contract verbs** (stems ending in ε) follows the pattern below. Once again, note the circumflex accent over the diphthongs which result from the vowel contractions.

		ST	+ V +	PAE	Contracted Form
Sing.	1st	ποιε	ω	-	ποιῶ
	2nd	ποιε	ει	ς	ποιεῖς
	3rd	ποιε	ει	-	ποιεῖ
Pl.	1st	ποιε	ο	μεν	ποιοῦμεν
	2nd	ποιε	ε	τε	ποιεῖτε
	3rd	ποιε	ου	σι (ν)	ποιοῦσι(ν)

The imperfect active indicative of epsilon contract verbs follows the paradigm below.

		A +	ST	+ V +	SAE	Contracted Form
Sing.	1st	ἐ	ποιε	ο	ν	ἐποιουν
	2nd	ἐ	ποιε	ε	ς	ἐποιεις
	3rd	ἐ	ποιε	ε	-	ἐποιει
Pl.	1st	ἐ	ποιε	ο	μεν	ἐποιοῦμεν
	2nd	ἐ	ποιε	ε	τε	ἐποιεῖτε
	3rd	ἐ	ποιε	ο	ν	ἐποιουν

The present active indicative of **omicron contract verbs** (stems ending in ο) follows the pattern below. Once again, note the circumflex accent over the diphthongs which result from the vowel contractions.

		ST	+ V +	PAE	Contracted Form
Sing.	1st	σταυρο	ω	-	σταυρῶ
	2nd	σταυρο	ει	ς	σταυροῖς
	3rd	σταυρο	ει	-	σταυροῖ
Pl.	1st	σταυρο	ο	μεν	σταυροῦμεν
	2nd	σταυρο	ε	τε	σταυροῦτε
	3rd	σταυρο	ου	σι (ν)	σταυροῦσι(ν)

The imperfect active indicative of omicron contract verbs follows the paradigm below.

		A +	ST	+ V	+ SAE	Contracted Form
Sing.	1st	ἐ	σταυρο	ο	ν	ἐσταυρουν
	2nd	ἐ	σταυρο	ε	ς	ἐσταυρους
	3rd	ἐ	σταυρο	ε	-	ἐσταυρου
Pl.	1st	ἐ	σταυρο	ο	μεν	ἐσταυροῦμεν
	2nd	ἐ	σταυρο	ε	τε	ἐσταυροῦτε
	3rd	ἐ	σταυρο	ο	ν	ἐσταυρουν

12.4 Vocabulary

Alpha Contract Verbs

221.	ἀγαπάω	I am loving	(143)
222.	ζάω, ζήσομαι	I am living	(140)
223.	ἐπιτιμάω	I am rebuking	(29)
224.	τιμάω	I am honoring	(21)
225.	νικάω	I am overcoming, conquering	(28)

Epsilon Contract Verbs

226.	αἰτέω	I am asking	(70)
227.	εὐλογέω	I am blessing (eulogy)	(42)
228.	εὐχαριστέω	I am giving thanks [dat. dir. obj.]	(38)
229.	μισέω	I am hating (misogynist)	(40)
230.	παρακαλέω	I am urging, exhorting, comforting	(109)
231.	ποιέω	I am making, doing (poet)	(568)
232.	φιλέω	I am loving (Philadelphia)	(25)
233.	φρονέω	I am thinking, having in mind	(26)

Omicron Contract Verbs

234.	δικαιόω	I am justifying, declaring righteous	(39)
235.	σταυρόω	I am crucifying	(46)

Liquid and Nasal Verbs

236.	ἀποκτείνω	I am killing	(74)
237.	ἐγείρω	I am raising	(144)
238.	κρίνω	I am judging (critic)	(114)

239.   παραγγέλλω   I am commanding, charging   (32)

240.   σπείρω   I am sowing   (52)

12.5 Form Identification - For each form, give the tense, voice, mood, person, number; the dictionary form, and a translation.

1. ἀγαπᾷ

2. εὐλογεῖτε

3. δικαιοῦμεν

4. ἐποιουν

5. ἐγερεῖ

6. νικῶσι

7. πεφιληκασι

8. ἐμισεις

9. αἰτῶ

10. ἐτιμησας

11. περιπατοῦμεν

12. ἠκολουθησα

13. ἀπεκτεινε

14. μαρτυρησεις

15. λαλεῖ

16. ἐζητουν

17. ἐσταυρου

18. ἠγειραν

19. ἠρε

20. παρακαλοῦσι

21. ἀπεστειλα

22. φρονεῖς

23. ζῶ

24. ἀρεῖς

25. ὁρᾶτε

12.6 Practice Exercises - Translate the following sentences. Parse all verbs (TVMPN - Dictionary form).

I myself have overcome the world.

1. ἐγω νενικηκα τον κοσμον.

they crucified the lord of glory

2. τον κυριον της δοξης ἐσταυρωσαν.

~~You have not said that the angels are judging?~~ *will*

3. οὐκ οἰδατε ὅτι ἀγγελους κρινοῦμεν;

You honor your father and ~~father~~ mother

4. τιμησεις τον πατερα σου και την μητερα.

You hate the work of the

5. μισεις τα ἐργα των Νικολαϊτων (Nicolaitans), ἃ κἀγω μισῶ.

You do the work of your ~~father~~

6. ὑμεις ποιειτε τα ἐργα του πατρος ὑμων.

3. Do you not know that we will judge angels?

Ask and you will recieve that you havent wrongly asked

7. αἰτεῖτε καὶ οὐ λαμβανετε ὅτι κακῶς (wrongly) αἰτεῖτε.

Jacob he hated loved Esau

*8. τὸν Ἰακωβ (Jacob) ἠγαπησα· τὸν Ἡσαυ (Esau) ἐμισησα.

You think not the things of God but the things of man

9. οὐ φρονεῖς τα (the things) τοῦ θεοῦ ἀλλα τα (the things) τῶν ἀνθρωπων.

The father himself loves you, because you loved me that you would love

10. αὐτος γαρ ὁ πατηρ φιλεῖ ὑμας, ὅτι ὑμεις ἐμε πεφιληκατε.

You love the lord your God with your whole heart

11. ἀγαπησεις κυριον τον θεον σου ἐν ὁλῃ (whole) τῃ καρδιᾳ σου.

i sent him to the world as he was fighting for the world

12. καθως ἐμε ἀπεστειλας εἰς τον κοσμον, κἀγω ἀπεστειλα αὐτους εἰς τον κοσμον.

And Jesus honored him and came to the man with the demon

13. και ὅτε ἐπετιμησεν αὐτῳ ὁ Ἰησους, ἠλθεν ἐκ του ἀνθρωπου το δαιμονιον.

We are always delighted about the Jesus Christ your father God

14. εὐχαριστοῦμεν τῳ θεῳ πατρι του κυριοῦ ἡμων Ἰησου Χριστου παντοτε (always) περι ὑμων.

15. λεγει τῳ Πετρῳ ὁ Ἰησους, ἀγαπᾳς με; λεγει αὐτῳ, συ οἰδας ὅτι φιλῶ σε.

came

16. τινες (some) δε ἐξ αὐτων ἠλθον προς τους Φαρισαιους (Pharisees) και εἰπαν αὐτοις ἃ ἐποιει Ἰησους.

17. τα ἐργα ἃ ποιῶ μαρτυρεῖ περι ἐμου ὅτι ὁ πατηρ με ἀπεσταλκεν.

18. ἐν τουτῳ (this) ἐστιν ἡ ἀγαπη· οὐχ ὅτι ἡμεις ἠγαπηκαμεν τον θεον, ἀλλ' ὅτι αὐτος ἠγαπησεν ἡμας και ἀπεστειλεν τον υἱον αὐτου ὡς ἱλασμον (propitiation) περι των ἁμαρτιων ἡμων.

19. ζῶ δε οὐκετι (no longer) ἐγω, ζῃ δε ἐν ἐμοι Χριστος· ἡ ζωη δε ἢν νυν (now) ζῶ ἐν σαρκι, πιστει ζῶ ἐν τῳ υἱῳ του θεου.

in the son of God. *by faith I live*

20. ἐν Κανα (Cana) τῆς Γαλιλαιας (Galilee) ἐποιησεν ὁ Ἰησους την ἀρχην των σημειων, και ἐφανερωσεν την δοξαν αὐτου και ἐπιστευσαν εἰς αὐτον οἱ μαθηται αὐτου.

7. you are asking and you are not receiving because you have asked wrongly

8. Jacob I loved, Esau I hated

12. Just as you sent me into the world, I also sent them into the world

13. And when Jesus rebuked him the demon came out of the man

14. we are giving thanks to God the father of our Lord Jesus Christ alway concerning

16. Some of them came to the Pharisees & spoke to them the things Jesus was doing

17. the works which im doing testify concerning me that the father sent me

GRAMMAR GRABBER: Passive Voice

ὅτι ὁ μὲν υἱὸς τοῦ ἀνθρώπου ὑπάγει καθὼς γέγραπται περὶ αὐτοῦ, οὐαὶ δὲ τῷ ἀνθρώπῳ ἐκείνῳ δι᾽ οὗ
ὁ υἱὸς τοῦ ἀνθρώπου παραδίδοται· καλὸν αὐτῷ εἰ
οὐκ ἐγεννήθη ὁ ἄνθρωπος ἐκεῖνος. (Mark 14:18-21)

Because, indeed, the Son of Man is departing just as it has been
written concerning Him, but woe to that man through whom the
Son of Man is being betrayed. {It would have been} good for him
if that man were not born.

Mark's account of Jesus' prediction of his betrayal at the Last Supper
table (Mark 14:18-21) demonstrates the versatility of Greek in relating subject
and action. Jesus first speaks in the active voice (the subject does the action)
of the one who "will betray him" (14:18). Then, as He gives a clue to the
identity of the betrayer, Jesus uses the middle voice (the subject does and
participates in the results of the action) to indicate that it is the "one who is
dipping for himself with me in the bowl" (14:20). Finally, He uses the
passive voice (the subject receives the verb's action) to seal both the Son of
Man's divinely predicted destiny and the betrayer's condemnation (14:21).

Jesus' use of the **passive voice** in verse 21 is striking. The *fact* of His
departure "has been written" (γέγραπται, perfect passive). By whom has
it been written? Although the agent is not explicitly stated, it is understood
to be God's Spirit through the Old Testament prophets. The Son of Man's
departure was in line with God's sovereign plan.

The *nature* of that departure, however, is also noteworthy. The Son of
Man "is being betrayed" (παραδίδοται, present passive; literally "is
being handed over into the power of another") "through" a friend (cf. Ps
41:9). The passive voice brings Jesus to the fore as the focus of the action. At
the same time, the use of an expressed agent makes clear Judas' responsibility in the action—a responsibility which Jesus emphasizes with a solemn
declaration.

Chapter 13

PRESENT, FUTURE, AND PERFECT MIDDLE/PASSIVE INDICATIVE

Previous lessons have introduced forms related to the active voice of the verb. Greek verbs, however, have middle and passive voice forms as well. After a brief discussion of the middle and passive voices in general, the middle and passive forms of the present, future, and perfect tenses will be explained.

13.1 Middle and Passive Voice

Voice is that element of a Greek verb which expresses how the subject relates to the action. There are three voices in Greek: active, middle, and passive. In the *active voice*, the subject produces the action (e.g., "Bill is writing the novel."). In the *middle voice*, the subject produces the action *and* participates in the results of the action. The middle voice has no exact parallel in English, but it is best translated using the reflexive pronoun, which reflects the action back to the subject (e.g., "Bill writing the novel *for himself*" . . . and he has a special interest in the final product). In the *passive voice*, the subject receives the action. The translation of the passive voice normally includes a form of the verb "to be." (e.g., "The novel is *being* written by Bill.").

13.2 Primary Middle/Passive Endings

In the same way that the active endings of the present, future, and perfect active indicative tenses could be grouped together, similar endings are used for the middle and passive voices of those tenses. The primary middle/passive endings are set out in the chart which follows.

Primary Middle/Passive Endings			
Singular		Plural	
1st	μαι	1st	μεθα
2nd	σαι	2nd	σθε
3rd	ται	3rd	νται

In the present and future tenses, the σ falls out of the second person singular ending (σαι) and the diphthong αι contracts with the theme vowel (ε) to produce ῃ. The basic ending, however, is σαι. For this reason, the perfect tense will be introduced first as the tense which best displays the basic endings.

13.3 Perfect Middle/Passive Indicative

The perfect tense is used to connote *completed-stative* action in *present* time. In order to reflect the completed action of the perfect tense, we will translate the perfect middle and passive indicative using the present perfect. The first person singular of the verb "to see" would thus be translated as "I have seen for myself" in the middle voice and "I have been seen" in the passive voice. The form of the perfect middle/passive indicative may be summarized by the following formula:

Reduplication + Stem + Primary Middle/Passive Endings
(R + ST + PM/PE)

- ▶ Reduplication: The initial letter/diphthong is added as a prefix to the verb stem in order to indicate completed-stative action.
- ▶ Stem: The perfect tense stem of a regular verb is found by removing the final ω of the dictionary form.
- ▶ Personal Endings: The perfect middle and passive indicative use the primary middle/passive endings discussed above. Note that these endings are attached directly to the verb stem, without either a tense sign or a theme vowel.

In the perfect tense the forms of the middle and passive voices are identical. The only difference is in the translation. Context must determine whether a form is translated as middle or as passive.

Middle		λυω (λυ-)		Translation
Sing. 1st	λε	λυ	μαι	I have loosed for myself.
2nd	λε	λυ	σαι	You have loosed for yourself.
3rd	λε	λυ	ται	He/she/it has loosed for him/her/itself.
Pl. 1st	λε	λυ	μεθα	We have loosed for ourselves.
2nd	λε	λυ	σθε	You have loosed for yourselves.
3rd	λε	λυ	νται	They have loosed for themselves.

Passive		λυω (λυ-)		Translation
Sing.	1st	λε λυ	μαι	I have been loosed.
	2nd	λε λυ	σαι	You have been loosed.
	3rd	λε λυ	ται	He/she/it has been loosed.
Pl.	1st	λε λυ	μεθα	We have been loosed.
	2nd	λε λυ	σθε	You have been loosed.
	3rd	λε λυ	νται	They have been loosed.

<u>Note</u>: It might be helpful at this point to review the idea of principal parts which was introduced in Chapter 10. Both the perfect middle and passive indicative are built on the *fifth* principal part. For completely regular verbs such as λυω and πιστευω the fifth principal part can be constructed using the formulas given. The fifth principal part of irregular verbs, however, must be memorized.

13.4 Present Middle/Passive Indicative

The present tense is used connote *progressive* action in *present* time. In order to reflect the continuing action of the present tense, we will translate the present middle and passive indicative using the progressive present. The first person singular of the verb "to see" would thus be translated as "I am seeing for myself" in the middle voice and "I am being seen" in the passive voice. The form of the present middle/passive indicative may be summarized by the following formula:

Stem + Theme Vowel + Primary Middle/Passive Endings
(ST +   V   +   PM/PE   )

► Stem: The present tense stem of a regular verb is found by removing the final ω of the dictionary form.
► Theme Vowel: The theme vowels follow the pattern *o-e-e-o-e-o*.
► Personal Endings: The present middle and passive indicative use the primary middle/passive endings discussed above.

As was true in the perfect tense, the forms of the present middle and passive voices are identical. The only difference is in the translation. Context must determine whether a form is translated as middle or as passive. In both paradigms, you should make special note of the contraction in the second person singular form.

Middle		λυω (λυ-)		Translation
Sing.	1st	λυ o	μαι	I am loosing for myself.
	2nd	λυ ε	σαι = η	You are loosing for yourself.
	3rd	λυ ε	ται	He/she/it is loosing for him/her/itself.
Pl.	1st	λυ o	μεθα	We are loosing for ourselves.
	2nd	λυ ε	σθε	You are loosing for yourselves.
	3rd	λυ o	νται	They are loosing for themselves.

Passive		λυω (λυ-)		Translation
Sing.	1st	λυ o	μαι	I am being loosed.
	2nd	λυ ε	σαι = η	You are being loosed.
	3rd	λυ ε	ται	He/she/it is being loosed.
Pl.	1st	λυ o	μεθα	We are being loosed.
	2nd	λυ ε	σθε	You are being loosed.
	3rd	λυ o	νται	They are being loosed.

Of course, when the theme vowel comes in contact with the vowel at the end of contract verbs, contraction takes place. The resulting forms are summarized below.

Alpha Contract	Epsilon Contract	Omicron Contract
ἀγαπ ῶ μαι	φιλ οῦ μαι	σταυρ οῦ μαι
ἀγαπ ᾷ	φιλ ῇ	σταυρ οῖ
ἀγαπ ᾶ ται	φιλ εῖ ται	σταυρ οῦ ται
ἀγαπ ώ μεθα	φιλ οῦ μεθα	σταυρ ού μεθα
ἀγαπ ᾶ σθε	φιλ εῖ σθε	σταυρ οῦ σθε
ἀγαπ ῶ νται	φιλ οῦ νται	σταυρ οῦ νται

13.5 Future Middle Indicative

The future tense is used connote *summary* action in *future* time. In order to reflect the summary action of the future tense, we will translate the future middle indicative using the simple future. The first person singular of the verb "to see" would thus be translated as "I shall see for myself" in the middle voice. The form of the future middle indicative may be summarized by the following formula:

Stem + Tense Sign + Theme Vowel + Primary Middle/Passive Endings
(ST +   S   +   V   +   PM/PE   )

▸ Stem: The present tense stem of a regular verb is found by removing the final ω of the dictionary form.
▸ Tense Sign: As in the future active indicative, the tense sign is σ.
▸ Theme Vowel: The theme vowels follow the pattern *o-e-e-o-e-o*.
▸ Personal Endings: The future middle indicative uses the primary middle/passive endings discussed above.

The paradigm of the future middle indicative of the verb λυω follows. You should make special note of the contraction in the second person singular form.

		λυω (λυ-)				Translation
Sing.	1st	λυ	σ	o	μαι	I shall loose for myself.
	2nd	λυ	σ	ε	σαι = η	You will loose for yourself.
	3rd	λυ	σ	ε	ται	He/she/it will loose for him/her/itself.
Pl.	1st	λυ	σ	o	μεθα	We shall loose for ourselves.
	2nd	λυ	σ	ε	σθε	You will loose for yourselves.
	3rd	λυ	σ	o	νται	They will loose for themselves.

<u>Note</u>: The future middle indicative is built on the *second* principal part. For completely regular verbs such as λυω and πιστευω the second principal part can be constructed using the formulas given. The second principal part of irregular verbs, however, must be memorized.

13.6 Future Passive Indicative

The future tense is used to connote *summary* action in *future* time. In order to reflect the summary action of the future tense, we will translate the future passive indicative using the simple future. The first person singular of the verb "to see" would thus be translated as "I shall be seen" in the passive voice. The form of the future passive indicative may be summarized by the following formula:

Stem + Tense Sign + Theme Vowel + Primary Middle/Passive Endings
(ST + S + V + PM/PE)

▸ Stem: The present tense stem of a regular verb is found by removing the final ω of the dictionary form.

▸ Tense Sign: Since the future passive actually related to the *aorist passive* rather than to the future active and middle (see the summary of principal parts), the tense sign is different. In the future passive indicative, the tense sign is θησ.

Theme Vowel: The theme vowels follow the pattern *o-e-e-o-e-o*.

▸ Personal Endings: The future middle indicative uses the primary middle/passive endings discussed above.

The paradigm of the future passive indicative of the verb λυω follows. You should make special note of the contraction in the second person singular form.

		λυω (λυ-)				Translation
Sing.	1st	λυ	θησ	o	μαι	I shall be loosed.
	2nd	λυ	θησ	ε	σαι = η	You will be loosed.
	3rd	λυ	θησ	ε	ται	He/she/it will be loosed.
Pl.	1st	λυ	θησ	o	μεθα	We shall be loosed.
	2nd	λυ	θησ	ε	σθε	You will be loosed.
	3rd	λυ	θησ	o	νται	They will be loosed.

Note: The future passive indicative is built on the *sixth* principal part. For completely regular verbs such as λυω and πιστευω the sixth principal part can be constructed using the formulas given. The sixth principal part of irregular verbs, however, must be memorized.

13.7 "Deponent" Verbs

Some verbs lack an active form in certain tenses. For whatever reason, the active form has fallen out of use, and the middle form has taken its place. These verb forms are called "deponent" forms. Such deponent forms can be readily identified in the verb's principal parts. **When a verb has a middle ending in a principal part which normally has an active form (#1-4), the verb is "deponent" in all of the tenses built on that principal part.** Some verbs are deponent in all of their forms; other verbs are deponent only in certain principal parts. In general, when only one form of a verb is listed in the vocabulary lists and it has the ending -ομαι, it will always be parsed as "deponent." When several forms for a verb are listed in the vocabulary lists, you must make a note of any middle endings in the first four principal parts. In those principal parts, that verb is "deponent." The following verbs will serve as examples.

The verb λυω is completely normal. It is not deponent in any of its principal parts.

PAI1S	FAI1S	AI1S	PfAI1S	PfM/PI1S	API1S
λυω	λυσω	ἔλυσα	λελυκα	λελυμαι	ἐλυθην

The verb δέχομαι is deponent in its first three principal parts.

PAI1S	FAI1S	AAI1S	PfAI1S	PfM/PI1S	API1S
δέχομαι	δέξομαι	ἐδεξάμην	none	δέδεγμαι	ἐδέχθην

The verb ἔρχομαι is deponent in its first and second principal parts, but not in its third and fourth.

PAI1S	FAI1S	AAI1S	PfAI1S	PfM/PI1S	API1S
ἔρχομαι	ἐλεύσομαι	ἦλθον	ἐλήλυθα	none	none

The verb ὁράω is deponent *only* in its second principal part.

PAI1S	FAI1S	AAI1S	PfAI1S	PfM/PI1S	API1S
ὁράω	ὄψομαι	εἶδον	ἑώρακα	ἕωραμαι	ὤφθην

It is important to remember the following concepts when dealing with deponent verbs:

1. All forms related to a deponent principal part will be deponent (e.g., if the *first* principal part is deponent, all voices, moods, and modes of the *present and imperfect* tenses will be deponent).
2. When a verbal form is deponent, (a) it will have a middle form, (b) it will be parsed as "deponent" (D), and (c) it will be translated as active (e.g., ἔρχεται is parsed as PDI3S and translated as "he/she/it **is coming**" . . . *not* "he/she/it is coming for him/her/itself")

13.8 The Future Tense of εἰμι

The future tense of the verb εἰμι was introduced in Chapter 3. It should now be clear why it is parsed as Future **Deponent** Indicative: it uses *middle* forms which are translated as *active*.

		εἰμι	Translation
Sing.	1st	ἐσομαι	I shall be.
	2nd	ἐσῃ	You will be.
	3rd	ἐσται	He/she/it will be.
Pl.	1st	ἐσομεθα	We shall be.
	2nd	ἐσεσθε	You will be.
	3rd	ἐσονται	They will be.

13.9 Vocabulary

Deponent Verbs

241.	ἅπτομαι	I am touching	(39)
242.	ἄρχομαι	I am beginning	(86)
243.	ἀσπάζομαι	I am greeting	(59)
244.	βούλομαι	I am wishing	(37)
245.	δέχομαι	I am receiving	(56)

(δέχομαι, δέξομαι, ἐδεξάμην,---, δέδεγμαι, ἐδέχθην)

246.	ἐργάζομαι	I am working	(41)
247.	εὐαγγελίζομαι	I am preaching the gospel	(54)
248.	ἡγέομαι	I am considering, regarding, leading	(28)
249.	ἰαόμαι	I am healing	(26)
250.	καυχάομαι	I am boasting	(37)
251.	λογίζομαι	I am considering	(40)
252.	μιμνήσκομαι	I am remembering	(23)

(6 = ἐμνήσθην)

253.	παραγίνομαι	I am coming, arriving, appearing	(37)
254.	πορεύομαι	I am coming, going	(153)

(6 = ἐπορεύθην)

255.	προσεύχομαι	I am praying	(85)
256.	προσκαλέομαι	I am summoning, calling to myself	(29)
257.	φοβέομαι	I am fearing (phobia)	(95)

(6 = ἐφοβήθην)

258.	χαρίζομαι	I am giving freely, granting	(23)
259.	ψεύδομαι	I am lying (pseudonym)	(12)

Additional Contract Verb

260. νοέω   I am understanding, perceiving   (14)

13.10 Form Identification - For each form given, identify its tense, voice, mood, person, and number; then write its dictionary form and a translation. One example is given

λυομαι   PM/PI1S   λυω   I am loosing for myself (middle)
                                I am being loosed (passive)

1. ἐσονται   14. πεπιστευσαι

2. πεπιστευμεθα   15. ἐξομεθα

3. γινεσθε   16. γραφησομαι

4. τιμῶνται   17. λυθησονται

5. γινωσκομαι   18. γινῃ

6. γεγραπται   19. λυεται

7. ἀκουσεσθε   20. ἐσται

8. βλεψομαι   21. πιστευσῃ

9. ὡμολογηνται   22. λελυμεθα

10. ἀπεσταλμαι   23. διδαξομαι

11. ἠγαπησθε   24. χαριζεται

12. ζησομαι   25. λειψῃ

13. ἐλευσεται

13.11 Practice Exercises - Translate the following sentences. Parse all verbs (TVMPN - Dictionary form).

1. οὐκ ψευδεσθε ἀνθρωποις ἀλλα τῳ θεῳ.

2. λογιζεται ἡ πιστις αὐτου αὐτῳ εἰς δικαιοσυνην (righteousness).

3. εἰ λεγεις λογον, ἰαθησεται ὁ δουλος μου.

4. ἀσπαζεται σε τα τεκνα της ἀδελφης (sister) σου.

5. εἰ δε πνευματι ἀγεσθε, οὐκ ἐστε ὑπο νομον.

6. και καυχωμεθα ἐπ' ἐλπιδι της δοξης του θεου.

7. και ὅσοι (as many as) ἐν νομῳ ἡμαρτον, δια νομου κριθησονται.

8. καθως γεγραπται ἐν τοις προφηταις, διδασκονται ὑπο θεου.

9. ἐγερθησεται γαρ ἐθνος ἐπ' ἐθνος και βασιλεια (kingdom) ἐπι βασιλειαν.

10. αὐτος δε ὃς ποιεῖ την ἀληθειαν ἐρχεται προς το φως.

11. ὅσα (as many things as) ἐν τῃ σκοτιᾳ εἰπατε ἐν τῳ φωτι ἀκουσθησεται.

12. καρδιᾳ γαρ πιστευεται εἰς δικαιοσυνην (righteousness), γλωσσῃ ὁμολογεῖται εἰς σωτηριαν (salvation).

13. και ἐσται ὁτι εἰ ἀνθρωπος καλεσει ἐπι τῳ ὀνοματι κυριου σωθησεται.

14. ὁτε ὁ Χριστος φανερωθησεται, τοτε (then) ὑμεις συν αὐτῳ φανερωθησεσθε ἐν δοξῃ.

15. αὐτος ὃς ἀγαπᾳ με ἀγαπηθησεται ὑπο του πατρος μου κἀγω ἀγαπησω αὐτον.

16. ὁ δε ᾽Ιησους εἰπεν αὐτοις, το βαπτισμα (baptism) ὃ ἐγω βαπτιζομαι βαπτισθησεσθε.

17. ἐξ ἐργων νομου οὐ δικαιωθησεται ἀνθρωπος ἐμπροσθεν αὐτου, δια γαρ νομου ἐστιν γνωσις ἀμαρτιας.

18. ὃ γεγεννηται ἐξ της σαρκος σαρξ ἐστιν, και ὃ γεγεννηται ἐκ του πνευματος πνευμα ἐστιν.

19. ἐλπις δε ἥ βλεπεται οὐκ ἐστιν ἐλπις· εἰ δε ὅ οὐ βλεπομεν ἐλπιζομεν (to hope for), δι' ὑπομονης (endurance) δεχομεθα αὐτην.

20. εἰ γαρ οἱ νεκροι (dead) οὐκ ἐγειρονται, οὐδε Χριστος ἐγηγερται· εἰ δε Χριστος οὐκ ἐγηγερται, ἐτι (still) ἐστε ἐν ταις ἁμαρτιαις ὑμων.

GRAMMAR GRABBER: Middle Voice

The **middle voice** is often difficult to translate with its full force. Sometimes it requires an entirely different word in English to convey it. In the active voice, for example, the verb ἅπτω means "to strike, so as to kindle a fire." This meaning is clearly seen in Luke 15:8 where the woman with the lost coin "lights a lamp" (ἅπτει λύχνον) to begin her search. In the middle voice, however, ἅπτω means "to touch, take hold of." Jesus' encounter with the hemorrhaging woman in Mark 5:27-32 revolves around the aorist middle form of ἅπτω:

ἀκούσασα περὶ τοῦ Ἰησοῦ, ἐλθοῦσα ἐν τῷ ὄχλῳ ὄπισθεν ἥψατο τοῦ ἱματίου αὐτοῦ· ἔλεγεν γὰρ ὅτι Ἐὰν ἅψωμαι κἂν τῶν ἱματίων αὐτοῦ σωθήσομαι . . . καὶ εὐθὺς ὁ Ἰησοῦς . . . ἔλεγεν, Τίς μου ἥψατο τῶν ἱματίων; καὶ ἔλεγον αὐτῷ οἱ μαθηταὶ αὐτοῦ, Βλέπεις τὸν ὄχλον συνθλίβοντά σε, καὶ λέγεις, Τίς μου ἥψατο; καὶ περιεβλέπετο ἰδεῖν τὴν τοῦτο ποιήσασαν.

When she heard about Jesus, the woman came up from behind and touched (ἥψατο, aorist middle indicative) Him, because she was saying to herself "If I might touch (ἅψωμαι, aorist middle subjunctive) even {the hem} of his garment, I will be healed." Jesus immediately queried the crowd, asking "Who touched (ἥψατο, aorist middle indicative) me?" When the disciples remonstrated with Jesus about the ridiculousness of the question "Who touched (ἥψατο) me?" given the press of the crowd, Jesus remained undeterred in his search. He kept on looking around for himself (περιεβλέπετο, imperfect middle indicative) to see who (feminine) had done this.

Not only does the repeated use of the aorist middle of ἅπτω in this passage point out the necessity of differentiating between the active and middle voice, the imperfect middle of περιβλέπω points out Jesus' persistence and personal involvement in seeking out the one who had touched Him.

Chapter 14

IMPERFECT, AORIST, AND PLUPERFECT MIDDLE/PASSIVE INDICATIVE

As the present, future, and perfect middle/passive forms may be grouped together as "primary" tenses, so may the imperfect, aorist, and pluperfect middle/passive forms be grouped together as "secondary" tenses. First, the secondary middle/passive endings will be presented, then the paradigms of each tense will be discussed.

14.1 Secondary Middle/Passive Endings

In the same way that the active endings of the imperfect, aorist, and pluperfect active indicative tenses could be grouped together, similar endings are used for the middle and passive voices of those tenses. These secondary middle/passive endings are set out below.

		Secondary Middle/Passive Endings
Singular	1st	μην
	2nd	σο
	3rd	το
Plural	1st	μεθα
	2nd	σθε
	3rd	ντο

In the imperfect and aorist tenses, the σ drops out of the second person singular ending (σο) and the ο contracts with the theme vowel. The basic ending, however, is σο. For this reason, the pluperfect tense will be introduced first as the tense which best displays the basic endings.

14.2 Pluperfect Middle/Passive Indicative

The pluperfect tense is used to connote *completed-stative* action in *past* time. In order to reflect the completed action of the pluperfect tense, we will translate the pluperfect middle and passive indicative using the past perfect.

The first person singular of the verb "to see" would thus be translated as "I had seen for myself" in the middle voice and "I had been seen" in the passive voice. The form of the pluperfect active indicative may be summarized by the following formula:

Augment + Reduplication + Stem + Secondary Middle/Passive Endings
(A   +   R   + ST +   SM/PE   )

▸ Augment: The prefix **ε** is added to indicate past time action.
▸ Reduplication: The initial letter/diphthong is added as a prefix to the verb stem in order to completed action.
▸ Stem: The perfect tense stem of a regular verb is found by removing the final **ω** of the dictionary form.
▸ Personal Endings: The pluperfect middle and passive indicative use the secondary middle/passive endings discussed above. Note that these endings are attached directly to the verb stem, without either a tense sign or a theme vowel.

The forms of the pluperfect middle and passive indicative are identical; the only difference is in the translation. Context must determine whether a form is translated as middle or as passive. Of the eighty-six occurrences of the pluperfect in the Greek New Testament, seventy-nine are in the active voice. The middle voice occurs only twice (John 9:33; Acts 26:32); the passive voice occurs only five times (Matt 7:25; Luke 4:29; 16:20; John 11:44; Acts 17:23). The paradigms which follow, therefore, should not be memorized, but they are helpful in understanding the way in which the pluperfect middle/passive is formed.

Middle		λυω (λυ-)		Translation
Sing.	1st	ἐ λε λυ μην		I had loosed for myself.
	2nd	ἐ λε λυ σο		You had loosed for yourself.
	3rd	ἐ λε λυ το		He/she/it had loosed for him/her/itself.
Pl.	1st	ἐ λε λυ μεθα		We had loosed for ourselves.
	2nd	ἐ λε λυ σθε		You had loosed for yourselves.
	3rd	ἐ λε λυ ντο		They had loosed for themselves.

Passive		λυω (λυ-)		Translation
Sing.	1st	ἐ λε λυ μην		I had been loosed.
	2nd	ἐ λε λυ σο		You had been loosed.
	3rd	ἐ λε λυ το		He/she/it had been loosed.
Pl.	1st	ἐ λε λυ μεθα		We had been loosed.
	2nd	ἐ λε λυ σθε		You had been loosed.
	3rd	ἐ λε λυ ντο		They had been loosed.

<u>Note</u>: Both the pluperfect middle and passive indicative are built on the *fifth* principal part. For completely regular verbs such as λυω and πιστευω the fifth principal part can be constructed using the formulas given. The fifth principal part of irregular verbs, however, must be memorized.

14.3 Imperfect Middle/Passive Indicative

The imperfect tense is used to connote *progressive* action in *past* time. In order to reflect the continuing action of the imperfect tense, we will translate the imperfect middle and passive indicative using the progressive past. The first person singular of the verb "to see" would thus be translated as "I was seeing for myself" in the middle voice and "I was being seen" in the passive voice.

It is helpful to remember that the imperfect tense, like the present tense, is built on the *first* principal part. The imperfect middle/passive, therefore, can always be constructed from the dictionary form using the following formula:

Augment + Stem + Theme Vowel + Secondary Middle/Passive Endings
(A   + ST +   V   +   SM/PE   )

- ▶ Augment: The prefix ε is added to indicate past time action.
- ▶ Stem: The imperfect tense stem of a regular verb is found by removing the final ω of the dictionary form.
- ▶ Theme Vowel: The theme vowels follow the pattern *o-e-e-o-e-o*.
- ▶ Personal Endings: The imperfect middle and passive indicative uses the secondary middle/passive endings discussed above.

The forms of the imperfect middle and passive indicative are identical. The only difference is in the translation. Context must determine whether a form is translated as middle or as passive. You should make special note of the contraction in the second person singular form.

Middle		λυω (λυ-)	Translation
Sing.	1st	ἐ λυ ο μην	I was loosing for myself.
	2nd	ἐ λυ ε σο = ου	You were loosing for yourself.
	3rd	ἐ λυ ε το	He/she/it was loosing for him/her/itself.
Pl.	1st	ἐ λυ ο μεθα	We were loosing for ourselves.
	2nd	ἐ λυ ε σθε	You were loosing for yourselves.
	3rd	ἐ λυ ο ντο	They were loosing for themselves.

Passive		λυω (λυ-)	Translation
Sing.	1st	ἐ λυ ο μην	I was being loosed.
	2nd	ἐ λυ ε σο = ου	You were being loosed.
	3rd	ἐ λυ ε το	He/she/it was being loosed.
Pl.	1st	ἐ λυ ο μεθα	We were being loosed.
	2nd	ἐ λυ ε σθε	You were being loosed.
	3rd	ἐ λυ ο ντο	They were being loosed.

Of course, when the theme vowel comes in contact with the vowel at the end of contract verbs, contraction takes place. The resulting forms are summarized below.

Alpha Contract	Epsilon Contract	Omicron Contract
ἠγαπ ω μην	ἐφιλ ου μην	ἐσταυρ ου μην
ἠγαπ ῶ	ἐφιλ οῦ	ἐσταυρ οῦ
ἠγαπ ᾶ το	ἐφιλ εῖ το	ἐσταυρ οῦ το
ἠγαπ ω μεθα	ἐφιλ ου μεθα	ἐσταυρ ου μεθα
ἠγαπ ᾶ σθε	ἐφιλ εῖ σθε	ἐσταυρ οῦ σθε
ἠγαπ ῶ ντο	ἐφιλ οῦ ντο	ἐσταυρ οῦ ντο

14.4 First Aorist Middle Indicative

The aorist tense is used to connote *summary* action in *past* time. In order to reflect the summary action of the aorist tense, we will translate the aorist middle indicative using the simple past. The first person singular of the verb "to see" would thus be translated as "I saw for myself" in the middle voice.

The form of the first aorist middle indicative may be summarized by the following formula:

Augment + Stem + Tense + Theme + Secondary Middle/Passive
Sign   Vowel   Endings
(A   + ST + S + V +   SM/PE   )

▶ Augment: The prefix ε is added to indicate past time action.
▶ Stem: The first aorist tense stem of a regular verb is found by removing the final ω of the dictionary form.
▶ Tense Sign: As in the future active indicative, the tense sign is σ.
▶ Theme Vowel: The theme vowel is α.
▶ Personal Endings: The first aorist middle indicative uses the secondary middle/passive endings discussed above.

The paradigm of the first aorist middle indicative of the verb λυω follows. Make special note of the contraction in the second person singular form. Understand also that the tense sign will contract with a labial, gutteral, or dental consonant at the end of a verb stem and will disappear when the verb stem ends in a liquid or nasal consonant.

[handwritten: Sigma + alpha endings]

		λυω (λυ-)	Translation
Sing.	1st	ἐ λυ σ α μην	I loosed for myself.
	2nd	ἐ λυ σ α σο = ω	You loosed for yourself.
	3rd	ἐ λυ σ α το	He/she/it loosed for him/her/itself.
Pl.	1st	ἐ λυ σ α μεθα	We loosed for ourselves.
	2nd	ἐ λυ σ α σθε	You loosed for yourselves.
	3rd	ἐ λυ σ α ντο	They loosed for themselves.

Note: The aorist middle indicative is built on the *third* principal part. For completely regular verbs such as λυω and πιστευω the third principal part can be always constructed using the formula given above.

14.5 Second Aorist Middle Indicative
As was true in the active voice, the middle voice of second aorist verbs is characterized by a stem change. This stem change is what distinguishes the second aorist middle from the imperfect middle, for the second aorist middle lacks a tense sign and uses a theme vowel pattern which is identical to the imperfect.

Like the first aorist tense, the second aorist is used to connote *summary* action in *past* time. There is no difference in *translation* (other than the lexical meaning) between a first aorist middle form and a second aorist middle form. Nor is there a difference in the *principal part* on which the first and second aorist tenses are formed; both are formed from the third principal part. The distinction between first and second aorist verbs is purely *formal*. Although the third principal part of a first aorist can be constructed from the dictionary form, the third principal part of a second aorist must be memorized. This difference may be summarized by the following formula for the second aorist middle indicative:

$$\text{Augment} + \text{Changed Stem} + \text{Theme Vowel} + \text{Secondary Middle/Passive Endings}$$
$$(\quad A \quad + \quad ST^* \quad + \quad V \quad + \quad SM/PE \quad)$$

▸ Augment: The prefix ε is added to indicate past time action.
▸ Stem: The second aorist tense stem must be memorized.
▸ Theme Vowel: The theme vowels follow the pattern *o-e-e-o-e-o*.
▸ Personal Endings: The second aorist middle indicative uses the secondary middle/passive endings discussed above.

The paradigm of the second aorist middle indicative of the verb βαλλω follows. You should make special note of stem change and of the contraction in the second person singular form.

Stem change + imperfect endings

irregular

		βαλλω (βαλ-)	Translation
Sing.	1st	ἐ βαλ ο μην	I threw for myself.
	2nd	ἐ βαλ ε σο = ου	You threw for yourself.
	3rd	ἐ βαλ ε το	He/she/it threw for him/her/itself.
Pl.	1st	ἐ βαλ ο μεθα	We threw for ourselves.
	2nd	ἐ βαλ ε σθε	You threw for yourselves.
	3rd	ἐ βαλ ο ντο	They threw for themselves.

14.6 Aorist Passive Indicative

The aorist tense is used to connote *summary* action in *past* time. In order to reflect the summary action of the aorist tense, we will translate the aorist passive indicative using the simple past. The first person singular of the verb "to see" would thus be translated as "I was seen" in the passive voice. The form of the aorist passive indicative may be summarized by the following formula:

Augment + Stem + Tense + Theme + Secondary **Active** Endings
Sign   Vowel
(A   + ST + S + V +   SAE   )

▶   Augment: The prefix ἐ is added to indicate past time action.
▶   Stem: The aorist tense stem of a regular verb is found by removing the final ω of the dictionary form. The aorist passive stem of an irregular verb is seen in the *sixth principal part* and must be memorized.
▶   Tense Sign: The tense sign is θ. Some verbs, however, omit the θ in the aorist passive. This omission is seen in the sixth principal part.
▶   Theme Vowel: The theme vowel is η.
▶   Personal Endings: The aorist passive indicative is unusual in that it uses the secondary *active* endings discussed in Chapter 7.

The paradigm of the aorist passive indicative of the verb λυω follows. Make special note of the *active* endings which are used.

stem + θ + η

		λυω (λυ-)					Translation
Sing.	1st	ἐ	λυ	θ	η	ν	I was loosed.
	2nd	ἐ	λυ	θ	η	ς	You were loosed.
	3rd	ἐ	λυ	θ	η	-	He/she/it was loosed.
Pl.	1st	ἐ	λυ	θ	η	μεν	We were loosed.
	2nd	ἐ	λυ	θ	η	τε	You were loosed.
	3rd	ἐ	λυ	θ	η	σαν	They were loosed.

<u>Note</u>: The aorist passive indicative is built on the *sixth* principal part. For completely regular verbs such as λυω and πιστευω the sixth principal part can be constructed using the formula given. The sixth principal part of irregular verbs, however, must be memorized.

14.7 "Deponent Passive" Forms
    Some verbs have lost entirely both their aorist active and aorist middle forms (e.g., μιμνησκομαι, πορεομαι, φοβεομαι). The aorist passive form of other verbs often has an active meaning (e.g., ἀποκρινομαι, γινομαι, ἐγειρω). With a verb such as γινομαι, for example, the aorist passive form (ἐγενήθην) *must* have an active sense, because a passive

sense simply does not fit the lexical meaning ("I was been"?). With the verb
ἐγείρω, however, only context will enable you to determine whether the
aorist passive form has a true passive sense (does ἠγέρθην mean "I arose"
or "I was raised"?).

When the aorist passive form of such a verb is translated with an active
sense, it is often referred to as a "deponent passive" in that it uses a *passive*
form (rather than the normal middle) to replace the active. The simplest way
to handle such verbs is to parse them as passive and then determine from
lexical meaning and context whether they should be translated as active.

14.8 Vocabulary

Verbs

261.	ἀναγινώσκω	I am reading	(32)
262.	ἀποθνήσκω	I am dying	(111)
	ἀποθνήσκω, ἀποθανοῦμαι, ἀπέθανον		
263.	ἄρχω	I am ruling [gen. dir. obj.]	(86)
264.	δοξάζω	I am glorifying (doxology)	(61)
265.	ἐκβάλλω	I am casting out, throwing out	(81)
266.	ἑτοιμάζω	I am preparing	(40)
267.	ἥκω	I have come [perfect]	(26)
268.	θεραπεύω	I am healing (therapeutic)	(43)
269.	κηρύσσω	I am preaching	(61)
270.	πείθω	I am trusting in, persuading	(52)
	(4 = πέποιθα)		
271.	ὑπάρχω	I am, exist	(60)

Nouns

272.	ἡ βασιλεία, -ας	kingdom, reign	(162)
273.	ἡ παρρησία, -ας	boldness, confidence	(31)
274.	ἡ σοφία, -ας	wisdom (sophisticated)	(51)
275.	ἡ σωτηρία, -ας	salvation (soteriology)	(46)
276.	ἡ χαρά, -ας	joy	(59)
277.	ἡ διδαχή, -ης	teaching (didactic)	(30)
278.	ἡ δικαιοσύνη, -ης	righteousness	(92)
279.	ἡ συκή, -ης	fig tree	(16)
280.	το δένδρον, -ου	tree (dendrology)	(25)

14.9 Verb Review - The principal parts for twenty-five important verbs that you already know are listed in the following chart. Since irregular verbs occur frequently, you should become as familiar with these verbs as possible.

	PAI1S	FAI1S	AAI1S	PfAI1S	PfM/PI1S	API1S
41	ἀγώ	ἄξω	ἤγαγον	ἦχα	ἦγμαι	ἤχθην
42	ἀκούω	ἀκούσω	ἤκουσα	ἀκήκοα	ἤκουσμαι	ἠκούσθην
43	-στελλω	-στελῶ	-εστειλα	-εστάλκα	-εστάλμαι	-εστάλην
46	γινώσκω	γνώσομαι	ἔγνων	ἔγνωκα	ἔγνωσμαι	ἐγνώσθην
49	λαμβάνω	λήμψομαι	ἔλαβον	εἴληφα	εἴλημμαι	ἐλήμφθην
58	γίνομαι	γενήσομαι	ἐγενόμην	γέγονα	γεγένημαι	ἐγενήθην
59	ἔρχομαι	ἐλεύσομαι	ἦλθον	ἐλήλυθα	------	------
78	λέγω	ἐρῶ	εἶπον	εἴρηκα	εἴρημαι	ἐρρέθην
103	αἴρω	ἀρῶ	ἦρα	ἦρκα	ἦρμαι	ἤρθην
106	εὑρίσκω	εὑρήσω	εὗρον	εὕρηκα	εὕρημαι	εὑρέθην
108	μένω	μενῶ	ἔμεινα	μεμένηκα	------	------
110	ὁράω	ὄψομαι	εἶδον	ἑώρακα	ἑώραμαι	ὤφθην
121	ἁμαρτάνω	ἁμαρτήσω	ἥμαρτον	ἡμάρτηκα	ἡμάρτημαι	ἡμαρτήθην
122	ἀνοίγω	ἀνοίξω	ἤνοιξα	ἀνέῳγα	ἀνέῳγμαι	ἀνεῴχθην
123	βάλλω	βαλῶ	ἔβαλον	βέβληκα	βέβλημαι	ἐβλήθην
125	ἔχω	ἕξω	ἔσχον	ἔσχηκα	------	------
126	λείπω	λείψω	ἔλιπον	λέλοιπα	λέλειμμαι	ἐλείφθην
128	πάσχω	πείσομαι	ἔπαθον	πέπονθα	------	------
129	φέρω	οἴσω	ἤνεγκα	ἐνήνοχα	------	ἠνέχθην
236	-κτείνω	-κτενῶ	-εκτεινα	------	------	-εκτάνθην
237	ἐγείρω	ἐγερῶ	ἤγειρα	ἐγήγερκα	ἐγήγερμαι	ἠγέρθην
238	κρίνω	κρινῶ	ἔκρινα	κέκρικα	κέκριμαι	ἐκρίθην
239	-αγγελλω	-αγγελῶ	-ηγγειλα	-ηγγελκα	-ηγγελμαι	-ηγγέλην
240	σπείρω	σπερῶ	ἔσπειρα	ἔσπαρκα	ἔσπαρμαι	ἐσπάρην
270	πείθω	πείσω	ἔπεισα	πέποιθα	πέπεισμαι	ἐπείσθην

14.10 Form Identification - For each form, give the tense, voice, mood, person, number, dictionary form, and a translation.

1. ἐθεραπευομην

2. ἐλυθησαν

3. ἐξεβαλετο

4. ἐτιμησαντο

5. ἐγενομην

6. ἐλαβεσθε

7. ἐσταυρουμην

8. ἐκηρυξω

9. ἐβαλλου

10. ἐβαλου

11. ἐμανθανεσθε

12. ἐμαθεσθε

13. ἀπελυθην   20. ἐδικαιωθην

14. ἠκουσαντο   21. ἠτησα

15. ἐπεπιστευσο   22. ἠτοιμαζετο

16. ἐλυσω   23. ἐτεθεραπευσο

17. ἐνικωμεθα   24. ἀπεστειλαμην

18. ἐδοξασθην   25. ἐπεμψαμεθα

19. ἐψευδοντο

14.11 Practice Exercises - Translate the following sentences. Parse all verbs (TVMPN - Dictionary form).

for grace we were saved
1. τῃ γαρ χαριτι ἐσωθημεν.

AND
2. και ὠφθη αὐτοις Μωϋσης (Moses) *AND* και Ἡλιας (Elijah).

Not me am here   *Just as said*
3. οὐκ ἐστιν ὡδε (here), ἠγερθη καθως εἰπεν.

AND Not ANSWER he Not one word
4. και οὐκ ἀπεκριθη αὐτῳ οὐδε ἐν (one) ῥημα.

AND Justifying or wisdom by of work his
5. και ἐδικαιωθη ἡ σοφια ἀπο των ἐργων αὐτης.

I am + + found death
6. ἐγω δε ἀπεθανον και εὐρεθη μοι ἡ ἐντολη εἰς θανατον.

7. ἐπιστευσεν δε ᾽Αβρααμ (Abraham) τῳ θεῳ και ἐλογισθη αὐτῳ εἰς δικαιοσυνην.

8. και ὁτε ἠλθεν εἰς Καφαρναουμ (Capernaum), ἠκουσθη ὁτι ἐν οἰκῳ ἠν.

9. και ὁ λογος σαρξ ἐγενετο και ἐθεασαμεθα την δοξαν αὐτου.

10. εἰ ἐβαπτισθημεν εἰς Χριστον ᾽Ιησουν, εἰς τον θανατον αὐτου ἐβαπτισθημεν.

11. και ὡμολογησεν και οὐκ ἠρνησατο ὁτι οὐκ εἰμι ὁ Χριστος.

12. και φωνη ἐγενετο ἐκ του οὐρανου, συ εἰ ὁ υἱος μου.

13. μη Παυλος (Paul) ἐσταυρωθη ὑπερ ὑμων, ἤ εἰς το ὀνομα Παυλου (Paul) ἐβαπτισθητε;

14. ἐκληθη δε και ὁ Ἰησους και οἱ μαθηται αὐτου εἰς τον γαμον (wedding).

15. λεγει Ἰησους, ἐδοξασθη ὁ υἱος του ἀνθρωπου, και ὁ θεος ἐδοξασθη ἐν αὐτῳ.

16. ἠκουσατε ὁτι ἐρρεθη, ἀγαπησεις τον πλησιον (neighbor) και μισησεις τον ἐχθρον (enemy) σου.

17. ὁτε οὐν ἠγερθη ἐκ νεκρων (dead), ἐμνησθησαν οἱ μαθηται αὐτου ὁτι τουτο (this) ἐλεγεν.

18. γινωσκετε το εὐαγγελιον ὁ εὐηγγελισαμην ὑμιν ὁ και παρελαβετε και δι' οὗ σωζεσθε.

19. και ἠλθεν Ἰησους ἀπο Ναζαρεθ (Nazareth) της Γαλιλαιας (Galilee) και ἐβαπισθη εἰς τον Ἰορδανου (Jordan) ὑπο Ἰωαννης (John).

20. ὁ Ἰησους ἠχθη εἰς την ἐρημον ὑπο του πνευματος και ἐπειρασθη ὑπο του διαβολου.

GRAMMAR GRABBER: Adjectives

We have delayed introducing **adjectives** (words which function to describe nouns) until now, because there are so few of them in our particular authors. In John 1:1-18, for example, there are only two adjectives used to modify nouns. Both help John clarify Jesus' revelatory role as the incarnate Word of God.

In verse 9 John makes it clear that Jesus is not just "*a* light"; he is "the *true* light." The adjective ἀληθινός carries the meaning of "real" or "genuine," and the construction John uses (τὸ φῶς τὸ ἀληθινόν, called the "restrictive attributive" use) places special emphasis on the adjective. There can be no doubt that Jesus is the genuine source of enlightenment for those who are seeking it.

ʾΗν τὸ φῶς τὸ ἀληθινόν, ὃ φωτίζει πάντα ἄνθρωπον, ἐρχόμενον εἰς τὸν κόσμον. (John 1:9)

He was the true light which enlightens every man by coming into the world.

In verse 18 John states that Jesus is "the unique" God. The adjective μονογενής combines two words — μονός (only) and γένος (kind) — and carries the sense of "the only one of its kind." This "one of a kind" God is at the Father's side — an idea which mirrors the way in which John began his prologue (1:1). There can be no doubt that Jesus' revelation of the Father is both unique and reliable.

θεὸν οὐδεὶς ἑώρακεν πώποτε· μονογενὴς θεὸς ὁ ὢν εἰς τὸν κόλπον τοῦ πατρὸς ἐκεῖνος ἐξηγήσατο. (John 1:18)

No one has seen God at any time. The unique God, who is in the bosom of the Father, that one has made Him known.

Chapter 15

FIRST AND SECOND DECLENSION ADJECTIVES

Closely related to nouns are adjectives. After a basic introduction to adjectives in general and Greek adjectives in particular, the paradigms for first and second declension adjectives will be presented. Then the use and comparison of Greek adjectives will be discussed.

15.1 English Adjectives

Adjectives are words which modify nouns. English has both *descriptive adjectives* which tell "what kind" (e.g., the young boy) and *limiting adjectives* which tell "which one" (e.g., that boy) or "how many" (e.g., the two boys). Some of the functions of English adjectives are represented in Greek by pronoun forms which will be introduced later.

In English, adjectives may be used in three ways. In the *attributive* use the adjective qualifies or limits the noun (e.g., The young boy hit the ball.). In the *predicate* use the adjective makes a statement about the noun (e.g., The boy is young.). In the *substantive* use the adjective stands alone and acts as a noun (e.g., The young one hit the ball.).

Adjectives can modify nouns in three degrees. The *positive* degree makes no comparison (e.g., the young boy). The *comparative* degree compares two persons or things (e.g., the younger boy). The *superlative* degree compares three or more persons or things (e.g., the youngest boy). In English, adjectives follow two patterns when moving from positive to comparative and/or superlative. Regular adjectives simply add "-er" for the comparative and "-est" for the superlative (e.g., small, smaller, smallest). Irregular adjectives may use entirely different words for each (e.g., good, better, best).

15.2 Greek Adjectives

Like nouns, adjectives also have gender, case, and number. Adjectives *must* agree with the nouns they modify in gender, case, and number. Greek adjectives may be grouped into two categories, depending on whether they have three or two ending patterns. *Three termination adjectives* have separate masculine, feminine, and neuter ending patterns.

1. The masculine follows the pattern of second declension masculine nouns.
2. The feminine follows the pattern of first declension feminine nouns. It may follow either the Alpha-pure or the Eta pattern of inflection.
3. The neuter follows the ending pattern of second declension neuter nouns.

Two termination adjectives have only two ending patterns.
1. Both the masculine and feminine follow the ending pattern of the second declension masculine nouns.
2. The neuter follows the ending pattern of second declension neuter nouns.

Although most adjectives follow the pattern of first and second declension nouns, several adjectives and numerals use first and third declension ending patterns. Since, however, the most common adjectives follow the pattern of first and second declension nouns, the discussion of third declension adjectives will be deferred until later.

15.3 First and Second Declension Adjectives

Although there are a few first and second declension adjectives with only two endings, most have three terminations. Paradigms for both three and two termination adjectives follow.

Three Termination		Gender			
		Masculine	Feminine (Eta)	Feminine (Alpha)	Neuter
Sing.	Nom.	ἀγαθ ός	ἀγαθ ή	ἀγί α	ἀγαθ όν
	Gen.	ἀγαθ οῦ	ἀγαθ ῆς	ἀγί ας	ἀγαθ οῦ
	Dat.	ἀγαθ ῷ	ἀγαθ ῇ	ἀγί ᾳ	ἀγαθ ῷ
	Acc.	ἀγαθ όν	ἀγαθ ήν	ἀγί αν	ἀγαθ όν
Pl.	Nom.	ἀγαθ οί	ἀγαθ αί	ἄγι αι	ἀγαθ ά
	Gen.	ἀγαθ ῶν	ἀγαθ ῶν	ἀγί ων	ἀγαθ ῶν
	Dat.	ἀγαθ οῖς	ἀγαθ αῖς	ἀγί αις	ἀγαθ οῖς
	Acc.	ἀγαθ ούς	ἀγαθ άς	ἀγί ας	ἀγαθ ά

Note that, in the feminine gender, an adjective follows *either* the Eta pattern *or* the Alpha pattern. For that reason, two different adjectives are included under the feminine in the chart above.

Adj must agree w/ Noun gender, case, #

Two Termination		Gender	
		Masculine/Feminine	Neuter
Sing.	Nom.	ἀδύνατος	ἀδύνατον
	Gen.	ἀδυνάτου	ἀδυνάτου
	Dat.	ἀδυνάτῳ	ἀδυνάτῳ
	Acc.	ἀδύνατον	ἀδύνατον
Pl.	Nom.	ἀδύνατοι	ἀδύνατα
	Gen.	ἀδυνάτων	ἀδυνάτων
	Dat.	ἀδυνάτοις	ἀδυνάτοις
	Acc.	ἀδυνάτους	ἀδύνατα

15.4 Use of Greek Adjectives

As is true in English, Greek adjectives may be used in any of three ways. Each use has a distinct syntactical form.

1. In the *attributive* use, the adjective qualifies or limits the noun ("the good man"). It always follows the article. *2nd attributive*

    1st attributive ὁ ἀγαθος ἀνθρωπος   ὁ ἀνθρωπος ὁ ἀγαθος
    the good man

2. In the *predicate* use, the adjective makes a statement about the noun ("the man is good"). It does not follow the article.

    ὁ ἀνθρωπος ἀγαθος   ἀγαθος ὁ ἀνθρωπος

3. In the *substantive* use, the adjective acts as a noun ("the good one"). It usually follows the article.

    ὁ ἀγαθος   ἡ ἀγαθη   το ἀγαθον

15.5 Comparison of Greek Adjectives

As is true in English, Greek adjectives can modify nouns in three degrees (positive, comparative, and superlative) and may follow either a regular or irregular pattern of inflection. Regular adjectives form their comparative by adding -τερος and their superlative by adding -τατος.

"more . . ."   *"most . . ."*

Positive	Comparative	Superlative
πιστος, η, ον	πιστοτερος, α, ον	πιστοτατος, η, ον
δικαιος, α, ον	δικαιοτερος, α, ον	δικαιοτατος, η, ον
σοφος, η, ον	σοφωτερος, α, ον	σοφωτατος, η, ον

grammatical agreement ≠ lexical agreement

The comparative and superlative of irregular adjectives must be memorized.

Positive	Comparative	Superlative
ἀγαθος, η, ον	κρεισσων, ον	κρατιστος, η, ον
μεγας, αλη, α	μειζων, ον	μεγιστος, η, ον
πολυς, η, υ	πλειων, ον	πλειστος, η, ον
μικρος, α, ον	ἐλασσων, ον	ἐλαχιστος, η, ον

15.6 Vocabulary

Three Termination Adjectives

281.	ἀγαθός, -η, -ον	good	(102)
282.	ἀγαπητός, -η, -ον	beloved	(61)
283.	ἔσχατος, -η, -ον	last (eschatology)	(52)
284.	καινός, -η, -ον	new	(42)
285.	κακός, -η, -ον	bad (cacophony)	(50)
286.	μόνος, -η, -ον	only, alone (monotheism)	(114)
287.	πιστός, -η, -ον	faithful	(67)
288.	πρῶτος, -η, -ον	first (prototype)	(155)
289.	σοφός, -η, -ον	wise (sophisticated)	(20)
290.	ἅγιος, -α, -ον	holy	(233)
291.	ἄξιος, -α, ον	worthy (axis)	(41)
292.	δεύτερος, -α, -ον	second (Deuteronomy)	(43)
293.	δίκαιος, -α, -ον	righteous, just	(79)
294.	ἔτερος, -α, -ον	other, different (heterosexual)	(98)
295.	ἴδιος, -α, -ον	one's own (idiosyncratic)	(114)
296.	ἰσχυρός, -α, -ον	strong	(29)
297.	μακάριος, -α, -ον	blessed	(50)
298.	μικρός, -α, -ον	small, little (microscope)	(46)
299.	νεκρός, -α, -ον	dead (necromancy)	(128)
300.	νεός, -α, -ον	new (neonatal)	(23)

15.8 Form Identification - For each form give the gender, case, number, dictionary form, and a translation. One example is provided.

καινη   FDS   καινος, η, ον   (to/for) new

1. πρωτα
2. ἀγιοι
3. ἀγαθη
4. νεους
5. ἰδια
6. μικρῳ
7. ἀπιστον
8. σοφοις
9. μονος
10. κακας
11. πιστην
12. νεκρων
13. ἀδυνατος

14. ἐσχαται
15. μακαριοι
16. ἀγαπητης
17. ἰσχυρος
18. ἀκαθαρτα
19. δικαιωτερος
20. ἑτερον
21. δευτερῳ
22. αἰωνιος
23. ἀγαθαι
24. πονηρων
25. ἀξιᾳ

1st attributive
art + adj + Noun

2nd attributive
art + noun + adj

15.9 Practice Exercises - Translate the following sentences. Parse all verbs (TVMPN - Dictionary form).

the man shall not live by bread alone
1. οὐκ ἐπ' ἀρτῳ μονῳ ζησεται ὁ ἀνθρωπος.

the last ones will be first and the first ones last
2. ἐσονται οἱ ἐσχατοι πρωτοι και οἱ πρωτοι ἐσχατοι.

Blessed is the man to whom the lord doesnt reckon
3. μακαριος ὁ ἀνηρ ᾧ οὐ λογιζεται ὁ κυριος ἁμαρτιαν. *sin*

His word will judge him @ the last day
4. ὁ λογος αὐτου κρινει αὐτον ἐν τῃ ἐσχατῃ ἡμερᾳ.

I am sending out from   prophets + wise +
5. ἐγω ἀποστελλω προς ὑμας προφητας και σοφους και γραμματεις. *writings / scripture*

he own came +   recieved
6. εἰς τα ἰδια ἠλθεν, και οἱ ἰδιοι αὐτον οὐ παρελαβον.

law holy + commandment
7. ὁ νομος ἁγιος και ἡ ἐντολη ἁγια και δικαια και ἀγαθη.

holy + ~~teaching~~ + love
just

8. μονῳ σοφῳ θεῳ δια Ἰησου Χριστου ἐστιν ἡ δοξα εἰς τους αἰωνας.

9. και ἐν τῃ συναγωγῃ ἠν ἀνθρωπος ὃς εἰχεν πνευμα δαιμονιου ἀκαθαρτου.

10. ἐπεμψα ὑμιν Τιμοθεον (Timothy), ὃς ἐστιν μου τεκνον ἀγαπητον και πιστον ἐν κυριῳ.

11. ἐλευσονται οἱ πονηροι εἰς κολασιν (judgment) αἰωνιον, οἱ δε δικαιοι εἰς ζωην αἰωνιον.

12. ἐντολην καινην διδωμι ὑμιν, ἱνα ἀγαπᾶτε ἀλληλους (one another), καθως ἠγαπησα ὑμας, και ὑμεις ἀγαπᾶτε ἀλληλους.

It was a 2nd sign which Jesus made

13. ἠν δευτερον σημειον ὃν ἐποιησεν ὁ Ἰησους ὁτε ἠλθεν ἐκ της Ἰουδαιος (Judea) εἰς την Γαλιλαιαν (Galilee).

14. δικαιοσυνη θεου ἐν τῳ εὐαγγελιῳ βλεπεται καθως γεγραπται, ὁ δε δικαιος ἐκ πιστεως ζησεται.

For Jesus said to them with men

15. ὁ δε Ἰησους εἰπεν αὐτοις, παρα ἀνθρωποις τουτο (this) ἀδυνατος ἐστιν, παρα δε θεῳ παντα (all things) δυνατα ἐστιν.

But God is faithful through whom you were called

16. πιστος δε ὁ θεος δι᾽ οὑ ἐκληθητε εἰς κοινωνιαν (fellowship) του υἱου αὐτου Ἰησου Χριστου κυριου ἡμων.

gen + comparison

17. ἐρχεται ὁ ἰσχυροτερος μου ὀπισω (μου) ἐγω ἐβαπτισα ὑδατι, αὐτος δε βαπτισει ὑμας ἐν πνευματι ἁγιῳ.

18. λεγω ὑμιν ὁτι ἐρχεται ὡρα και νυν (now) ἐστιν ὁτε οἱ νεκροι ἀκουσουσιν της φωνης του υἱου του θεου και ζησουσιν.

19. εἰ γὰρ ἄνθρωπος ἔρχεται και ἕτερον Ἰησοῦν κηρύσσει ὃν οὐκ ἐκηρύξαμεν, ἢ πνεῦμα ἕτερον λαμβάνετε ὃ οὐκ ἐδέξασθε, αὐτὸν παραλαμβάνετε καλως (splendidly).

20. τὸ μωρον (foolishness) τοῦ θεοῦ σοφώτερον των ἀνθρώπων ἐστιν καὶ τὸ ἀσθενες (weakness) του θεου ἰσχυρότερον των ἀνθρωπων.

14.13a. The righteousness of God has been seen just as it is written in the gospel

17. he who is stronger than me comes after me, I baptize with with water but he will baptize you in the spirit

GRAMMAR GRABBER: *Participles*

κἀγὼ οὐκ ᾔδειν αὐτόν, ἀλλ' ὁ πέμψας με βαπτίζειν ἐν ὕδατι ἐκεῖνός μοι εἶπεν, Ἐφ' ὃν ἂν ἴδῃς τὸ πνεῦμα καταβαῖνον καὶ μένον ἐπ' αὐτόν, οὗτός ἐστιν ὁ βαπτίζων ἐν πνεύματι ἁγίῳ. (John 1:33)

And I did not know him but the one who sent me to baptize with water, that one said to me, "On whomever you see the Spirit descending and abiding on him, this one is the one who is baptizing with the Holy Spirit."

Greek is a language of action. Most Greek clauses and sentences revolve around verbs. **Participles** are hybrid verb forms which combine the action aspect of verbs (tense and voice) with the descriptive power of adjectives. Participles thus enable a Greek writer with one word to communicate an *embodiment* of action and/or apply an action *description* to a noun.

Look at the way John uses participles to present God the Father, God the Son, and God the Holy Spirit in his narrative of the Baptist's identification of Jesus in John 1:33:

▸   The Father is the embodiment of action: ὁ <u>πέμψας</u> με βαπτίζειν ἐν ὕδατι. He is "the one [who] sent me to baptize with water."

▸   The Spirit is modified by two participles: τὸ πνεῦμα <u>καταβαῖνον</u> καὶ <u>μένον</u> ἐπ' αὐτόν. He is the "descending and abiding on him" Spirit.

▸   The Son embodies the action of dispensing eschatological salvation blessings: ὁ <u>βαπτίζων</u> ἐν πνεύματι ἁγίῳ "the one (who) baptizes with the Holy Spirit."

In Greek, then, nouns not only do actions, they *are* actions and are characterized by actions.

Chapter 16

ACTIVE PARTICIPLES

"-ing"
"-ed"

The Greek participle is a verbal mode which combines the descriptive power of an adjective with the action aspect of a verb. Simply stated, a participle is a verb with adjective endings, or a **verbal adjective**. The Greek participle is, therefore, considerably more complex than the English participle. After a brief review of English participles, basic concepts related to Greek participles will be discussed. This chapter will focus on the *form* of the active voice of participles in the present, aorist, and perfect tenses. The *translation* of participles is closely tied to their function and their context, and it is helpful to master the forms participles can take before considering the complexities involved in translating them.

16.1 English Participles

There are two participles in English: the *present participle* ends in –ing; the *past participle* ends in –ed. Since English participles most commonly occur in conjunction with helping verbs (e.g., am loving; have loved), their principle use is to form the progressive and completed-stative tenses of verbs (progressive: I am <u>loving</u>; completed-stative: I have <u>loved</u>). English participles are sometimes used as adjectives (e.g., the <u>loving</u> wife).

16.2 Greek Participles   Verbal adjective

Since Greek participles combine the descriptive power of adjectives with the action aspect of verbs they share some of the characteristics of both. As a verb, a participle (a) has tense and voice, (b) may have a subject and/or an object, and (c) may have modifiers. As an adjective, a participle (a) has gender, case, and number, (b) may act as a noun, and (c) may have modifiers.

The primary idea in the tense of a participle is *kind* (not time) of action. Present tense participles indicate *progressive* action. Aorist tense participles indicate *summary* action. Perfect tense participles indicate *completed-stative* action.

Although participles do not have inherent *time* value, their relationship to their context usually involves a temporal significance. It is impossible to

tense, voice, gender, case, #

present "ing"
aorist "ed"
perfect - both

state those relationships absolutely, but general tendencies may be observed. The action of a present participle is often *simultaneous* with the main verb's action (e.g., Rom 6:13). The action of an aorist participle is often *antecedent* to (one stage before) the main verb's action (e.g., Rom 6:9). The action of a perfect participle is regularly *complete* at the time of the main verb's action (e.g., John 7:10). The action of a future participle is regularly *subsequent* to (one stage after) the main verb's action. These ideas will be developed at greater length in Chapters 18-20.

[handwritten margin note: only applies to ad-verbial participles]

A Greek participle may function in any of four ways. A **substantival** participle functions as a noun. An **adjectival participle** modifies a noun. An **adverbial** participle modifies a verb. A **verbal participle** either (a) functions as the main verb in a sentence, (b) completes the action of another verb, or (c) emphasizes duration in conjunction with the verb εἰμί. Although the first three functions are common, the verbal function is comparatively rare.

[handwritten margin note: ✳✳✳]

16.3 Active Participle Endings

Active participles follow third declension noun endings in the masculine, first declension noun endings in the feminine, and third declension noun endings in the neuter. For reasons that will become obvious in the paradigms related to the various tenses, feminine participles follow the *alpha-impure* pattern in the present and aorist tenses, but they follow the *alpha-pure* pattern in the perfect tense. The basic ending patterns are set out in the table below.

Number	Case	Masculine	Feminine		Neuter
			Gender		
Sing.	Nom.	ν, ς	α	α	ν
	Gen.	ος	ης	ας	ος
	Dat.	ι	η	ᾳ	ι
	Acc.	α	αν	αν	ν
Pl.	Nom.	ες	αι		α
	Gen.	ων	ων		ων
	Dat.	σι	αις		σι
	Acc.	ας	ας		α

[handwritten notes at bottom of page]
1 Substantival - Noun
→ definite article usually in front
2 adjectival - maybe or maybe not artial
3 adverb - No article

16.4 Present Active Participles

The primary idea conveyed by the present participle is *progressive* action. The precise way in which this idea will be translated depends on the context, as will be seen in later chapters. As a general rule of thumb, however, present participles—*and only present participles*—will be translated using "–ing." The form of present active participles may be summarized by the following formula:

Stem + Theme Vowel + Participle Morpheme + Active Endings
(ST + V + M + AE)

▸ Stem: The stem of the present tense participle is found by removing the final ω of the dictionary form.
▸ Theme Vowel: The theme vowel is o in the masculine and neuter forms, and the dipthong ου in the feminine.
▸ Participle Morpheme: In the masculine and neuter, ντ is inserted between the theme vowel and the endings. In the feminine, σ is inserted.
▸ Active Endings: The present active participle uses the endings set out above. Because the participle morpheme is σ in the feminine, the alpha-impure pattern applies.

The full paradigm for the present active participle of the verb λυω follows.

present active

	Masculine				Feminine				Neuter			
	ST	V	M	AE	ST	V	M	AE	ST	V	M	AE
N.	λυ	ω	-	ν	λυ	ου	σ	α	λυ	ο	-	ν
G.	λυ	ο	ντ	ος	λυ	ου	σ	ης	λυ	ο	ντ	ος
D.	λυ	ο	ντ	ι	λυ	ου	σ	η	λυ	ο	ντ	ι
A.	λυ	ο	ντ	α	λυ	ου	σ	αν	λυ	ο	-	ν
N.	λυ	ο	ντ	ες	λυ	ου	σ	αι	λυ	ο	ντ	α
G.	λυ	ο	ντ	ων	λυ	ου	σ	ων	λυ	ο	ντ	ων
D.	λυ	ου	-	σι	λυ	ου	σ	αις	λυ	ου	-	σι
A.	λυ	ο	ντ	ας	λυ	ου	σ	ας	λυ	ο	ντ	α

Note that in the masculine and neuter dative plural the participle morpheme ντ drops out and the theme vowel lengthens to ου in order to compensate. The resulting forms are identical to the present active indicative third person plural. The correct parsing of this ambiguous form must be determined from the context in which it occurs.

16.5 Present Active Participles of Contract Verbs

As would be expected, when the vowel at the end of the stem of a contract verb comes in contact with the theme vowel of the present tense, vowel contraction takes place (see the discussion and chart in Chapter 12). This contraction is most often accompanied by a circumflex accent. Representative forms are summarized below.

Alpha Contracts		
	Masculine	Feminine	Neuter

	Masculine	Feminine	Neuter
Nom.	ἀγαπ - ῶν	ἀγαπ - ῶσα	ἀγαπ - ῶν
Gen.	ἀγαπ - ῶντος	ἀγαπ - ῶσης	ἀγαπ - ῶντος

Epsilon Contracts			
	Masculine	Feminine	Neuter
Nom.	ποι - ῶν	ποι - οῦσα	ποι - οῦν
Gen.	ποι - οῦντος	ποι - οὔσης	ποι - οῦντος

Omicron Contracts			
	Masculine	Feminine	Neuter
Nom.	δηλ - ῶν	δηλ - οῦσα	δηλ - οῦν
Gen.	δηλ - οῦντος	δηλ - οὔσης	δηλ - οῦντος

16.6 First Aorist Active Participles

The primary idea conveyed by the aorist participle is *summary* action. The precise way in which this idea will be translated depends on the context, as will be seen in later chapters. The form of first aorist active participles may be summarized by the following formula:

Stem + Tense + Theme + Participle + Active Endings
Sign   Vowel   Morpheme
(ST + S + V + M + AE)

▶ Stem: The first aorist stem of a regular verb is found by removing the final ω of the dictionary form.
▶ Tense Sign: The tense sign is σ.
▶ Theme Vowel: The theme vowel is α.
▶ Participle Morpheme: In the masculine and neuter, ντ is inserted between the theme vowel and the endings. In the feminine, σ is inserted.
▶ Active Endings: The present active participle uses the endings set out above. Because the participle morpheme is σ in the feminine, the alpha-impure pattern applies.

The full paradigm for the aorist active participle of the verb λυω follows. Note that in the masculine and neuter dative plural the participle morpheme ντ drops out.

alpha endings   *sigma*   aorist active Participle

	Masculine					Feminine					Neuter				
	ST	S	V	M	AE	ST	S	V	M	AE	ST	S	V	M	AE
N.	λυ	σ	α	-	ς	λυ	σ	α	σ	α	λυ	σ	α	-	ν
G.	λυ	σ	α	ντ	ος	λυ	σ	α	σ	ης	λυ	σ	α	ντ	ος
D.	λυ	σ	α	ντ	ι	λυ	σ	α	σ	η	λυ	σ	α	ντ	ι
A.	λυ	σ	α	ντ	α	λυ	σ	α	σ	αν	λυ	σ	α	-	ν
N.	λυ	σ	α	ντ	ες	λυ	σ	α	σ	αι	λυ	σ	α	ντ	α
G.	λυ	σ	α	ντ	ων	λυ	σ	α	σ	ων	λυ	σ	α	ντ	ων
D.	λυ	σ	α	-	σι	λυ	σ	α	σ	αις	λυ	σ	α	-	σι
A.	λυ	σ	α	ντ	ας	λυ	σ	α	σ	ας	λυ	σ	α	ντ	α

No epsilon

16.7 Second Aorist Active Participles

The primary idea conveyed by the second aorist participle is identical to that of the first aorist active participle: *summary* action. As was true in the indicative mood, the difference between the first and second aorist is purely one of form. Once again the key formal characteristic of the second aorist participle is the *stem change* which occurs. It should also be noted that the second aorist active participle uses the same theme vowels and endings as the present active participle. The recognition of the changed stem, then, is doubly important. The form of second aorist active participles may be summarized by the following formula:

Changed Stem + Theme Vowel + Participle Morpheme + Active Endings
(　　ST*　　+　　V　　+　　M　　+　　AE　　)

▸ Changed Stem: The stem of the second aorist active participle must be memorized from the third principal part.
▸ Theme Vowel: The theme vowel is O in the masculine and neuter forms, and the dipthong OU in the feminine.
▸ Participle Morpheme: In the masculine and neuter, ντ is inserted between the theme vowel and the endings. In the feminine, σ is inserted.
▸ Active Endings: The first aorist active participle uses the endings set out above.

The full paradigm for the (second) aorist active participle of the verb βαλλω follows. Note that in the masculine and neuter dative plural the participle morpheme ντ drops out and the theme vowel lengthens to OU in order to compensate.

stem change 2nd Aorist active

present endings

	Masculine				Feminine				Neuter			
	ST*	V	M	AE	ST*	V	M	AE	ST*	V	M	AE
N.	βαλ	ω	-	ν	βαλ	ου	σ	α	βαλ	ο	-	ν
G.	βαλ	ο	ντ	ος	βαλ	ου	σ	ης	βαλ	ο	ντ	ος
D.	βαλ	ο	ντ	ι	βαλ	ου	σ	η	βαλ	ο	ντ	ι
A.	βαλ	ο	ντ	α	βαλ	ου	σ	αν	βαλ	ο	-	ν
N.	βαλ	ο	ντ	ες	βαλ	ου	σ	αι	βαλ	ο	ντ	α
G.	βαλ	ο	ντ	ων	βαλ	ου	σ	ων	βαλ	ο	ντ	ων
D.	βαλ	ου	-	σι	βαλ	ου	σ	αις	βαλ	ου	-	σι
A.	βαλ	ο	ντ	ας	βαλ	ου	σ	ας	βαλ	ο	ντ	α

No episilon
time comes from verb/noun /adj

16.8 Perfect Active Participles

The primary idea conveyed by the perfect active participle is *completed-stative* action. The precise way in which this idea will be translated depends on the context, as will be seen in later chapters. The form of the perfect active participle is characterized by the use of reduplication and the tense sign κ. A further characteristic is that the masculine and neuter genders lack the ν normally found in the active participle morpheme. The form of the perfect active participle may be summarized by the following formula:

Reduplication + Stem + Tense + Theme + Participle + Active Endings
　　　　　　　　　　　　　　Sign　　Vowel　 Morpheme
(　　R　　+ ST + 　S　 + 　V　 + 　M　 + 　　AE　　)

- ▶ Reduplication: The initial letter/diphthong is added as a prefix to the verb in order to indicate completed-stative action.
- ▶ Stem: The perfect tense stem of a regular verb is found by removing the final ω of the dictionary form. The perfect tense stem of irregular verbs must be memorized from the fourth principal part.
- ▶ Tense Sign: The tense sign is κ.
- ▶ Theme Vowel: In masculine and neuter perfect participles, the theme vowel is o. In feminine participles, it is the diphthong $\upsilon\iota$.
- ▶ Participle Morpheme: The masculine and neuter forms insert the morpheme τ. There is no morpheme inserted in the feminine form.
- ▶ Active Endings: The perfect active participle uses the endings set out above. Because the diphthong which precedes the endings in the feminine ends in ι, the alpha-pure pattern applies.

The full paradigm for the perfect active participle of $\lambda\upsilon\omega$ follows. Note that in the masculine and neuter dative plural the participle morpheme τ drops out.

KAPPA　　　　　　　　*Perfect Active*

Masculine						Feminine					Neuter					
R	ST	S	V	M	AE	R	ST	S	V	AE	R	ST	S	V	M	AE
λε	λυ	κ	ω	-	ς	λε	λυ	κ	υι	α	λε	λυ	κ	ο	-	ς
λε	λυ	κ	ο	τ	ος	λε	λυ	κ	υι	ας	λε	λυ	κ	ο	τ	ος
λε	λυ	κ	ο	τ	ι	λε	λυ	κ	υι	ᾳ	λε	λυ	κ	ο	τ	ι
λε	λυ	κ	ο	τ	α	λε	λυ	κ	υι	αν	λε	λυ	κ	ο	-	ς

tense

λε λυ κ ο τ ες	λε λυ κ υι αι	λε λυ κ ο τ α
λε λυ κ ο τ ων	λε λυ κ υι ων	λε λυ κ ο τ ων
λε λυ κ ο - σι	λε λυ κ υι αις	λε λυ κ ο - σι
λε λυ κ ο τ ας	λε λυ κ υι ας	λε λυ κ ο τ α

16.9 Vocabulary

Nouns

301.	ἡ διαθήκη, -ης	covenant	(33)
302.	ἡ θυγάτηρ, θυγατρός	daughter	(28)
303.	ἡ κεφαλή, -ης	head (encephalitis)	(75)
304.	ὁ μισθός, -ου	wages, hire, reward	(29)
305.	ἡ οἰκία, -ας	house	(93)
306.	ἡ ὀργή, -ης	anger, wrath	(36)
307.	τό ὄρος, -ους	mountain	(63)
308.	ἡ περιτομή, -ης	circumcision	(36)
309.	ὁ πρεσβύτερος, -ου	elder	(66)
310.	ἡ προσευχή, -ης	prayer	(85)
311.	ἡ ὑπομονή, -ης	endurance, steadfastness	(32)
312.	ὁ ὑποκριτής, -ου	hypocrite	(17)

Adjectives

313.	ἄλλος, -η, -ον	other, another (of the same kind)	(155)
314.	δυνατός, -η, -ον	powerful, possible (dynamic)	(32)
315.	ἕκαστος, -η -ον	each, every	(82)
316.	ὅλος, -η, -ον	whole, all, complete	(109)
317.	καλός, -η, -ον	good, beautiful	(100)
318.	τρίτος, -η, -ον	third	(56)

Conjunctions

319.	τε	and [postpositive coordinate]	(215)
320.	τε ... καί	both ... and	

16.11 Form Identification - For each form given, identify its tense, voice, whether it is a participle, gender, case, and number; then write its dictionary form. One example is given.

Form	Parsing	Dictionary Form
λυσαση	AAPtcFDS	λυω

1. βαλων *throwing*
2. πιστευον *believing*
3. ἐληλυθοτες *commandment*
4. λελυκυιαν *losing*
5. βλεπουσι *seeing*
6. γραψαντος *writing*
7. λυσαντας *loosing*
8. λεγουσα *saying*
9. πιστευσαντων
10. βαλλοντα
11. ἐχοντος
12. λυουσαις
13. μενοντα
14. λαβοντες *receiving*
15. ἐλθων
16. τεθεραπευκυιᾳ
17. φερουσης *bearing*
18. λαλουντα
19. ἀπεσταλκοσι *sending out*
20. ἰδοντες *seeing*

21. πεπιστευκυιαις
22. εἰπων
23. ζητοῦντες *seeking*
24. ἐλθοντων
25. κηρυξας *preaching*
26. γεγραφοτας
27. ἀκουσασα *hearing*
28. πεποιθως
29. ἐγειρας *raising*
30. λαλησαντι
31. λελοιπος
32. ἀγαγων *loving*
33. γνοντι *knowing*
34. λιπον
35. πιπτοντος

GRAMMAR GRABBER: Middle/Passive Participles

ἐξῆλθεν ὁ τεθνηκὼς δεδεμένος τοὺς πόδας καὶ τὰς χεῖρας κειρίαις, καὶ ἡ ὄψις αὐτοῦ σουδαρίῳ περιεδέδετο. λέγει αὐτοῖς ὁ Ἰησοῦς, Λύσατε αὐτὸν καὶ ἄφετε αὐτὸν ὑπάγειν. (John 11:44)

The one who has died came out, having been bound hand and foot with cloth strips, and his face was bound around with a cloth. Jesus says to them, "Loose him and let him go!"

As is true with finite verbs, participles can communicate action using passive or middle voice. When John describes the great miracle of the raising of Lazarus, he uses both an active participle and a passive participle to characterize him.

He begins with an perfect active participle used as a noun. The Lazarus who comes out is ὁ τεθνηκὼς "the one who has died." He has been a corpse, who embodies the entering into the state of death and continuing there, but here he comes shuffling out of the tomb!

John then uses a perfect passive participle to point out that Lazarus' condition, with reference to his feet and hands, is one of δεδεμένος— "having been bound." His body had been lifeless, yet lovingly cared for by others who remain unnamed. Now, most properly, this condition must be reversed in obedience to Jesus' command, "Loose him and let him go!"

Chapter 17

MIDDLE AND PASSIVE PARTICIPLES

Just as verbs in the indicative mood may occur in active, middle, or passive voice, so participles may occur in all three voices. This chapter will focus on the *form* of middle and passive participles. The *translation* of participles is closely tied to their function and their context, and it is helpful to master the forms participles can take before considering the complexities involved in translating them. As was true in the indicative, the middle and passive forms of the present tense are identical, as are the middle and passive forms of the perfect tense. These forms will be discussed before the aorist tense. The aorist tense has separate middle and passive forms, as well as the possibility of the verb being a first or second aorist.

17.1 Basic Concepts

The primary idea in the tense of a participle is kind (not time) of action. A present tense participle indicates *progressive* action. An aorist tense participle indicates *summary* action. A perfect tense participle indicates *completed-stative* action.

Although participles do not have inherent *time* value, their relationship to their context usually involves a temporal significance. It is impossible to state those relationships absolutely, but general tendencies may be observed. The action of a present participle is often *simultaneous* with the main verb's action. The action of an aorist participle is often *antecedent* to (one stage before) the main verb's action. The action of a perfect participle is regularly *complete* at the time of the main verb's action. The action of a future participle is regularly *subsequent* to (one stage after) the main verb's action. These ideas will be developed at greater length in Chapters 18-20.

Voice has the same significance in participles as it does in verbs in the indicative mood. In the *active* voice the subject produces the action. In the *middle* voice the subject both produces and participates in the results of the action. The middle voice has no exact parallel in English, but it is best translated using the reflexive pronoun ("-self"), which reflects the action back to the subject. In the passive voice the subject receives the action. The translation of the passive voice normally includes a form of the verb "to be."

17.2 Middle/Passive Participle Endings

Middle/passive participle endings follow normal noun endings. The masculine and neuter forms follow the pattern of second declension masculine and neuter nouns; the feminine form follows the pattern of first declension *eta* nouns. The chart below summarizes the middle/passive participle endings. These endings, however, do *not* apply to the aorist passive participle.

Number	Case	Masculine	Feminine	Neuter
Sing.	Nom.	ος	η	ον
	Gen.	ου	ης	ου
	Dat.	ῳ	ῃ	ῳ
	Acc.	ον	ην	ον
Pl.	Nom.	οι	αι	α
	Gen.	ων	ων	ων
	Dat.	οις	αις	οις
	Acc.	ους	ας	α

17.3 Present Middle/Passive Participles

The primary idea conveyed by the present participle is *progressive* action. The precise way in which this idea will be translated depends on the context, as will be seen in later chapters. As a general rule of thumb, however, present participles—*and only present participles*—will be translated using "–ing." The form of present middle/passive participles may be summarized by the following formula:

Stem + Theme Vowel + Participle Morpheme+ Middle/Passive Endings
(ST + V + M + M/PE)

- ▶ Stem: The stem of the present tense participle is found by removing the final ω of the dictionary form.
- ▶ Theme Vowel: The theme vowel is ο
- ▶ Participle Morpheme: The middle passive participle morpheme is μεν.

▶ Middle/Passive Endings: The present middle/passive participle follows the endings set out above.

The full paradigm for the present middle/passive participle of λυω follows. Context must determine whether the form is middle or passive.

Present M/P

	Masculine				Feminine				Neuter			
	ST	V	M	E	ST	V	M	E	ST	V	M	E
N.	λυ	ο	μεν	ος	λυ	ο	μεν	η	λυ	ο	μεν	ον
G.	λυ	ο	μεν	ου	λυ	ο	μεν	ης	λυ	ο	μεν	ου
D.	λυ	ο	μεν	ῳ	λυ	ο	μεν	η	λυ	ο	μεν	ῳ
A.	λυ	ο	μεν	ον	λυ	ο	μεν	ην	λυ	ο	μεν	ον
N.	λυ	ο	μεν	οι	λυ	ο	μεν	αι	λυ	ο	μεν	α
G.	λυ	ο	μεν	ων	λυ	ο	μεν	ων	λυ	ο	μεν	ων
D.	λυ	ο	μεν	οις	λυ	ο	μεν	αις	λυ	ο	μεν	οις
A.	λυ	ο	μεν	ους	λυ	ο	μεν	ας	λυ	ο	μεν	α

Present Nom: ΛVOΜΕVOS: "the one who looses for himself"

17.4 Present Middle/Passive Participles of Contract Verbs

As would be expected, when the vowel at the end of the stem of a contract verb comes in contact with the theme vowel of the present tense, vowel contraction takes place (see the discussion and chart in Chapter 12). Representative forms are summarized below.

Alpha Contracts		
	Masculine	Feminine	Neuter
Nom. Gen.	ἀγαπ - ω - μενος ἀγαπ - ω - μενου	ἀγαπ - ω - μενη ἀγαπ - ω - μενης	ἀγαπ - ω - μενον ἀγαπ - ω - μενου

Epsilon Contracts		
	Masculine	Feminine	Neuter
Nom. Gen.	ποι - ου - μενος ποι - ου - μενου	ποι - ου - μενη ποι - ου - μενης	ποι - ου - μενον ποι - ου - μενου

Omicron Contracts		
	Masculine	Feminine	Neuter
Nom.	δηλ - ου - μενος	δηλ - ου - μενη	δηλ - ου - μενον
Gen.	δηλ - ου - μενου	δηλ - ου - μενης	δηλ - ου - μενου

17.5 Perfect Middle/Passive Participles

The primary idea conveyed by the perfect participle is *completed-stative* action. The precise way in which this idea will be translated depends on the context, as will be seen in later chapters. The form of the perfect participle is characterized by the use of reduplication. As was true in the indicative mood, the middle/passive participle morpheme is attached directly to the verb stem, without a tense sign or theme vowel. The form of perfect middle/passive participles may be summarized by the following formula:

Reduplication + Stem + Participle Morpheme + Middle/Passive Endings
(R   +   ST   +   M   +   M/PE   )

▸   Reduplication: The initial letter/diphthong is added as a prefix to the verb in order to indicate completed-stative action.
▸   Stem: The perfect stem of a regular verb is found by removing the final ω of the dictionary form. The perfect stem of irregular verbs must be memorized from the fourth principal part.
▸   Participle Morpheme: The middle/passive participle morpheme is μεν.
▸   Middle/Passive Endings: The present middle/passive participle follows the endings set out above.

The full paradigm for the perfect middle/passive participle of λυω follows. The context must determine whether the form is middle or passive. *Perfect m/p*

	Masculine				Feminine				Neuter			
	R	ST	M	E	R	ST	M	E	R	ST	M	E
N.	λε	λυ	μεν	ος	λε	λυ	μεν	η	λε	λυ	μεν	ov
G.	λε	λυ	μεν	ου	λε	λυ	μεν	ης	λε	λυ	μεν	ου
D.	λε	λυ	μεν	ῳ	λε	λυ	μεν	η	λε	λυ	μεν	ῳ
A.	λε	λυ	μεν	ov	λε	λυ	μεν	ην	λε	λυ	μεν	ov

N.	λε	λυ	μεν	οι	λε	λυ	μεν	αι	λε	λυ	μεν	α
G.	λε	λυ	μεν	ων	λε	λυ	μεν	ων	λε	λυ	μεν	ων
D.	λε	λυ	μεν	οις	λε	λυ	μεν	αις	λε	λυ	μεν	οις
A.	λε	λυ	μεν	ους	λε	λυ	μεν	ας	λε	λυ	μεν	α

17.6 First Aorist Middle Participles

The primary idea conveyed by the aorist participle is *summary* action. Characteristic of first aorist middle participles is the presence of σα immediately preceding the participle morpheme. The form of first aorist middle participles may be summarized by the following formula:

Stem + Tense Sign + Theme Vowel + Participle + Middle/Passive
Morpheme   Endings
(ST +   S   +   V   +   M   +   M/PE   )

▸ Stem: The aorist stem of a regular verb is found by removing the final ω of the dictionary form.
▸ Tense Sign: The tense sign is σ.
▸ Theme Vowel: The theme vowel is α.
▸ Participle Morpheme: The middle/passive participle morpheme is μεν.
▸ Middle/Passive Endings: The first aorist middle participle uses the middle/passive endings set out above.

The full paradigm for the aorist middle participle of the verb λυω follows:

aorist Middle

	Masculine					Feminine					Neuter				
	ST	S	V	M	E	ST	S	V	M	E	ST	S	V	M	E
N.	λυ	σ	α	μεν	ος	λυ	σ	α	μεν	η	λυ	σ	α	μεν	ον
G.	λυ	σ	α	μεν	ου	λυ	σ	α	μεν	ης	λυ	σ	α	μεν	ου
D.	λυ	σ	α	μεν	ῳ	λυ	σ	α	μεν	ῃ	λυ	σ	α	μεν	ῳ
A.	λυ	σ	α	μεν	ον	λυ	σ	α	μεν	ην	λυ	σ	α	μεν	ον
N.	λυ	σ	α	μεν	οι	λυ	σ	α	μεν	αι	λυ	σ	α	μεν	α
G.	λυ	σ	α	μεν	ων	λυ	σ	α	μεν	ων	λυ	σ	α	μεν	ων
D.	λυ	σ	α	μεν	οις	λυ	σ	α	μεν	αις	λυ	σ	α	μεν	οις
A.	λυ	σ	α	μεν	ους	λυ	σ	α	μεν	ας	λυ	σ	α	μεν	α

17.7 Second Aorist Middle Participles

The primary idea conveyed by the second aorist participle is identical to that of the first aorist participle: *summary* action. As was true in the indicative mood, the difference between the first and second aorist is purely one of form. Once again the key formal characteristic of the second aorist participle is the *stem change* which occurs. It should also be noted that the second aorist middle participle uses the same theme vowels and endings as the present middle/passive participle. The recognition of the changed stem, then, is doubly important. The form of second aorist middle participles may be summarized by the following formula:

Changed Stem + Theme Vowel + Participle + Middle/Passive
Morpheme Endings
(ST* + V + M + M/PE)

- ▸ Changed Stem: The stem of the second aorist middle participle must be memorized from the third principal part.
- ▸ Theme Vowel: The theme vowel is O.
- ▸ Participle Morpheme: The middle/passive participle morpheme is μεν.
- ▸ Middle/Passive Endings: The second aorist middle participle uses the middle/passive endings set out above.

The full paradigm for the aorist middle participle of the verb βαλλω follows:

2 aorst Middle

	Masculine				Feminine				Neuter			
	ST*	V	M	E	ST*	V	M	E	ST*	V	M	E
N.	βαλ	ο	μεν	ος	βαλ	ο	μεν	η	βαλ	ο	μεν	ον
G.	βαλ	ο	μεν	ου	βαλ	ο	μεν	ης	βαλ	ο	μεν	ου
D.	βαλ	ο	μεν	ῳ	βαλ	ο	μεν	η	βαλ	ο	μεν	ῳ
A.	βαλ	ο	μεν	ον	βαλ	ο	μεν	ην	βαλ	ο	μεν	ον
N.	βαλ	ο	μεν	οι	βαλ	ο	μεν	αι	βαλ	ο	μεν	α
G.	βαλ	ο	μεν	ων	βαλ	ο	μεν	ων	βαλ	ο	μεν	ων
D.	βαλ	ο	μεν	οις	βαλ	ο	μεν	αις	βαλ	ο	μεν	οις
A.	βαλ	ο	μεν	ους	βαλ	ο	μεν	ας	βαλ	ο	μεν	α

2 aorist takes present endings

17.8 Aorist Passive Participles

The primary idea conveyed by the aorist participle is *summary* action. Characteristic of most aorist passive participles is the presence of θε immediately preceding the participle morpheme. There are, however, some verbs which omit the θ. The absence of the θ will be easily noted in the sixth principle part of the verb. As was true in the indicative mood, aorist passive participles take *active* endings. The form of aorist passive participles may be summarized by the following formula:

Stem + Tense Sign + Theme Vowel + Participle + Active Endings
Morpheme
(ST +   S   +   V   +   M   +   AE   )

▶ Stem: The stem of the aorist passive participle of a regular verb is found by removing the final ω of the dictionary form. The stem of the aorist passive participle of irregular verbs must be memorized from the sixth principal part.

▶ Tense Sign: The tense sign is θ

▶ Theme Vowel: The theme vowel is ε in the masculine and neuter and the diphthong ει in the feminine.

▶ Participle Morpheme: In the masculine and neuter, ντ is inserted between the theme vowel and the endings. In the feminine, σ is inserted.

▶ Active Endings: The aorist passive participle uses the active endings set out in Chapter 16. Because the participle morpheme is σ in the feminine, the alpha-impure pattern applies.

The full paradigm for the aorist passive participle of the verb λυω follows:

aorist passive

	Masculine					Feminine					Neuter				
	ST	S	V	M	AE	ST	S	V	M	AE	ST	S	V	M	AE
N.	λυ	θ	ει	-	ς	λυ	θ	ει	σ	α	λυ	θ	ε	-	ν
G.	λυ	θ	ε	ντ	ος	λυ	θ	ει	σ	ης	λυ	θ	ε	ντ	ος
D.	λυ	θ	ε	ντ	ι	λυ	θ	ει	σ	η	λυ	θ	ε	ντ	ι
A.	λυ	θ	ε	ντ	α	λυ	θ	ει	σ	αν	λυ	θ	ε	-	ν
N.	λυ	θ	ε	ντ	ες	λυ	θ	ει	σ	αι	λυ	θ	ε	ντ	α
G.	λυ	θ	ε	ντ	ων	λυ	θ	ει	σ	ων	λυ	θ	ε	ντ	ων
D.	λυ	θ	ει	-	σι	λυ	θ	ει	σ	αις	λυ	θ	ει	-	σι
A.	λυ	θ	ε	ντ	ας	λυ	θ	ει	σ	ας	λυ	θ	ε	ντ	α

17.9 Participles of Deponent Verbs

The idea of "deponent" verbs was introduced in Chapter 13. Verbs which were deponent in the indicative will also be deponent in their participial form. It will be helpful to review the basic definition of a deponent form: **When a verb has a middle ending in a principal part which normally has an active form (#1-4), the verb is "deponent" in all of the tenses, moods, and modes built on that principal part.** If, for example, the first principal part of a verb (PAI1S) is deponent, the present participle will also be deponent. Some verbs are deponent in all of their forms; other verbs are deponent only in certain principal parts. It is important to remember the following concepts when dealing with deponent verbs:

1. All forms related to a deponent principal part will be deponent (e.g., if the *first* principal part is deponent, all moods and modes of the *present and imperfect* tenses—including the present participle—will be deponent).

2. When a verbal form is deponent, it will (a) have a middle form, (b) be parsed as "deponent" (D), and (c) be translated as active (e.g., ἐρχομενην is parsed as PDPtcFAS and translated as **"(is) coming,"** *not* "(is) coming for him/her/itself").

17.10 Vocabulary

Nouns

321.	ὁ ἀγρός, -ου	field (agrarian)	(36)
322.	τό βιβλίον, -ου	book (bibliography)	(34)
323.	ὁ διάβολος, -ου	slanderer, devil (diabolic)	(37)
324.	ὁ ἐχθρός, -ου	enemy	(32)
325	ὁ ἥλιος, -ου	sun	(32)
326	τό ἱμάτιον, -ου	cloak, garment	(60)
327.	ὁ καιρός, -ου	time, occasion	(85)
328.	ὁ καρπός, -ου	fruit	(66)
329.	ὁ λαός, -ου	people (laity)	(142)
330.	ὁ ναός, -ου	temple, sanctuary	(45)
331.	τό παιδίον, -ου	child (pediatrics)	(52)
332.	ὁ τυφλός, -ου	blind man	(50)
333.	ὁ φίλος, -ου	friend (philanthropic)	(29)

Conjunction and Adverbs

334.	διό	therefore [coordinate. conjunction]	(53)
335.	ἔτι	yet, still	(93)
336.	καλῶς	rightly, well	(37)

337.	νῦν	now	(147)
338.	οὐκέτι	no longer	(47)
339.	σήμερον	today	(41)
340.	τότε	then	(160)

17.11 Form Identification - For each form, identify its tense, voice, whether it is a participle, gender, case, and number; then write its dictionary form. One example is given.

Form	Parsing	Dictionary Form
ἐχομενος	PM/PPtcMNS	ἐχω

1. γενομενης
2. πεπιστευμενον
3. ἀγαγομενας
4. λυθεντος
5. βαλομενη
6. πιστευομεναι
7. λελυμενοις
8. λεγομενου
9. λυσαμεναις
10. βαλλομενην
11. πιστευθεισαν
12. λυθεις
13. γεγραμμενοι
14. γνωσθεντα
15. ἀπεσταλμενην
16. ἀγαγομενος
17. βαλομενον
18. λαλουμεναις
19. δικαιωθεντες
20. βλεψαμενων

21. βεβλημενον
22. γραφεισῃ
23. αἰρομενους
24. δοξασαμεναι
25. τεθεραπευμενα
26. κηρυξαμενος
27. βληθεν
28. ἠγαπημενοι
29. λογιζομενων
30. δεχθεντος
31. μισουμενης
32. δεδικαιωμενον
33. εὐλογηθεισα
34. λυομενας
35. ἐκβληθεν

GRAMMAR GRABBER: Substantival Participles

ὁ πιστεύων εἰς τὸν υἱὸν ἔχει ζωὴν αἰώνιον· ὁ δὲ
ἀπειθῶν τῷ υἱῷ οὐκ ὄψεται ζωήν, ἀλλ' ἡ ὀργὴ τοῦ
θεοῦ μένει ἐπ' αὐτόν. (John 3:36)

The one who is believing in the Son is having eternal life; but the
one who is not obeying/believing the son shall not see life, but the
wrath of God is abiding on him.

Greek is a language of action. Nowhere do we see that fact more clearly
than in the way this language takes a verbal form, the participle, and uses
it as a noun (i.e., substantivally). In English, we turn verbs into nouns by
adding an "r" (e.g., believe, believer; love, lover), but we lack the capability
to continue to represent fully all aspects of the verb's action. In Greek,
however, an author or speaker can present a person or thing as fully
embodying an action. Look at the two substantival participles in John 3:36.
    The first present active participle (ὁ πιστεύων) with its progressive
action shows us what characterizes, indeed continues to characterize, those
who possess the salvation blessing of eternal life: they are "the ones who *keep
on believing*," Similarly, the second participle (ὁ ἀπειθῶν) shows us what
marks those who will not enter that life but will continue to experience
God's wrath: they are "the ones who *keep on disobeying*." We learn that a
person who possesses eternal life is one who has done more than simply
shown faith in a conversion experience. He/she *embodies* faith by manifesting
a settled condition of a life of believing.

Present — ongoing
Aorist • completed
Perfect •——x completed w/ continuing results

(Future)-vane

Chapter 18

SUBSTANTIVAL USES OF PARTICIPLES

Participles may function in several different ways. The most common uses are substantival, adjectival, and adverbial. This chapter will introduce the substantival use; Chapters 19-20 will introduce adjectival and adverbial participles.

18.1 The Substantival Use of the Participle

A substantival participle is usually preceded by a definite article which agrees with the participle in gender, case, and number. The substantival use of the participle may be readily distinguished from the adjectival use because the substantival participle has no noun which it modifies. It is best translated by a clause introduced by a relative pronoun: "(the one) who . . ." or "(that) which . . ." The substantival participle may serve in any of the ways a noun serves: subject, predicate nominative, direct object, indirect object, object of preposition, noun in apposition. In the following example, the participle serves as the indirect object

John 5:10   ἐλεγον οὐν οἱ Ἰουδαιοι τῳ τεθεραπευμενῳ . . .
Then the Jews were saying *to the one who had been healed* . . .

18.2 Translating Participles

Because the translation of participles is based on multiple factors, little has been said about it so far. At this point it will be helpful to set out some initial guidelines. Although these guidelines are general, not absolute, they should be applied as consistently as possible. The basic principle behind the guidelines is that a participle should be translated as *an indicative verb in its own clause, with tense indicating the kind of action and voice indicating how the subject relates to the action.*

1.   Every participle occurs in a specific *tense.* The most frequently occurring tenses are Present, Aorist, and Perfect. The primary factor indicated by tense is the *kind* of action.

a. **Present tense** indicates progressive action. This progressive action is best indicated by the use of "–ing" in combination with the helping verb "to be."

b. **Aorist tense** indicates summary action. This summary action is best indicated by the verb alone, apart from any helping verbs.

c. **Perfect tense** indicates completed-stative action. This completed-stative action is best indicated in combination with the helping verb "to have."

2. Participles also have *voice*. The translation of voice in participles is similar to that in the indicative.

a. In the **active voice**, the subject produces the action. Translating the active voice requires no helping words other than those necessary to distinguish the kind of action.

b. In the **middle voice**, the subject produces the action and participates in the results of the action. It is best translated using a reflexive pronoun (e.g., himself, themselves) which reflects the action back to the subject.

c. In the **passive voice**, the subject receives the action. The translation of the passive voice normally includes an "extra" form of the verb "to be."

3. *Time* of action is the most complex factor in the translation of participles, because it is *relative*. That is, the participle usually exists in a temporal relationship to the main verb in the sentence or clause.

a. **Present tense** often indicates progressive action *at the same time as* the main verb. It can, however, also indicate progressive action one step prior to the main verb.

b. **Aorist tense** often indicates summary action *one step in time prior to* the main verb. It can, however, also indicate summary action at the same time as the main verb.

c. **Perfect tense** regularly indicates completed-stative action *one step in time prior to* the main verb with continuing results *at the same time as* the main verb.

d. The few (thirteen) **future tense** participles in the New Testament regularly indicate simple action *one step in time subsequent to* the main verb.

These temporal relationships may be summarized in the chart on the next page.

		Relationship to Main Verb Time		
		Antecedent	Contemporaneous	Subsequent
Participle Tense	Present	sometimes	often	
	Aorist	often	sometimes	
	Perfect	regularly		
	Future			regularly

If context so indicates, it might be necessary to reflect the relative time relationship in your translation by adjusting the way in which you represent the tense. The chart below offers a basic overview. For example, if the context indicates that the action of a present tense participle is contemporaneous with an aorist tense main verb, the participle will be translated as if it were an indicative verb in the *imperfect* tense.

		Main Verb Tense		
		Imperfect Aorist Pluperfect	Present Perfect	Future
Present Tense	**Contemporaneous**	Imperfect	Present	Progressive Future
	Antecedent	-----	Imperfect	Present
Aorist Tense	**Antecedent**	Pluperfect	Aorist	Simple Present
	Contemporaneous	Aorist	Simple Present	Future
Perfect Tense	**Antecedent with Contemporaneous Results**	Pluperfect	Perfect	Future Perfect
Future Tense	**Subsequent**	Simple Present	Future	-----

The preceding discussion means that the translation of each participle must take into account multiple factors. Those factors include (a) the function of the participle (i.e., substantival, adjectival, adverbial, or verbal), (b) the tense of the participle, (c) the voice of the participle, and (d) the contextual relationship of the participle to the main verb.

18.3 Translating Substantival Participles

A mentioned above, a substantival participle is best translated as an indicative verb in a relative clause (e.g., "the one who . . ." or "that which . . ."). The following chart provides an initial reference point, reflecting the kind of action most often indicated by the three most frequently occurring tenses and the subject's relationship to the action as indicated by the active, middle, and passive voices.

	Present	Aorist	Perfect
Active	ὁ λυων the one who is loosing	ὁ λυσας the one who looses	ὁ λελυκως the one who has loosed
Middle	ὁ λυομενος the one who is loosing for himself	ὁ λυσαμενος the one who looses for himself	ὁ λελυμενος the one who has loosed for himself
Passive	ὁ λυομενος the one who is being loosed	ὁ λυθεις the one who is loosed	ὁ λελυμενος the one who has been loosed

Since participles (like nouns) have *case*, it is to be expected that when they function as nouns the genitive or dative case will be reflected in the helping words used.

του λυοντος (genitive)   = **of** the one who is loosing

τῳ λυοντι (dative)   = **to/for/in/by/with** the one who is loosing

18.3 Vocabulary

Conjunction and Adverbs

341.	ἐπεί	since, because [subord. conjunction]	(26)
342.	ἐγγύς	near	(31)
343.	ἐκεῖ	there, in that place	(105)
344.	ἔξω	outside	(63)
345.	εὐθύς, εὐθέως	immediately, at once	(44)
346.	οὕτως	thus, so, in this manner	(208)
347.	πάντοτε	always	(41)
348.	πότε	when?	(19)
349.	ὧδε	here, in this place	(61)

Prepositions

350.	ἄχρι + gen.	until, up to	(49)
351.	ἕνεκα, ἕνεκεν + gen.	because of, for the sake of	(26)
352.	ἕως + gen.	until, up to	(146)

Nouns

353.	ὁ τόπος, -ου	place (topography)	(94)
354.	ἡ χρεία, -ας	need	(49)

Verbs

355.	ἀπόλλυμι	I am destroying	(90)
356.	ἐντέλλομαι	I am commanding	(15)
357.	ἐπιλαμβάνομαι	I am seizing, taking hold of	(19)
358.	προσκυνέω	I am worshiping	(60)
359.	προσέρχομαι	I am approaching	(86)
360.	τηρέω	I am keeping	(70)

18.4 Practice Exercises - Translate the following sentences. Parse all verbal forms (TVMPN or TVPtcGCN - Dictionary form).

M 1. συ εἶ ὁ ἐρχόμενος;   *coming*
   asking   *about*   *bc of*
2. ἐρωτῶ περι των πιστευόντων δια του λογου αὐτων.
              brother   *light   abiding*
3. ὁ ἀγαπῶν τον ἀδελφον αὐτου ἐν τω φωτι μενει.
              righteouss   *God*
4. ὁ ποιῶν την δικαιοσυνην ἐξ θεου γεγεννηται.
   doing   *beggetting*
   making   *giving birth*

5. οὐ ζητῶ τον θελημα μου ἀλλα το θελημα του πεμψαντος με.

will (handwritten above θελημα)

6. τελος (end) γαρ νομου Χριστος εἰς δικαιοσυνην τω πιστευοντι.

7. ὁ ὢν ἐκ του θεου τα ῥηματα του θεου ἀκουει.

8. ὁ ποιῶν την ἀμαρτιαν δουλος ἐστιν της ἀμαρτιας.

9. ὁ ἐχων τον υἱον ἐχει ζωην· ὁ μη ἐχων τον υἱον του θεου την ζωην οὐκ ἐχει.

10. και ὁ τηρῶν τας ἐντολας αὐτου ἐν αὐτῳ μενει και αὐτος ἐν αὐτῳ.

11. ὁ γινωσκων τον θεον ἀκουει ἡμων· ὃς οὐκ ἐστιν ἐκ του θεου οὐκ ἀκουει ἡμων. *He who is not of God does not hear us* (handwritten)

12. ὁ ἀγαπῶν ἐκ θεου γεγεννηται και γινωσκει τον θεον.

13. και ὁ ἐωρακως μεμαρτυρηκεν, και ἀληθινη (true) ἐστιν ἡ μαρτυρια αὐτου.

14. ὁ θεος ἀγαπη ἐστιν, και ὁ μενων ἐν τη ἀγαπη ἐν τω θεω μενει και ὁ θεος ἐν αὐτῳ μενει.

15. ἐγραψα ὑμιν τοις πιστευουσιν εἰς το ὀνομα του υἱου θεου.

16. ὁ καταβας αὐτος ἐστιν και ὁ ἀναβας εἰς τους οὐρανους.

17. Ἰησους ἐστιν ὁ αἰρων την ἀμαρτιαν του κοσμου. *Jesus himself is the one who is taking away the sin* (handwritten)

18. ὁ ἀγαπῶν τον γεννησαντα ἀγαπᾳ και τον γεγεννημενον ἐξ αὐτου.

19. ἐλεγον οὐν οἱ Ἰουδαιοι (Jews) τω τεθεραπευμενῳ, Σαββατον ἐστιν.

20. οἰδαμεν ὅτι ὁ ἐγειρας τον κυριον Ἰησουν και ἡμας συν Ἰησου ἐγερεῖ.

21. ὁ ποιῶν την ἁμαρτιαν ἐκ του διαβολου ἐστιν, ὁτι ἀπ' ἀρχης ὁ διαβολος ἁμαρτανει.

22. οὐ γαρ ὑμεις ἐστε οἱ λαλοῦντες, ἀλλα το πνευμα του πατρου ὑμων ἐστιν το λαλοῦν ἐν ὑμιν.

23. ὁ πιστευων εἰς αὐτον οὐ κρινεται· ὁ δε μη πιστευων ἠδη κεκριται ὁτι οὐ πεπιστευκεν εἰς το ὀνομα του υἱου του θεου.

24. το γεγεννημενον ἐκ της σαρκος σαρξ ἐστιν, και το γεγεννημενον ἐκ του πνευματος πνευμα ἐστιν.

25. ὁ δε Ἰησους εἰπεν, ὁ πιστευων εἰς ἐμε οὐ πιστευει εἰς ἐμε ἀλλα εἰς τον πεμψαντα με, και τα ἐργα ἃ ἐγω ποιῶ ποιησει.

GRAMMAR GRABBER: Adjectival Participles

ἐγώ εἰμι ὁ ἄρτος τῆς ζωῆς. οἱ πατέρες ὑμῶν ἔφαγον
ἐν τῇ ἐρήμῳ τὸ μάννα καὶ ἀπέθανον· οὗτός ἐστιν ὁ
ἄρτος ὁ ἐκ τοῦ οὐρανοῦ καταβαίνων, ἵνα τις ἐξ αὐτοῦ
φάγῃ καὶ μὴ ἀποθάνῃ. ἐγώ εἰμι ὁ ἄρτος ὁ ζῶν ὁ ἐκ
τοῦ οὐρανοῦ καταβάς. (John 6:48-51a)

I am the bread of life. Your fathers ate the manna in the wilderness
and died; this is the "coming down from heaven" bread, in order
that anyone who should eat of him and should not die. I am the
"living, the come down from heaven" bread.

By definition the participle, as a verbal adjective, can function like other
adjectives to modify nouns. This quality again brings verbal action to bear
on Greek nouns. It contributes to the dynamism of the Biblical message. In
the acted parable of feeding the five thousand, Jesus creates a strong parallel
to the provision of manna to Israel in the wilderness, but he immediately
goes on to contrast that temporal sustenance with the eternal life he offers.

John gives us Jesus' point not only in descriptive genitives, "bread of
life," but also in dynamic adjectival participles, which preserve all the action
in Jesus' accomplishment of salvation. He is the bread which is "alive" (ὁ
ἄρτος ὁ ζῶν); he is that proactive, "coming down from heaven" bread
(ὁ ἄρτος ὁ ἐκ τοῦ οὐρανοῦ καταβαίνων, present participle); in
fact, viewed summatively, he is the "come down from heaven" bread (ὁ
ἄρτος ὁ ἐκ τοῦ οὐρανοῦ καταβάς, aorist participle). That is the kind
of dynamic "bread" he is!

Chapter 19

ADJECTIVAL USES OF PARTICIPLES

Participles are verbal adjectives. It should come as no surprise, therefore, to discover that they can be used to modify nouns in the same ways that adjectives do. The syntax and function of adjectival participles corresponds exactly with that of adjectives studied previously. The translation of participles used in this way is (in most instances) similar to that of substantival participles.

19.1 The Adjectival Use of the Participle

An adjectival participle always modifies a noun with which it agrees in gender, case, and number. Usually (but not always) an adjectival participle follows the noun it modifies, and usually (but not always) it is accompanied by a definite article. Adjectival participles are often best translated using a clause introduced by a relative pronoun: "(the one) who . . ." or "(that) which . . ."

19.2 The Syntax of Adjectival Participles

Chapter 15 introduced three uses of the Greek adjective: attributive, predicate, and substantive. The syntax of participles may be understood similarly. Since the preceding chapter discussed the substantival use of participles at some length, this chapter will concentrate on attributive and predicate constructions.

A participle in the **attributive** position qualifies or limits a noun in some way. There are three common attributive constructions.

1.   The *ascriptive attributive* construction (article-participle-noun) attributes a quality to the noun modified. With regard to participles, this construction is comparatively rare.

Rom 3:25   . . . δια την παρεσιν των <u>προγεγονοτων</u> ἁμαρτηματων

. . . because of the overlooking of the sins <u>which had happened previously</u>

2. The *restrictive attributive* construction (article-noun-article-participle)
draws special attention to a distinctive characteristic of the noun modified.
With regard to participles, this construction occurs most frequently.

Col 1:25   ... την οἰκονομιαν την δοθεισαν μοι.
... the administration of God <u>which was given</u> to me.

<u>Note</u>: Although it is possible to view the participle in this construction as a
substantival participle in apposition to the noun, it is best to treat it as
adjectival unless the context provides a compelling reason to do otherwise.

3. The *anarthrous attributive* construction (noun-participle) assigns a
general quality to the noun it modifies. With regard to participles, this
construction is comparatively common.

John 4:10   ... και ἐδωκεν ἀν σοι ὑδωρ <u>ζῶν</u>.
... and He would have given to you <u>living</u> water.

<u>Note</u>: Care must be taken to distinguish this construction from the adverbial
participle, since the adverbial participle frequently follows a noun with
which it agrees in gender, case, and number. A key to identifying the
adjectival construction is that *it usually occurs in a case other than the
nominative*, while adverbial participles usually are in the nominative case.

A participle in the **predicate** position makes a statement about a noun.
There are two common predicate constructions.

1. The *predicate adjective* construction involves the use of a linking ("to
be") verb. With regard to participles, this construction is comparatively
common.

Gal 1:22   ἠμην δε <u>ἀγνοουμενος</u> τῳ προσωπῳ ταις
ἐκκλησιαις
But I was <u>unknown</u> by face to the churches.

2. The *verbless predicate* construction may take either of two forms
(participle-article-noun <u>or</u> article-noun-participle). In neither form is the
participle preceded by an article.

Matt 14:9   και <u>λυπηθεις</u> ὁ βασιλευς δια τους ὁρκους.
And the king was <u>grieved</u> because of the oaths.

Luke 24:2   εὑρον δε τον λιθον <u>ἀποκεκυλισμενον</u> ἀπο
του μνημειου.
And they found the stone <u>which had been rolled away</u>
from the tomb.

<u>Note</u>: Care must be taken to distinguish both verbless predicate forms from
the adverbial participle, since the adverbial participle regularly occurs in
similar constructions. The first is easily identified by the absence of a verb

in the sentence. The second is most common in John's Gospel and usually occurs in a case other than the nominative.

19.3 Translating Adjectival Participles

As was true with substantival participles, an adjectival participle is best translated as an indicative verb in a relative clause (e.g., "the one who . . ." or "that which . . ."). There are instances (e.g., John 4:10 above) when it will be necessary to resort to either the English present participle (ending in –ing) or the English past participle (ending in –ed) in translating a Greek adjectival participle, but that option should be avoided if possible.

19.4 Vocabulary

Nouns

361.	ἡ ἀκοή, -ης	hearing, report	(24)
362.	τό ἔτος, -ους	year	(49)
363.	τό πλῆθος, -ους	multitude, crowd (plethora)	(31)
364.	τό πῦρ, πυρός	fire (pyromaniac)	(71)
365.	τό σπέρμα, -ατος	seed, descendant (sperm)	(43)
366.	τό στόμα, -ατος	mouth	(78)

Verbs

367.	εἰσέρχομαι	I am entering	(194)
368.	ἐκπορεύομαι	I am coming out, going out	(33)
369.	ἐπερωτάω	I am asking, asking for	(56)
370.	ἐπιστρέφω	I am returning, turning back	(36)
371.	παρέρχομαι	I am passing, passing by	(29)

Conjunctions

372.	ἄρα	therefore [coordinate]	(49)
373.	μηδέ, μητέ	nor, and not, not even [coordinate]	(90)
374.	μὲν . . . δέ	on the one hand . . . on the other hand	
375.	οἱ μὲν . . . οἱ δέ	some . . . others	
376.	οὐδὲ . . . οὐδέ	neither . . . nor	

Adverbs

377.	ἤδη	already	(61)
378.	ὅπου	where	(82)
379.	οὔπω	not yet	(26)
380.	πάλιν	again	(141)

19.5 Practice Exercises - Translate the following sentences. Parse all verbal forms.

1. ἔχεις το ὕδωρ το ζῶν. *You have the living one*

2. Ἰησουν ζητεῖτε τον Ναζαρηνον (Nazarene) τον ἐσταυρω-
   μενον. *You are seeking Jesus the Nazarene the one who has been crucified*

3. ὁ μη ἀκουων τον υἱον οὐ ἀκουει τον πατερα τον
   πεμψαντα αὐτον.

4. ἀρα οὖν οὐ ἐστιν του θελοντος ἀλλα του ἐλεῶντος θεου. *So then it isnt of the one who will but the mercifal Go*

5. τουτο (this) δε ἐστιν το ῥημα το εὐαγγελισθεν εἰς ὑμας.

6. και ὄψονται τον υἱον του ἀνθρωπου ἐρχομενον μετα
   δυναμεως και δοξης.

7. οὗτος (this one) ἐστιν ἀληθως (truly) ὁ προφητης ὁ
   ἐρχομενος εἰς τον κοσμον.

8. καθως ἀπεστειλεν με ὁ ζῶν πατηρ κἀγω ζῶ δια τον
   πατερα.

9. και οἱ γραμματεις οἱ ἀπο Ἱεροσολυμων (Jerusalem)
   ἐρχομενοι ἐλεγον ὅτι Βεελζεβουλ (Beelzebul) ἔχει και ὅτι
   ἐν τῳ ἀρχοντι των δαιμονιων ἐκβαλλει τα δαιμονια.

10. ἐπιστευε ἐπι τῳ θεῳ τῳ ἐγειροντι τους νεκρους.

11. ζῶ δε οὐκετι ἐγω, ζῃ δε ἐν ἐμοι Χριστος· ὃ δε νυν ζῶ
    ἐν σαρκι, ζῶ ἐν πιστει του υἱου του θεου του ἀγαπη-
    σαντος με.

12. θεος ἤγειρεν ἐκ των νεκρων Ἰησουν τον σωζοντα
    ἡμας ἐκ της ὀργης της ἐρχομενης.

13. εὐχαριστοῦμεν τῳ θεῳ τῳ καλοῦντι ὑμας εἰς την
    βασιλειαν και δοξαν αὐτου.

14. συ εἶ ὁ Χριστος ὁ υἱος του θεου του ζῶντος.

15. οὐκ ἐπ' ἀρτῳ ζησεται ὁ ἀνθρωπος ἀλλ' ἐπι των λογων ἐκπορευομενων δια στοματος θεου.

16. και ἐμαρτυρησεν Ἰωαννης, τεθεαμαι το πνευμα καταβαινον ὡς περιστερα ἐξ οὐρανου και μενον ἐπ' αὐτον.

17. ἠλπικαμεν ἐπι θεῳ ζῶντι, ὃς ἐστιν σωτηρ ἡμων.

18. και ἐχει ἐπι το ἱματιον ὀνομα γεγραμμενον βασιλευς βασιλεων και κυριος κυριων.

19. ἐμαρτύρει οὐν ὁ ὀχλος ὁ ὠν μετ' αὐτου ὀτε τον Λαζα-ρον (Lazarus) ἐφωνησεν ἐκ του μνημειου (tomb) και ἠγειρεν αὐτον ἐκ νεκρων.

20. και λεγει αὐτῳ ἀμην ἀμην λεγω ὑμιν, ὀψεσθε τον οὐρανον ἀνεῳγοτα και τους ἀγγελους του θεου ἀναβαινοντας και καταβαινοντας ἐπι τον υἱον του ἀνθρωπου.

GRAMMAR GRABBER: Adverbial Participles

πορευθέντες οὖν μαθητεύσατε πάντα τὰ ἔθνη,
βαπτίζοντες αὐτοὺς εἰς τὸ ὄνομα τοῦ πατρὸς καὶ τοῦ
υἱοῦ καὶ τοῦ ἁγίου πνεύματος, διδάσκοντες αὐτοὺς
τηρεῖν πάντα ὅσα ἐνετειλάμην ὑμῖν. (Matthew 28:19-20a)

Going, therefore, make disciples of all the ethnic groups, baptizing
them in the name of the Father and the Son and the Holy Spirit,
teaching them to be keeping all which I commanded you . . .

In the Greek New Testament, speakers and writers often delight in
treating the main verb as the "sun" and placing participles "in orbit" around
it. This approach not only keeps the attention on the main verb's action but
also relates it to other important actions. Take Jesus' commission in
Matthew 28 as an example.

Jesus' statement contains four verbal forms. One is the main command:
"make disciples of all the ethnic groups" (μαθητεύσατε πάντα τὰ
ἔθνη). The other three forms are adverbial participles which further
characterize that action: "going . . . baptizing . . . teaching" (πορευθέντες
. . . βαπτίζοντες . . . διδάσκοντες). There are eight possible ways in
which these adverbial participles could be related to the verb they modify
(see the discussion in Chapter 20). These adverbial participles, then, become
a challenge for interpreters.

For example, some interpreters would take πορευθέντες ("going")
as *temporal*: "While you are going" (i.e., wherever you are) make disciples.
For them this verse ceases to be a special call to cross-cultural missionary
service. Others understand the same participle as one of *manner*: what
characterizes the making of disciples, particularly among πάντα τὰ ἔθνη
"all the people groups," must include a "going" to them.

The adverbial participle itself will not tell you which relationship the
writer intends, but there will be clues which will help you as you interpret.
Those clues can come from a comparison of the lexical meaning of the
participle and the verb it modifies as well as from the immediate context.
Here, because of the international nature of the targets of disciple making,
the "going" — as well as the "baptizing" and "teaching" — is probably a
necessary characteristic of what it means to "make disciples."

Chapter 20

ADVERBIAL USES OF PARTICIPLES

The substantival and adjectival uses reflect the adjective side of participles. The adverbial and verbal uses reflect their verb side. Although the verbal use is relatively rare, the adverbial use is quite common. This chapter will introduce the eight common nuances which can be expressed by adverbial participles.

20.1 The Adverbial Use of the Participle

The adverbial use of the participle is made complex by the many possible nuances which can be expressed. English sentences often have a similar ambiguity. A simple example is the sentence, "Having finished his work Bill went shopping." The phrase "Having finishing his work" might indicate the *reason* ("Because he had finished his work . . .") Bill was free to shop, or it might indicate the *time* ("After he had finished his work . . .") he hit the mall.

In the same way, Greek adverbial participles are open to a number of possible interpretations. Familiarity with an author's style is often helpful, but context is the determining factor in deciding which nuance an adverbial participle communicates. As was the case in the English example above, it is desirable to render the participle as precisely as possible using a subordinate clause.

An adverbial participle *never* has the definite article; it usually occurs in the nominative case (70% of the time); and there is always another "finite" verb (a verb in the indicative, subjunctive, or imperative) for it to modify. The subject of the participle is the same as that of the verb which it modifies. Adverbial participles are best translated as part of a subordinate clause introduced by the appropriate connector. Examples are given below.

20.2 Nuances of the Adverbial Participle

modifies main verb

An adverbial participle may modify the verb in any one of eight ways. The options below are listed in order of frequency. Where possible, clues to identifying each category are included.

1. **Manner** (or "Modal"): the participle describes the emotion, attitude, or style in which the action takes place. The adverbial participle of manner usually *follows* its verb and is often in the present tense.
2. **Means** (or "Instrumental"): the participle describes the physical or mental means by which the action takes place. The adverbial participle of means usually *follows* its verb and is often in the present tense.
3. **Time**: the participle describes an event before (aorist tense), during (present tense), or after (future tense) which the action takes place.
4. **Cause**: the participle describes the cause, reason, or ground on which the action takes place. The adverbial participle of cause usually *precedes* its verb and is often in the perfect or aorist tense.
5. **Condition**: the participle describes the condition under which the action takes place. The adverbial participle of condition usually *follows* its verb and is often in the aorist or present tense.
6. **Concession**: the participle describes the condition in spite of which the action takes place. The adverbial participle of concession usually *precedes* its verb and is often in the perfect or aorist tense.
7. **Purpose** (or "Telic"): the participle describes the aim for which the action takes place. The adverbial participle of purpose usually *follows* its verb and is often in the future or present tense.
8. **Attendant Circumstances** (or "Circumstantial"): the participle describes an event loosely related to the action. Since all adverbial participles describe circumstances related to the action of the main verb, this category should be viewed as a "last resort" once it clear that none of the other seven categories would be preferable. The adverbial participle of attendant circumstances (a) usually *precedes* it verb, (b) usually is in the aorist tense, (c) usually occurs in conjunction with an aorist tense verb, and (d) most frequently occurs in narrative literature.

20.3 Time in Adverbial Participles

As is true with regard to participles in general, the time of an adverbial participle is relative to that of the verb it modifies. Nevertheless, certain general tendencies may be observed. They are set out in the following chart.

Antecedent	Contemporaneous	Subsequent
Time (aorist tense)	Time (present tense)	Time (future tense)
Cause	Manner	Purpose
Condition	Means	
Concession	Attendant Circumstances	

20.4 Translating Adverbial Participles

As mentioned above, an adverbial participle is best translated as part of a subordinate clause introduced by the appropriate connector. The examples which follow demonstrate this process.

Manner: **"In a manner which shows that ..."**

Heb 13:13　ἐξερχωμεθα... τον ὀνειδισμον <u>φεροντες</u>.

Let us go out . . . <u>in a manner which shows that we are bearing</u> his reproach.

Means: **"By ..."**

Matt 6:27　τις δε ἐξ ὑμων <u>μεριμνων</u> δυναται προσθειναι ἐπι την ἡλικιαν αὐτου πηχυν ἑνα;

Who among you <u>by being anxious</u> is being able to add to his stature one cubit?

Time: **"After ..."** (aorist tense); **"While ..."** (present tense)

Matt 2:10　<u>ἰδοντες</u> δε τον ἀστερα ἐχαρησαν χαραν μεγαλην σφοδρα.

And <u>after they had seen</u> the star they rejoiced with exceedingly great joy.

Matt 4:18　<u>περιπατῶν</u> δε παρα την θαλασσαν...εἰδεν δυο ἀδελφους.

And <u>while he was walking</u> beside the sea . . . he saw two brothers.

Cause: **"Because ..."**

Rom 5:1　<u>δικαιωθεντες</u> οὑν ἐκ πιστεως εἰρηνην ἐχομεν προς τον θεον.

Therefore <u>because we are justified</u> by faith we are having peace with God.

Condition: **"If ..."**

Gal 6:9　θερισομεν μη <u>ἐκλυομενοι</u>.

We will reap <u>if we are not fainting</u>.

Concession: **"Although ..."**

Heb 5:12　και γαρ <u>ὀφειλοντες</u> εἰναι διδασκαλοι... παλιν χρειαν ἐχετε του διδασκειν ὑμας τινα.

For <u>although you ought</u> to be teachers . . . you are having need again for someone to be teaching you.

Purpose: **"In order to . . ."**
   Matt 27:49 ἰδωμεν εἰ ἐρχεται ῾Ηλιας <u>σωσων</u> αὐτον.
     Let us see if Elijah is coming <u>in order to save</u> him.

Attendant Circumstances: **"and . . ."**
   Mark 16:20 ἐκεινοι δε <u>ἐξελθοντες</u> ἐκηρυξαν πανταχου.
     They <u>went out and</u> preached everywhere.

20.5 The Absolute Use   *independent*
   A special kind of adverbial participle is the **absolute** use. It defines the circumstances in which the action of the verb in the main clause occurs, but its subject is grammatically separate from the subject of the main clause. It usually is adverbial of *time*. The absolute use of the participle never uses a definite article, and it occurs with a noun or pronoun in the same case. The noun or pronoun is translated as the subject of the participle, and the participle is translated as a verb in a subordinate clause.

   A *genitive absolute* has the participle and its subject in the genitive case.
   Matt 9:33 και <u>ἐκβληθεντος του δαιμονιου</u> ἐλαλησεν ὁ κωφος.
     And <u>after</u> (aorist tense) <u>the demon was cast out</u>, the mute one spoke.

p165 chart

   An *accusative absolute* has the participle and its subject in the accusative case.
   Eph 2:5 και <u>ὀντας ἡμας νεκρους</u> τοις παραπτωμασιν συνεζωοποιησεν τω Χριστω.
     And <u>while</u> (present tense) <u>we were being dead</u> in our trespasses, he made (us) alive together with Christ.

20.6 Vocabulary

		Nouns	
381.	τό γράμμα, -ατος	letter	(14)
382.	ἡ θλίψις, -εως	tribulation, affliction	(45)
383.	τό κρίμα, -ατος	judgment	(27)
384.	τό μέλος, -ους	member	(34)
385.	ἡ παράκλησις, -εως	encouragement, comfort	(29)
386.	ὁ πούς, ποδός	foot (podiatrist, podium)	(93)
387.	ἡ συνείδησις, -εως	conscience	(30)
388.	τό τέλος, -ους	end	(40)

Verbs

389.	ἀναβλέπω	I am looking up, regaining sight	(25)
390.	ἀσθενέω	I am being weak, sick	(33)
391.	βλασφημέω	I am blaspheming, reviling	(34)
392.	διακονέω	I am serving, ministering	(37)
393.	δοκέω	I am thinking, supposing	(62)
394.	δουλόω	I am enslaving	(8)
395.	ἐγγίζω	I am approaching, coming near	(42)
396.	ἐλευθερόω	I am setting free	(7)
397.	ἐπικαλέω	I am calling upon	(30)
398.	κερδαίνω	I am gaining, profiting	(17)
399.	μνημονεύω	I am remembering	(21)
400.	πλανάω	I am deceiving, leading astray	(39)

20.7 Practice Exercises - Translate the following sentences. Parse all verbal forms.

1. ἀπελθόντες δε εὖρον καθως εἶπεν αὐτοις.

2. ἁμαρτια δε οὐκ λογιζεται μη ὀντος νομου.

3. εἰδοτες οὖν τον φοβον του κυριου ἀνθρωπους πειθομεν.

4. ἁμαρτωλων ὀντων ἡμων Χριστος ὑπερ ἡμων ἀπεθανεν.

5. και εὐθυς τοις σαββασιν εἰσελθων εἰς την συναγωγην ἐδιδασκεν.

6. νυνι δε πορευομαι εἰς Ἰερουσαλημ (Jerusalem) διακονων τοις ἁγιοις.

7. ἐλευθερωθεντες δε ἀπο της ἁμαρτιας ἐδουλωθητε τη δικαιοσυνη.

8. ἐλθουσης δε της πιστεως οὐκετι ὑπο παιδαγωγον (tutor) ἐσμεν.

contemp.
temporal

9. περιπατων δε παρα την θαλασσαν της Γαλιλαιας
εἶδεν δυο ἀδελφους Σιμωνα και Ἀνδρεαν.

walking + from sea Galilee
saw two brother Simon + Andrew

10. δυναμενοι εἰναι ὡς Χριστου ἀποστολοι ἐγενηθημεν
ἡπιοι (gentle) ἐν μεσῳ ὑμων.

Power to be as christ apostle became your

11. και ἐλθοντες εἰς τον οἰκον εἰδον το τεκνον μετα
Μαριας της μητρας αὐτου.

And come Middle house saw watched child with
Mary womb

12. και ἀκουσαντες οἱ ἀρχιερεις και οἱ Φαρισαιοι (Pharisees)
τας παραβολας αὐτου ἐγνωσαν ὁτι περι αὐτων λεγει.

And Heard priest And
parables the saying

13. και εὐθυς ἀναβαινων ἐκ του ὑδατος εἰδεν το πνευμα
ὡς περιστεραν καταβαινον εἰς αὐτον.

1 time
And immediately regain sight out of water spirit
done coming down as

14. ὁ δε Ἰωσηφ ἐγερθεις ἐλαβεν το παιδιον και την
μητερα αὐτου και ἀπηλθεν εἰς Αἰγυπτον (Egypt).

+ rise took received child +
Mother went

15. του δε Ἰησου γεννηθεντος ἐν Βηθλεεμ (Bethlehem) της
Ἰουδαιας (Judea) βασιλεις παρεγενοντο εἰς Ἰεροσολυμα
(Jerusalem).

+ Jesus born
time kings came arrived

16. ἠλθεν ὁ Ἰησους εἰς την Γαλιλαιαν (Galilee) κηρυσσων
το εὐαγγελιον του θεου και λεγων ὁτι ἠγγικεν ἡ
βασιλεια του θεου.

came Jesus Preaching
purpose gospel said Near draw
kings

17. και ἠλθεν κηρυσσων ἐν ταις συναγωγαις αὐτων και
τα δαιμονια ἐκβαλλων.

+ came Preach synagogue +
Attended demon Casting

18. και οἱ ὀχλοι ἐπιστευσαν εἰς το ὀνομα αὐτου
θεωρουντες αὐτου τα σημεια ἁ ἐποιει.

+ crowd believed name
saw behold him/his signs doing temporal cause
n/s/i

19. και ἀποκριθεις ὁ Ἰησους ἐλεγεν διδασκων ἐν τῳ
ναῳ, Πως λεγουσιν οἱ γραμματεις ὁτι ὁ Χριστος υἰος
Δαυιδ (David) ἐστιν;

answered Jesus saying teaching
At temple now

20. νυνι δε χωρις νομου δικαιοσυνη θεου πεφανερωται
μαρτυρουμενη ὑπο του νομου και των προφητων.

now + without law Serve God appeared
witnessed law prophet

21. και ἐλθοντος αὐτου εἰς τον ναον προσηλθον αὐτῳ οἱ
ἀρχιερεις και οἱ πρεσβυτεροι του λαου.

+ under w/s/it temple came him/his
gen abs cheif + elders people

22. δικαιωθέντες οὖν ἐκ πίστεως εἰρηνην ἔχομεν πρὸς
τὸν θεον διὰ τοῦ κυριου ἡμων Ἰησου Χριστου.

23. εὐχαριστῶ οὖν τῷ θεῷ ἀκούσας τὴν πιστιν ὑμῶν ἐν
τῷ κυριῳ Ἰησου καὶ τὴν ἀγαπην ὑμων εἰς τους ἁγιους.

24. ἤκουσεν Ἰησους ὅτι ἐξέβαλον αὐτὸν ἐκ τῆς συναγω-
γης, καὶ εὑρὼν αὐτὸν εἶπεν, Σὺ πιστευεις εἰς τον
υἱον του ἀνθρωπου;

25. ἔχοντες δὲ τὸ αὐτὸ πνεῦμα τῆς πιστεως κατα το
γεγραμμενον, ἐπιστεύσα διο ἐλαλησα, καὶ ἡμεις
πιστευομεν διο και λαλουμεν.

24. Jesus heard that they cast him out the
synagogue and when he found him he said,
" do you believe in the son of man? "

25. Now having the same spirit of faith according
to that which has been written, I believed
therefore I speak and we believed therefore
we spoke

GRAMMAR GRABBER: Demonstrative Pronouns

λέγω ὑμῖν, κατέβη οὗτος δεδικαιωμένος εἰς τὸν οἶκον
αὐτοῦ παρ᾽ ἐκεῖνον· ὅτι πᾶς ὁ ὑψῶν ἑαυτὸν
ταπεινωθήσεται, ὁ δὲ ταπεινῶν ἑαυτὸν ὑψωθήσεται.
(Luke 18:14)

I say to you, this one went down to his house justified, rather than
that one. Because everyone who exalts himself will be humbled, but
the one who humbles himself will be exalted.

The "Parable of the Pharisee and the Tax Collector" (Luke 18:9-14) is a
study in contrasts. With deft literary touches, which utilize **near and far
demonstrative pronouns**, Jesus makes a strong theological point about who
is truly "near God." In verses 11-12, the Pharisee is center stage, declaring
in much detail his spiritual and moral superiority. The tax collector, by
contrast, stands "afar off," repentantly grieving over his sin (18:13).

In a dramatic twist, Jesus climaxes the parable with an evaluation
(18:14). Referring to the tax collector with a near demonstrative pronoun
(οὗτος) and the Pharisee with a far demonstrative pronoun (ἐκεῖνον) our
Lord says, "I say to you, This one went down to his house, justified, rather
than that one." With this reversal of perspective via these pronouns, we
learn an important truth about God's way of looking at persons. Those who
think they are near God by their own efforts, are really far away; those who
know how far their sins distance them from God and are repentant, God
bids come near. Indeed, as Jesus makes explicit, "Everyone who exalts
himself will be humbled, but the one who humbles himself will be exalted."

Chapter 21

DEMONSTRATIVE PRONOUNS

Demonstrative pronouns point out particular persons or objects. There are two categories. The **Near Demonstrative Pronoun** ("this, these") points to persons or objects which are close to the speaker. The **Far Demonstrative Pronoun** ("that, those") points to persons or objects which are farther away. The near/far distinction can relate to any of three contexts: (1) the literary context, (2) the speaker/author's mental context, or (3) the audience's historical context. After the paradigms of each category are presented, the basic syntax related to demonstrative pronouns will be explained.

21.1 The Near Demonstrative Pronoun

The endings of the near demonstrative pronoun are identical to those of the third person personal pronoun. The complete paradigm follows. Note the absence of the τ in the masculine and feminine nominative forms as well as the rough breathing marks on those same forms. Notice also that the diphthong in the pronoun stem varies in accordance with the vowel of the ending (i.e., ου with ο/ω and αυ with α/η).

rough breathing

		Masculine		Feminine		Neuter	
Singular	Nom	ουτ	ος	αυτ	η	τουτ	ο
	Gen	τουτ	ου	ταυτ	ης	τ ουτ	ου
	Dat	τουτ	ῳ	ταυτ	ῃ	το υτ	ῳ
	Acc	τουτ	ον	ταυτ	ην	τουτ	ο
Plural	Nom	ουτ	οι	αυτ	αι	ταυτ	α
	Gen	τουτ	ων	τουτ	ων	τουτ	ων
	Dat	τουτ	οις	ταυτ	αις	τουτ	οις
	Acc	τουτ	ους	ταυτ	ας	ταυτ	α

21.2 The Far Demonstrative Pronoun

The endings of the far demonstrative pronouns are also identical to those of the third person personal pronoun. The complete paradigm follows.

		Masculine		Feminine		Neuter	
Singular	Nom	ἐκειν	ος	ἐκειν	η	ἐκειν	ο
of the	Gen	ἐκειν	ου	ἐκειν	ης	ἐκειν	ου
to/for	Dat	ἐκειν	ῳ	ἐκειν	ῃ	ἐκειν	ῳ
	Acc	ἐκειν	ον	ἐκειν	ην	ἐκειν	ο
Plural	Nom	ἐκειν	οι	ἐκειν	αι	ἐκειν	α
	Gen	ἐκειν	ων	ἐκειν	ων	ἐκειν	ων
	Dat	ἐκειν	οις	ἐκειν	αις	ἐκειν	οις
	Acc	ἐκειν	ους	ἐκειν	ας	ἐκειν	α

21.3 The Syntax of Demonstrative Pronouns

Demonstrative pronouns can occur in either of two syntactical arrangements: adjectival or substantival. The *near* demonstrative pronoun occurs more frequently as a substantive (70% of the time) than as an adjective (30 % of the time). In contrast, the *far* demonstrative pronoun occurs more frequently as an adjective (60% of the time) than as a substantive (40% of the time).

In the **adjectival** use, the pronoun stands with an article and a noun in the same gender, case, and number and modifies the noun. The pronoun normally follows the article and the noun (75% of the time), but it will *never* occur between the article and the noun.

ἡ ἀγγελια αὐτη	=	this promise
αὐτη ἡ ἀγγελια	=	this promise

Note carefully that, although the pronoun stands in what would be the *predicate* position for an adjective, it is not translated as making a statement about the noun ("this is the promise") but as qualifying/limiting it ("this promise").

In the **substantival** use, the pronoun stands alone and acts a pronoun. In translating the substantival use, it is sometimes helpful to supply a gloss which specifies the antecedent more precisely.

αὐτη = this one (woman)

The substantival use can also occur with a "to be" verb—usually εἰμι—as part of a statement.

αὐτη ἐστιν ἡ ἀγγελια = This is the promise.

21.4 Vocabulary

Demonstrative Pronouns

401.	ἐκεῖνος, -η, -ο	that [far demonstrative]	(265)
402.	οὗτος, αὕτη, τοῦτο	this [near demonstrative]	(1388)

Verbs

403.	δεῖ	it is necessary	(101)

(impersonal verb, actually PAI3S of δέω, I am binding)

404.	ἔξεστι(ν)	it is lawful	(31)

(impersonal verb, actually PAI3S of ἔξειμι, I am departing)

405.	θεωρέω	I am seeing, perceiving (theory)	(58)
406.	κρατέω	I am grasping, taking hold of	(47)
407.	μέλλω	I am about to	(109)
408.	μετανοέω	I am repenting	(34)
409.	οἰκοδομέω	I am building (up), edifying	(40)
410.	πληρόω	I am filling, fulfilling	(86)
411.	τελειόω	I am perfecting, completing	(23)

Nouns

412.	ὁ ἄνεμος, -ου	wind (anemometer)	(31)
413.	τό ἀρνίον, -ου	lamb	(30)
414.	ὁ οἶνος, -ου	wine	(34)
415.	το ποτήριον, -ου	cup	(31)
416.	τό πρόσωπον, -ου	face	(76)
417.	τό συνέδριον, -ου	council (Sanhedrin)	(22)

Adjective, Preposition, Conjunction

418.	λοιπός, -η, -ον	rest, remaining	(55)
419.	πρίν	before	(13)
420.	ὥστε	so that [subordinate conjunction]	(83)

21.5 Form Identification - For each form give gender, case, number, dictionary form, and a translation. One example is provided.

ταυτης	FGS	αὐτη	of this one (woman)

1. ἐκεινο   3. ταυτη

2. τουτω   4. ἐκεινους

5. ἐκειναι

6. αὑτη

7. ταυτα

8. ταυτην

9. ἐκεινων

10. τουτο

11. ἐκεινας

12. ταυταις

13. ἐκεινα

14. οὑτος

15. ἐκεινου

16. τουτου

17. ἐκεινος

18. ἐκεινη

19. ἐκεινην

20. οὑτοι

21. τουτῳ

22. τουτοις

23. ἐκεινῳ

24. αὑται

25. ταυτης

21.6 Practice Exercises - Translate the following sentences. Parse all verbal forms.

~~the woman~~ the commandment received from with father
1. ταυτην την ἐντολην ἐλαβον παρα του πατρος μου.

the Kingdom   out   it   of the world of this
2. ἡ βασιλεια μου οὐκ ἐστιν ἐκ του κοσμου τουτου.

this   the man   son God
3. οὑτος ὁ ἀνθρωπος υἱος θεου ἠν.

+ of the apostles   the name   this
4. των δε ἀποστολων τα ὀνοματα ἐστιν ταυτα.

the word of the faith   preaching
5. τουτ' ἐστιν ὁ λογος της πιστεως ὁ κηρυσσομεν.

+
6. και ἐξηλθεν ἡ ἀκοη αὑτη εἰς ὁλην την γην ἐκεινην.

this   know blessed   making
7. εἰ ταυτα οἰδατε, μακαριοι ἐστε ὀτε ποιειτε αὐτα.   doing

this   the words   +
8. οὑτος ἐστιν ὁ τον λογον μου ἀκουων και ποιων αὐτον.

of this of the world   I am out
9. ὑμεις ἐκ τουτου του κοσμου ἐστε, ἐγω οὐκ εἰμι ἐκ του κοσμου τουτου.

out   with God this the man
10. οὐκ ἐστιν παρα θεου οὑτος ὁ ἀνθρωπος, ὁτι το σαββατον οὐ τηρει.
keeping

11. ἐκ δε τῆς πολεως ἐκεινης ἐπιστευσαν εἰς αὐτον οἱ
Σαμαριτοι (Samaritans) διa τον λογον της γυναικος.

12. ἐν ἐκεινη τῃ ἡμερᾳ γνωσεσθε ὑμεις ὁτι ἐγω ἐν τῳ
πατρι μου εἰμι και ὑμεις ἐν ἐμοι καγω ἐν ὑμιν.

13. ὁ λογος ἐκεινος ὃν ἐλαλησα κρινει αὐτον ἐν τῃ
ἐσχατη ἡμερᾳ.

14. διa τουτο γαρ ἐρχεται ἡ ὀργη του θεου ἐπι τους υἱους
της περιτομης.

15. ὁ ποιῶν την δικαιοσυνην δικαιος ἐστιν, καθως ἐκεινος δικαιος ἐστιν.

16. ἐχομεν παρρησιαν ἐν τῃ ἡμερᾳ της κρισεως ὁτι καθως
ἐκεινος ἐστιν και ἡμεις ἐσμεν ἐν τῳ κοσμῳ τουτῳ.

17. τα ἐργα ἃ ἐγω ποιῶ ἐν τῳ ὀνοματι του πατρος μου
ταυτα μαρτυρει περι ἐπου.

18. ταυτα εἰπεν ἐν συναγωγῃ διδασκων ἐν Καφαρναουμ
(Capernaum).

19. ἀκουσαντες οὐν των λογων τουτων ἐλεγον, οὑτος
ἐστιν ἀληθως (truly) ὁ προφητης.

20. ἐγενετο δε ἐν ταις ἡμεραις ταυταις ὁτι ἐξηλθεν εἰς
το ὀρος και προσηυξατο

GRAMMAR GRABBER: Infinitives

κατὰ τὴν ἀποκαραδοκίαν καὶ ἐλπίδα μου, ὅτι ἐν
οὐδενὶ αἰσχυνθήσομαι ἀλλ᾽ ἐν πάσῃ παρρησίᾳ ὡς
πάντοτε καὶ νῦν μεγαλυνθήσεται Χριστὸς ἐν τῷ
σώματί μου, εἴτε διὰ ζωῆς εἴτε διὰ θανάτου. ἐμοὶ
γὰρ τὸ ζῆν Χριστὸς καὶ τὸ ἀποθανεῖν κέρδος.
(Phil 1:20-21)

... according to my earnest expectation and hope, that in nothing
I will be ashamed, but with all boldness, as always, even now,
Christ will be magnified in my body whether through life or
through death. For to me to be living is Christ and to die is gain.

As in English, Greek contains a form of the verb—the **infinitive**—which
has the qualities of both a verb and a noun. This feature of the Greek
language enables the New Testament writer to communicate realities in a
dynamic, action-oriented way.

As Paul speaks of the passion which drives him in Phil 1:20-21, he begins
with nouns: "Christ will be magnified ... whether through life (διὰ ζωῆς)
or through death (διὰ θανάτου)." He then continues his explanation with
infinitives: "For to me to be living (τὸ ζῆν) is Christ, and to die (τὸ
ἀποθανεῖν) is gain."

With clarity and impact, Paul declares his perspective on life. Using a
present active infinitive (*progressive* action), he makes it clear that as he lives
his whole life its meaning is summed up in one person, Christ. Then, as he
views death comprehensively through the eyes of faith—using an aorist
active infinitive (*summary* action)—he is able to conclude that it can only be
viewed as gain.

to loose
to be loosing   to loose
to be loosed

to have been loosed

Chapter 22

INFINITIVES

An infinitive is a verbal mode which combines the designative power of a noun with the action aspect of a verb. Simply stated, an infinitive is a **verbal noun**. As a noun, an infinitive may have a definite article and may be qualified by adjectives. As verb, an infinitive has tense and voice, may have a subject and/or an object, and may adverbial qualifiers. After a brief review of English infinitives, Greek infinitives will be discussed at some length.

22.1 English Infinitives

There are two infinitives in English. The *present infinitive* is the dictionary form. The *past infinitive* adds the suffix -ed. English infinitives are formed by using the preposition "to" (e.g., to walk; to have walked). The English infinitive is most commonly used as part of an infinitival phrase in one of three ways: as a **noun** (e.g., His goal is to hit the ball.), as an **adjective** (e.g., I have a plan to suggest.), or as an **adverb** (e.g., We waited to see him.)

22.2 Greek Infinitives

All Greek infinitives have tense and voice. The primary idea in the tense of an infinitive is *kind* (not time) of action. Present tense indicates *progressive* action. Aorist tense indicates *summary* action. Perfect tense indicates *completed-stative* action. There are three basic infinitive endings.

Active: ειν, ναι   Middle/Passive: σθαι

simple indefinite

Voice	Present (λυω) 1PP = λυω ongoing	1st Aorist (λυω) 3PP = ἐλυσα 6PP = ἐλυθην	2nd Aorist (βαλλω) 3PP = ἐβαλον 6PP = ἐβληθην	Perfect (λυω) 4PP = λελυκα 5PP = λελυμαι
Act.	λυ-ειν	λυ-σ-αι	βαλ-ειν	λε-λυ-κ-ε-ναι
Mid.	λυ-ε-σθαι	λυ-σ-α-σθαι	βαλ-ε-σθαι	λε-λυ-σθαι
Pass.	λυ-ε-σθαι	λυ-θ-η-ναι	βλη-θ-η-ναι	λε-λυ-σθαι

22.3 Uses of the Infinitive

The uses of infinitives may be thought of as fitting into four categories. An **adjectival infinitive** modifies a noun or an adjective. A **substantival infinitive** functions as a noun. A **verbal infinitive** functions as the main verb in a sentence. An **adverbial infinitive** modifies a verb. The statistics cited in the following discussion are derived from J. L. Boyer, "The Classification of Infinitives: A Statistical Study," *Grace Theological Journal* 6 (1985): 3-27 and D. B. Wallace, *Greek Grammar Beyond the Basics*, (Grand Rapids: Zondervan, 1996), 587-611.

An **adjectival infinitive** modifies a noun or adjective, usually a word denoting time, fitness, readiness, ability, power, authority, need, or hope. The adjectival infinitive is usually *not* accompanied by a definite article. (Boyer identifies 88 infinitives which limit nouns and 42 which limit adjectives.)

- Used to modify a **noun**

  John 1:12   ἐδωκεν αὐτοις <u>ἐξουσιαν</u> τεκνα θεου <u>γενε-</u>
  <u>σθαι</u>

  He gave them authority <u>to become</u> children of God.

- Used to modify an **adjective**

  Mark 1:7   ... οὐκ εἰμι ἰκανος <u>λυσαι</u>

  ... I am not worthy <u>to loose</u>.

A **substantival infinitive** functions as a noun in one of three basic roles: subject, object, or appositive.

- When used as a **subject**, the infinitive is that of which something is said or asserted. About one-third of the time, it is accompanied by a neuter definite article. (Boyer identifies 316 subject infinitives; 202 of them are anarthrous.)

  Rom 7:18   το γαρ <u>θελειν</u> παρακειται μοι

  For <u>to will</u> (or "the willing") is present with me.

- When used as an **object**, the infinitive receives or completes the action of the verb.

  a.   The most common use is that of *complementary object*. Verbs which regularly take complementary objects include those expressing beginning, wishing, being able, willing, being about to, and being obligated. Only rarely is the infinitive accompanied by a definite article. (Boyer identifies 892 infinitives used as complementary objects; 876 of them are anarthrous.)

  Acts 1:1   ... ὡν ἠρξατο ὁ 'Ιησους <u>ποιειν</u> τε και
  <u>διδασκειν</u>

  ... which Jesus began both <u>to be doing</u> and <u>to be</u>
  <u>teaching</u>

b. There only a few instances of the infinitive serving as a *direct object*. All but one of them have the definite article. (Boyer classifies two infinitives as direct objects: 2 Cor 8:11; Phil 4:10. Wallace adds three more: John 5:26; Phil 2:6; 2:13).

    Phil 2:6   οὐχ ἁρπαγμον ἡγησατο το <u>εἰναι</u> ἰσα θεῳ

          He did not consider <u>equality</u> with (or "the being equal to") God as something to be grasped.

▸ When used as an **appositive**, the infinitive explains or describes another noun or a pronoun more fully. (Boyer classifies six infinitives as standing in apposition to nouns and 24 as standing in apposition to pronouns.)

    Jas 1:27   θρησκεια καθαρα και ἀμιαντος . . . αὐτη ἐστιν <u>ἐπισκεπτεσθαι</u> ὀρφανους και χηρας

          Pure and undefiled religion . . . is this, <u>to visit</u> orphans and widows.

▸ A special use of the substantival infinitive is **indirect discourse**: "When an infinitive stands as the object of a verb of mental perception or communication and expresses the content or the substance of the thought or of the communication it is classed as being in indirect discourse" (Boyer, 7). Only rarely is the infinitive accompanied by a definite article. (Boyer classifies 362 infinitives as being used in indirect discourse; 353 of them are anarthrous).

    Mark 12:18   Σαδδουκαιοι οἵτινες λεγουσιν ἀναστα-σιν μη <u>εἰναι</u>

          Sadducees . . . who are saying <u>there is</u> no resurrection.

3   A **verbal infinitive** functions as the main verb in a sentence to give a *command* or *prohibition*. It never has a definite article and is clearly unrelated to a main verb or to a noun. According to Wallace (p.608) and Blass-Debrunner-Funk (§389) there are only three verbal uses of the verbal infinitive in the New Testament: Rom 12:15 (twice) and Phil 3:16.

    Phil 3:16   εἰς ὃ ἐφθασαμεν, τῳ αὐτῳ <u>στοιχειν</u>

          To that which we attained, by this <u>be living</u>.

4   An **adverbial infinitive** modifies the action of another verb. It is usually introduced by a conjunction, a preposition + an article, or the genitive definite article (τοῦ). An adverbial infinitive may modify the verb in any of four primary ways. Specific forms that each category can take and the best way to translate each will be given below.

1. **Purpose**: the infinitive states the aim for which the action in the main clause takes place.

2. **Result**: the infinitive states the consequences of the action in the main clause taking place.
3. **Time**: the infinitive describes an event before, during, or after which the action in the main clause takes place.
4. **Cause**: the infinitive states the ground on or the source out of which the action in the main clause takes place.

22.4 Identifying and Translating Adverbial Infinitives

Several of the adverbial uses of the infinitive are represented by more than one structural form. In most instances, it will be helpful to memorize the most frequently occurring forms so as to speed both translation and exegesis.

As was true in the case of adverbial participles, an adverbial infinitive is best translated as part of a subordinate clause introduced by the appropriate subordinate conjunction. The examples which follow demonstrate this process.

Purpose: **"In order to/that . . ."**

Forms: simple infinitive (over 200 occurrences)
εἰς τo + infinitive (71 occurrences)
τoυ + infinitive (46 occurrences)
πρoς τo + infinitive (11 occurrences)
ὥστε + infinitive (6 occurrences - Matt 10:1 [twice]; 15:33; 27:1; Luke 4:29; 20:20)
ὡς + infinitive (twice - Luke 9:52; Acts 20:24)

Examples:

Matt 5:17   μη νομισητε ὁτι ἠλθον <u>καταλυσαι</u> τον νομον.

Do not suppose that I came in order <u>to abolish</u> the law.

Phil 1:10   . . . εἰς το <u>δοκιμαζειν</u> ὑμας τα διαφεροντα
. . . in order that you <u>might be approving</u> the things that are excellent.

Result: **"So that . . ."**

Forms: ὥστε + infinitive (56 occurrences)
τoυ + infinitive (5 occurrences - Matt 21:32; Luke 24:16; Acts 20:30; Rom 1:24; 7:3)
simple infinitive (5 occurrences - Eph 6:19; Heb 6:10; 11:8; Rev 2:20 [twice])

Examples:

Matt 8:24   . . . ὥστε το πλοιον <u>καλυπτεσθαι</u> ὑπο των κυματων.
. . . so that the boat <u>was being covered</u> by the waves.

Mark 2:12   . . . ὥστε ἐξιστασθαι παντας και δοξαζειν
τον θεον.

. . . so that all <u>were being amazed</u> and <u>were glorifying</u>
God.

③ Antecedent Time: "After . . ."
Form: μετα το + infinitive (15 occurrences)
Examples:
Matt 26:32 μετα το ἐγερθηναι με . . .
After I <u>have been raised</u> . . .
Acts 15:13 μετα δε το σιγησαι αὐτους ἀπεκριθη
Ἰακωβος.
And after they <u>became silent</u>, James answered.

<u>Note</u>: In this construction the action of the infinitive is *antecedent* to that
of the main verb. In other words, first the action of the infinitive takes
place; then the action of the main verb occurs. The action of the main
verb thus takes place *after* that of the infinitive.

Contemporaneous Time: "While . . ."
Form: ἐν τῳ + infinitive (56 occurrences)
Examples:
Matt 13:4   και ἐν τῳ σπειρειν αὐτον . . .
And while he <u>was sowing</u> . . .
Luke 24:51 και ἐγενετο ἐν τῳ εὐλογειν αὐτον αὐτους
διεστη ἀπ' αὐτων.
And it came to pass while he <u>was blessing</u> them, he
was parted from them.

<u>Note</u>: In this construction the action of the infinitive is *contemporaneous*
with that of the main verb. In other words, the action of the infinitive
takes place at the same time that the action of the main verb occurs. The
action of the main verb thus takes place *while* that of the infinitive
happens.

Subsequent Time: "Before . . ."
Forms: πριν (ἡ) + infinitive (11 occurrences)
πρo τoυ + infinitive (9 occurrences)
Examples:
Mark 14:30 . . . πριν ἡ δις ἀλεκτορα φωνησαι
. . . before the cock <u>crows</u> twice.

John 1:48　　προ του σε Φιλιππον <u>φωνησαι</u>...ειδον σε.
　　　　　　　Before Philip <u>called</u> you . . . I saw you.

Note: In this construction the action of the infinitive is *subsequent* to that of the main verb. In other words, first the action of the main verb takes place; then the action of the infinitive occurs. The action of the main verb thus takes place *before* that of the infinitive.

Cause: **"Because of . . ."**
　　Forms: δια το + infinitive (32 occurrences)
　　　　　εκ του + infinitive (3 occurrences - Rom 9:21; 1 Cor 9:14;
　　　　　　　2 Cor 5:8)
　　　　　ενεκεν του + infinitive (once - 2 Cor 7:12)
　　Examples:
　　　　Matt 13:5　ευθεως ξανατειλεν δια το μη <u>εχειν</u>
　　　　　　　　　βαθος γης
　　　　　　　　　Immediately it sprang up because it <u>was having</u> no
　　　　　　　　　depth of earth.
　　　　Phil 1:7　... δια το <u>εχειν</u> με εν τη καρδια υμας.
　　　　　　　　　... because I <u>am having</u> you in my heart.

22.5 Additional Adverbial Constructions

　　Three additional adverbial constructions involving the infinitive occur in the New Testament. Since they are so infrequent, it is enough simply to note them.
　　Means: **"By . . ."**
　　　εν τω + infinitive (twice - Acts 3:26; 4:30)
　　Substitution: **"Instead of . . ."**
　　　αντι του + infinitive (once - Jas 4:15)
　　Place: **"As far as . . ."**
　　　εως του + infinitive (once - Acts 8:40)

22.6 Vocabulary

		Adjectives	
421.	πτωχός, -η, -ον	poor	(34)
422.	φιλός, -η, -ον	friendly	(29)
		Nouns	
423.	ἡ εὐδοκία, -ας	good will, pleasure, favor	(9)
424.	τό θηρίον, -ου	wild beast	(46)
425.	τό πρόβατον, -ου	sheep	(39)

426.	ὁ τύπος, -ου	mark, type, example	(15)
		Verbs	
427.	διώκω	I am pursuing, persecuting	(45)
428.	ἐνεργέω	I am working, operating	(21)
429.	ἐπιγινώσκω	I am coming to know, recognize	(222)
		Pronouns	
430.	ἀλλήλων	one another	(100)
431.	ἑαυτοῦ, -ης	himself, herself, itself	(319)
432.	ἐμαυτοῦ, -ης	myself	(37)
433.	ἐμός, -η, -ον	my, mine	(76)
434.	ἡμέτερος, -α, -ον	our	(7)
435.	ὅστις, ἥτις, ὅ τι	who, whoever, which, whichever	(153)
436.	σεαυτοῦ, -ης	yourself	(43)
437.	σός, σή, σόν	your (sing.)	(27)
438.	τίς, τί	who? which? what? why?	(555)
439.	τις, τι	someone, anyone, a certain one	(525)
440.	ὑμέτερος, -α, -ον	your (pl.)	(11)

22.7 Form Identification - For each form give the tense, voice, dictionary form, and a translation. One example is provided.

λυειν   PAInf   λυω   to be loosing

1. λυσαι
2. λελυκεναι
3. βαλεσθαι
4. ἐρχεσθαι
5. βληθηναι
6. γραψασθαι
7. ἀγαγειν
8. λυσασθαι
9. ἐλθειν
10. βλεψαι
11. λυθηναι
12. ἀγαπᾶν
13. βαλειν
14. γεγραφεναι
15. ἀκουσαι
16. λεγειν
17. βαλλεσθαι
18. ἀγειν
19. τεθεραπευκεναι
20. λυεσθαι

*subject of infinitive is in accusative case

21. γενεσθαι   23. ἐσθιειν

22. ἰδειν   24. πιστευσασθαι

underline infinitives

22.8 Practice Exercises - Translate the following sentences. Parse all verbal forms.

1. καὶ παλιν ἠρξατο <u>διδασκειν</u> παρα την θαλασσαν.
   teaching by the sea

2. καὶ ἀπεστειλεν αὐτους <u>κηρυσσειν</u> την βασιλειαν του θεου.
   preaching the kingdom of God

3. ἐπεμψα εἰς το <u>γνωναι</u> την πιστιν ὑμων.
   making known the faith   some

4. ὁ υἱος του ἀνθρωπου οὐκ ἠλθεν <u>διακονηθηναι</u> ἀλλα <u>διακονησαι</u>.
   the son of men out truth righteous but

5. ἐμοι γαρ το <u>ζῆν</u> Χριστος και <u>το ἀποθανειν</u> κερδος (gain).
   for the life Christ +

6. μετα δε το <u>ἐγερθηναι</u> (με) ἀξω προ ὑμας εἰς την Γαλιλαιαν.
   accusative

7. και οὐ δυναται <u>ἁμαρτανειν</u> ὁτι ἐκ του θεου γεγεννηται.
   + never possible powerful sin be of God born

8. και λεγει αὐτοις, ἐξεστιν ἀγαθον <u>ποιησαι</u> ἠ ψυχην <u>σωσαι</u>;
   + saying it is lawful yield life save?

9. οὐκ ἐδεξαντο την ἀγαπην της ἀληθειας εἰς το <u>σωθηναι</u> αὐτους.
   out recieved the love the truth saved

10. οὐχι δει <u>παθειν</u> τον Χριστον και <u>εἰσελθειν</u> εἰς την δοξαν αὐτου;
    Not must suffer Christ + enter glory

11. ὁ Πετρος λεγει τω Ἰησου, ῥαββι καλον ἐστιν ἡμας ὡδε <u>εἰναι</u>.
    Peter saying rabbi good you us/me have

12. θεος γαρ ἐστιν ὁ ἐνεργων ἐν ὑμιν και το <u>θελειν</u> και το <u>ἐνεργειν</u> ὑπερ της εὐδοκιας.
    God for works you + will + good

13. ἐπεμψε ὁ θεος τον υἱον αὐτου εἰς το <u>εἰναι</u> αὐτον δικαιον και δικαιουντα τον ἐχοντα πιστιν ἐν Ἰησου.
    sent God the son be/is servant + righteous having faith Jesus

14. ἔγραψα οὖν ἃ εἶδον καὶ ἃ εἰσιν καὶ ἃ μελλει γενεσθαι.

wrote (over ἔγραψα) *going* (over μελλει)

15. εἰ ἄνθρωπος ἐρχεται προς με καὶ οὐ μισεῖ τον πατερα καὶ την μητερα οὐ δυναται εἶναι μου μαθητης.

16. δει πληρωθηναι τα γεγραμμενα ἐν τῳ νομῳ Μωϋσεως (Moses) καὶ τοις προφηταις περι ἐμου.

17. μελλει γαρ Ἡρῳδης (Herod) ζητειν το παιδιον του ἀποκτεῖναι αὐτο.

18. λεγω γαρ ὑμιν ὅτι ὁ θεος ἐκ των λιθων τουτων δυναται ἐγεῖραι τεκνα τῳ Ἀβρααμ.

19. ὁ δε ἀποκριθεις εἶπεν, οὐκ ἐστιν καλον λαβειν τον ἀρτον των τεκνων καὶ βαλειν τοις κυναριοις (dogs).

20. ὑμιν ἐχαρισθη το ὑπερ Χριστου, οὐ μονον το εἰς αὐτον πιστευειν ἀλλα και το ὑπερ αὐτου πασχειν.

1. And he began to teach by the sea

2. And he sent them in order to preach the kingdom of God

3. I sent in order to know of your faith

4. the son of man did not come in order to be served but to serve

5. For me to live is Christ and to die is gain

6. After I am raised I will go before you into Galilee

GRAMMAR GRABBER: Pronouns

Καὶ προσκαλεσάμενος τὸν ὄχλον σὺν τοῖς μαθηταῖς αὐτοῦ εἶπεν αὐτοῖς, Εἴ τις θέλει ὀπίσω μου ἀκολουθεῖν, ἀπαρνησάσθω ἑαυτὸν καὶ ἀράτω τὸν σταυρὸν αὐτοῦ καὶ ἀκολουθείτω μοι. ὃς γὰρ ἐὰν θέλῃ τὴν ψυχὴν αὐτοῦ σῶσαι ἀπολέσει αὐτήν· ὃς δ' ἂν ἀπολέσει τὴν ψυχὴν αὐτοῦ ἕνεκεν ἐμοῦ καὶ τοῦ εὐαγγελίου σώσει αὐτήν. τί γὰρ ὠφελεῖ ἄν-θρωπον κερδῆσαι τὸν κόσμον ὅλον καὶ ζημιω-θῆναι τὴν ψυχὴν αὐτοῦ; (Mark 8:34-36)

And summoning the crowd with his disciples, he said to them, "If someone is desiring to be following me, let him deny himself and take up his cross and be following me. For whoever should be desiring to save his life will lose it; and whoever shall lose his life on account of me and the gospel will save it. For what is it benefitting a person to gain the whole world and forfeit his life?"

Pronouns have many uses. Most commonly, they stand in the place of nouns (personal), point out nouns they modify (demonstrative), and introduce adjectival clauses (relative). At other times, however, they can stand for an indefinite something or someone (indefinite), indicate the someone who both does and receives the action (reflexive), express a plural subject which passes the action back and forth (reciprocal), or ask questions (interrogative).

Jesus puts a variety pronouns to good use in His call for radical discipleship (Mark 8:34-36). They help highlight three aspects of the call to follow Him:

1. His call is universal (8:34b): "If someone, anyone (τις = indefinite pronoun) is desiring to be following me . . ."
2. His call must be responded to personally and completely (8:34c): ". . . let him deny himself (ἑαυτὸν = reflexive pronoun)."
3. His call engages us to make value judgments according to a true set of values (8:36): "What (τί = interrogative pronoun) is it benefitting a person to gain the whole world and forfeit his own soul?"

Chapter 23

ADDITIONAL PRONOUNS

To this point personal, relative, and demonstrative pronouns have been introduced. There are several additional types of pronouns. They are the **Interrogative, Indefinite, Indefinite Relative, Reflexive,** and **Reciprocal** pronouns. Each type will be discussed briefly below. As was true for personal and demonstrative pronouns, these pronouns also have gender, case, and number, and their endings will resemble noun endings.

23.1 Interrogative Pronouns

Interrogative pronouns ask questions. They refer to persons ("Who, whose, whom ...?") or to places and things ("Which, what ...?"). Interrogative pronouns follow the pattern of third declension nouns. Be certain to note the accent marks, which distinguish the interrogative pronoun from the indefinite pronoun which follows below.

interrogative		Masculine	Feminine	Neuter
Singular	Nom.	τίς	τίς	τί
	Gen.	τίν - ος	τίν - ος	τίν - ος
	Dat.	τίν - ι	τίν - ι	τίν - ι
	Acc.	τίν - α	τίν - α	τί
Plural	Nom.	τίν - ες	τίν - ες	τίν - α
	Gen.	τίν - ων	τίν - ων	τίν - ων
	Dat.	τί - σι	τί - σι	τί - σι
	Acc.	τίν - ας	τίν - ας	τίν - α

23.2 Indefinite Pronouns

Indefinite pronouns refer to no particular person, place, or thing. In English, the indefinite pronouns is frequently translated using the suffixes "–one," "–body, or "–thing" (e.g., anyone, somebody, everything). Indefinite pronouns also follow the pattern of third declension nouns and are identical to the interrogative pronouns with the exception that the accent is missing.

indefinite

		Masculine	Feminine	Neuter
Singular	Nom.	τις	τις	τι
	Gen.	τιν - ος	τιν - ος	τιν - ος
	Dat.	τιν - ι	τιν - ι	τιν - ι
	Acc.	τιν - α	τιν - α	τι
Plural	Nom.	τιν - ες	τιν - ες	τιν - α
	Gen.	τιν - ων	τιν - ων	τιν - ων
	Dat.	τι - σι	τι - σι	τι - σι
	Acc.	τιν - ας	τιν - ας	τιν - α

Technically speaking, the indefinite pronoun is "enclitic." That is, it throws its accent back on to the preceding word. For this reason, the indefinite pronouns *can* occur with an accent on its second syllable, but it will *never* have an accent on its first syllable.

23.3 Indefinite Relative Pronouns

Relative pronouns relate the clause in which they occur (the relative clause) to a noun or a pronoun in another clause (the antecedent). There are two sub-categories of relative pronouns: definite relative pronouns and indefinite relative pronouns. Definite relative pronouns were introduced in Chapter 11. **Indefinite relative pronouns** are formed by combining the relative pronoun and the indefinite pronoun. *Both* parts of the resulting composite pronoun will inflect, each according to its own paradigm.

Indefinite relative

		Masculine	Feminine	Neuter
Singular	Nom.	ὅσ - τις	ἥ - τις	ὅ - τι
	Gen.	οὗ - τινος	ἧσ - τινος	οὗ - τινος
	Dat.	ᾧ - τινι	ᾗ - τινι	ᾧ - τινι
	Acc.	ὅν - τινα	ἥν - τινα	ὅ - τι
Plural	Nom.	οἵ - τινες	αἵ - τινες	ἅ - τινα
	Gen.	ὧν - τινων	ὧν - τινων	ὧν - τινων
	Dat.	οἷσ - τισι	αἷσ - τισι	οἷσ - τισι
	Acc.	οὗσ - τινας	ἅσ - τινας	ἅ - τινα

23.4 Reflexive Pronouns

Reflexive pronouns always refer the action back to the subject. They will never serve as the subject of a sentence and, therefore, have no nominative form. They are translated using the suffixes "–self" (singular) and "–selves" (plural):

First person	Myself, ourselves
Second person	Yourself, yourselves
Third person	Himself, herself, itself, themselves

Although there are separate forms for the first and second person singular, the first and second person plural forms are identical to those of the third person plural. Context will be the determining factor in translating any ambiguous forms. Be certain to note the rough breathing marks on the singular forms of the third person and on all plural forms.

reflexive

First Person		Masculine	Feminine
Singular	Nom.	—	—
	Gen.	ἐμαυτ - ου	ἐμαυτ - ης
	Dat.	ἐμαυτ - ῳ	ἐμαυτ - ῃ
	Acc.	ἐμαυτ - ον	ἐμαυτ - ην
Plural	Nom.	—	
	Gen.	ἑαυτ - ων	ἑαυτ - ων
	Dat.	ἑαυτ - οις	ἑαυτ - αις
	Acc.	ἑαυτ - ους	ἑαυτ - ας

Second Person		Masculine	Feminine
Singular	Nom.	—	—
	Gen.	σεαυτ - ου	σεαυτ - ης
	Dat.	σεαυτ - ῳ	σεαυτ - ῃ
	Acc.	σεαυτ - ον	σεαυτ - ην
Plural	Nom.	—	—
	Gen.	ἑαυτ - ων	ἑαυτ - ων
	Dat.	ἑαυτ - οις	ἑαυτ - αις
	Acc.	ἑαυτ - ους	ἑαυτ - ας

Third Person		Masculine	Feminine	Neuter
Singular	Nom.	—	—	—
	Gen.	ἑαυτ - ου	ἑαυτ - ης	ἑαυτ - ου
	Dat.	ἑαυτ - ῳ	ἑαυτ - ῃ	ἑαυτ - ῳ
	Acc.	ἑαυτ - ον	ἑαυτ - ην	ἑαυτ - ον
Plural	Nom.	—	—	—
	Gen.	ἑαυτ - ων	ἑαυτ - ων	ἑαυτ - ων
	Dat.	ἑαυτ - οις	ἑαυτ - αις	ἑαυτ - οις
	Acc.	ἑαυτ - ους	ἑαυτ - ας	ἑαυτ - ους

23.5 Reciprocal Pronouns

Reciprocal pronouns denote the interchange of action among more than one subject. They are best translated using the phrase "one another." They occur only in the plural, and they have no nominative form.

reciprocal

		Pronoun	Translation
Plural	Nom.	—	—
	Gen.	ἀλληλ - ων	of one another
	Dat.	ἀλληλ - οις	to/for one another
	Acc.	ἀλληλ - ους	one another

23.6 Vocabulary

Verbs

441.	ἀπαγγέλλω	I am announcing, reporting	(45)
442.	ἀπέρχομαι	I am departing	(117)
443.	ἐξέρχομαι	I am coming/going out	(218)
444.	κατοικέω	I am dwelling, inhabiting	(44)
445.	πίνω	I am drinking	(73)
446.	πίπτω	I am falling	(90)
447.	προφητεύω	I am prophesying	(28)

Numeral, Nouns, Correlative Pronoun

448.	ἑπτά	seven	(88)
449.	το μνημεῖον, -ου	tomb, monument	(40)
450.	ὅσος, -η, -ον	as great as, as many as	(110)
451.	ἡ φυλακή, -ης	guard, prison, watch	(47)

		Particles	
452.	ἄν	-ever	(167)
453.	ἐάν	if [moods other than indicative]	(351)
454.	ἐάν μη	except, unless	
455.	ἐνώπιον + gen.	before	(94)
456.	ἰνα μη	lest, in order that not	
457.	μᾶλλον	more, rather	(81)
458.	ὅταν	whenever	(123)
459.	ὅπως	that, in order that [with subjunctive]	(53)
460.	οὐ μη	never [with subjunctive]	

23.7 Form Identification - For each form below give the type of pronoun, the gender (if applicable), case, number, dictionary form, and a translation. One example is given.

ἥτις   indef. rel.   FNS   ἥτις   whoever, whatever

1. ἀλλήλους
2. ἄτινα
3. ἐαυτου
4. αἵτινες
5. ἐμαυτον
6. ἀλλήλοις
7. τινα
8. τί
9. σεαυτῃ
10. ἐαυτους
11. τισι
12. ὅστις
13. ἐμαυτης
14. τίνι
15. σεαυτη

16. οἵτινες
17. ἐαυτην
18. τίνων
19. σεαυτον
20. ἀλλήλων
21. τινος
22. αἵτινες
23. ἐαυτῳ
24. τίς
25. ἐμαυτης

23.8 Practice Exercises - Translate the following sentences. Parse all verbal forms.

1. ἀκουσαντες δε οἱ μαθηται ἐλεγον, τίς ἀρα δυναται σωθηναι;

2. ὅστις οὖν ἀκουει μου τους λογους τουτους και ποιεῖ αὐτους ἀνηρ σοφος ἐστιν.

3. διο δεχεσθε ἀλληλους καθως και ὁ Χριστος ἐδεξατο ὑμας εἰς δοξαν του θεου.

4. ὁ οὖν διδασκων ἑτερον, σεαυτον οὐ διδασκεις;

5. εἰ δε τις πνευμα Χριστου οὐκ ἐχει, οὐκ ἐστιν αὐτου.

6. και ἐρχονται Σαδδουκαιοι (Sadducees) προς αὐτον οἵτινες λεγουσιν ἀναστασιν μη εἰναι.

7. τῃ γαρ ἐλπιδι ἐσωθημεν· ἐλπις δε βλεπομενη οὐκ ἐστιν ἐλπις· ὃ γαρ βλεπει τίς ἐλπιζει;

8. ἀλλα δια της ἀγαπης διακονεῖτε ἀλληλους.

9. εἰ συ πιστιν ἐχεις, κατα σεαυτον ἐχεις ἐνωπιον θεου.

10. εἰ δε τις ἀγαπᾷ τον θεον, οὗτος ἐγνωσται ὑπ' αὐτου.

11. ὅστις οὐ φερει τον σταυρον ἑαυτου και ἐρχεται ὀπισω μου, οὐ δυναται εἰναι μου μαθητης.

12. ἐκρινα γαρ ἐμαυτῳ τουτο, του μη παλιν ἐν ὀργῃ προς ὑμας ἐλθειν.

13. ἀλλα τί λεγει ἡ γραφη; ἐγγυς σου ὁ λογος ἐστιν ἐν τῳ στοματι σου και ἐν τῃ καρδιᾳ σου, τουτ' ἐστιν ὁ λογος της πιστεως ὃ κηρυσσομεν.

14. εἰτε (whether) οὖν ἐσθιετε εἰτε (or) πινετε εἰτε (or) τι ποιεῖτε, εἰς δοξαν θεου ποιεῖτε.

15. ὁ δε ἀποκριθεις εἶπεν τω λεγοντι αὐτω, Τίς ἐστιν ἡ μητηρ μου και τίνες εἰσιν οἱ ἀδελφοι μου;

16. εἰ οὕτως ὁ θεος ἠγαπησεν ἡμας, και ἡμας δει ἀλληλους ἀγαπᾶν.

17. και γαρ ὁτε ἦμεν προς ὑμας τουτο παρηγγελλομεν ὑμιν, ὁτι εἰ τις οὐ θελει ἐργαζεσθαι μηδε ἐσθιει.

18. ὁ δε θελων δικαιωσαι ἑαυτον εἶπεν προς τον Ἰησουν, Και τίς ἐστιν μου πλησιον (neighbor);

19. οὕτως και ὑμεις λογιζεσθε ἑαυτους εἶναι νεκρους μεν τη ἁμαρτιᾳ ζωντας δε τω θεω ἐν Χριστω Ἰησου.

20. ἐλθων δε ὁ Ἰησους εἰς τα μερη Καισαρειας (Caesarea) της Φιλιππου (Philippi) ἠρωτα τους μαθητας αὐτου λεγων, Τίνα λεγουσιν οἱ ἀνθρωποι εἶναι τον υἱον του ἀνθρωπου;

GRAMMAR GRABBER: Subjunctive Mood

ὅταν λέγωσιν, εἰρήνη καὶ ἀσφάλεια, τότε αἰφνίδιος
αὐτοῖς ἐφίσταται ὄλεθρος... καὶ οὐ μὴ ἐκφύγωσιν.
ὑμεῖς δέ, ἀδελφοί, οὐκ ἐστὲ ἐν σκότει, ἵνα ἡ ἡμέρα
ὑμᾶς ὡς κλέπτης καταλάβῃ... ἄρα οὖν μὴ καθεύδωμεν ὡς οἱ λοιποί ἀλλὰ γρηγορῶμεν καὶ νήφωμεν.
(1 Thess 5:3-6)

Whenever they *might be saying*, "Peace and security, then suddenly destruction comes upon them ... and they *are by no means escaping*. But you, brothers, are not in darkness, so that the day *might overtake* you as a thief ... Therefore, *let us not be being asleep* as the rest, but *let us be being watchful and be being sober.*

New Testament Greek, as well as English, has the ability to tell us what the speaker thinks about the "reality" of a verb's action. Is he affirming it to be actual, probable on certain conditions, possible, or merely potential? This property we label the verb's "mood." So far, we have been dealing in one mood, the indicative. By it, the speaker presents the action as actually occurring. Now we meet a second mood — the subjunctive.

In the subjunctive mood the speaker presents the verb's action as probable when certain conditions obtain. Look at the subjunctives in 1 Thessalonians 5:3-6. Can you guess why Paul has presented each action as probable rather than as actually occurring?

First, Paul uses the subjunctive to speak of a general, indefinite, situation in the future — "whenever they might be saying" (ὅταν λέγωσιν). Then, he uses a subjunctive to make an emphatic denial of what is yet to take place — "they are by no means escaping" (οὐ μὴ ἐκφύγωσιν). Next, he speaks of something which is yet to take place, if indeed it will, in their case — "so that the day might overtake you" (ἵνα ἡ ἡμέρα ὑμᾶς ... καταλάβῃ) — again with the subjunctive. Finally, with a subjunctive first person plural, he gives an exhortation whose probable occurrence depends on the will of the hearers — "Let us not be being asleep... but let us be being watchful and let us be being sober" (μὴ καθεύδωμεν ... ἀλλὰ γρηγορῶμεν καὶ νήφωμεν). In each instance, the action is probable but not yet actual and, so, is properly expressed by the subjunctive.

Chapter 24

SUBJUNCTIVE

To this point one mood (indicative) and two modes (participle and infinitive) have been introduced. There are, however, three additional Greek moods. In this chapter the Subjunctive mood will be introduced. In the next chapter the Optative and Imperative moods will be explained.

24.1 Mood

Mood portrays the speaker's affirmation of whether he views the action or state as actual, probable, possible, or potential. Greek verbs may, therefore, occur in any of four moods. In the **indicative** mood the speaker presents the action as *actual*. In the **subjunctive** mood the speaker presents the action as *probable* but contingent on existing and known circumstances. In the **optative** mood the speaker presents the action as *possible* without reference to existing and known circumstances. In the **imperative** mood the speaker presents the action as *potential* but dependent on the volitional response of the hearer.

24.2 The Greek Subjunctive Mood

The subjunctive mood is the mood of *probability*. The speaker asserts that the action is probable, but contingent on existing (but often unstated) circumstances. In English, the subjunctive is most often expressed by the helping verbs "might" (e.g., The boy *might* hit the ball.) or "were ... would" (e.g., If the boy *were* a good batter, he *would* hit the ball.)

In Greek, the subjunctive mood occurs only in the present and aorist tenses. The general time orientation is futuristic (contingent or possible action). The primary emphasis of tense is on the *kind* (not time) of action. The **present tense** is used to indicate *progressive* action; the **aorist tense** is used to indicate *summary* action.

There is no augment in the aorist subjunctive because there is no time of action in the subjunctive. The subjunctive uses *primary endings* in both tenses. The key characteristic of the subjunctive is the presence of long theme vowels (ω, η).

24.3 Present Subjunctive

The basic idea of the present subjunctive is *progressive* action which is *probable but contingent*. In order to express the incomplete action when translating, "–ing" should be used; in order to indicate the contingency it is often desirable to use the helping verb "might." The present active subjunctive first person singular would thus be "I might be loosing," the present middle subjunctive first person singular would be "I might be loosing for myself," and the present passive subjunctive first person singular would be "I might be being loosed." The form of the Present Subjunctive may be summarized by the following formula.

Stem + Theme Vowel + Personal Endings
(ST   +   V   +   PE   )

▶   Stem: The present tense stem is found by removing the -ω from the dictionary form of the verb.
▶   Theme Vowel: The theme vowels are long, but they follow the pattern *o-e-e-o-e-o* (ω-η-η-ω-η-ω).
▶   Personal Endings: The present subjunctive uses the primary endings in all three voices.

The full paradigm of the present subjunctive of the verb λυω follows. Note that the iota-subscript in certain forms reflects vowel contraction.

Active		λυω	Translation
Sing.	1st	λυ-ω	I might be loosing.
	2nd	λυ-η-ς	You might be loosing.
	3rd	λυ-η	He/she/it might be loosing.
Pl.	1st	λυ-ω-μεν	We might be loosing.
	2nd	λυ-η-τε	You might be loosing.
	3rd	λυ-ω-σι(ν)	They might be loosing.

Middle		λυω	Translation
Sing.	1st	λυ-ω-μαι	I might be loosing for myself.
	2nd	λυ-η	You might be loosing for yourself.
	3rd	λυ-η-ται	He/she/it might be loosing for him/her/itself.
Pl.	1st	λυ-ω-μεθα	We might be loosing for ourselves.
	2nd	λυ-η-σθε	You might be loosing for yourselves.
	3rd	λυ-ω-νται	They might be loosing for themselves.

Passive		λυω	Translation
Sing.	1st	λυ-ω-μαι	I might be being loosed.
	2nd	λυ-η	You might be being loosed.
	3rd	λυ-η-ται	He/she/it might be being loosed.
Pl.	1st	λυ-ω-μεθα	We might be being loosed.
	2nd	λυ-η-σθε	You might be being loosed.
	3rd	λυ-ω-νται	They might be being loosed.

24.4 First Aorist Subjunctive

The basic idea of the aorist subjunctive is *summary* action which is *probable but contingent*. Again, the helping verb "might" is often useful in translating. The aorist active subjunctive first person singular would thus be "I might loose," the aorist middle subjunctive first person singular would be "I might loose for myself," and the aorist passive subjunctive first person singular would be "I might be loosed."

As was true in the indicative, some verbs follow the first aorist pattern; others follow the second aorist pattern. In both instances, the active and middle voices are built on the third principal part; the passive voice is built on the sixth principal part. The form of the **first aorist subjunctive** may be summarized by the following formula.

$$\text{Stem + Tense Sign + Theme Vowel + Personal Endings}$$
$$(\text{ ST } + \quad \text{S} \quad + \quad \text{V} \quad + \quad \text{PE} \quad)$$

- ▶ Stem: The first aorist stem is found by removing the ω from the dictionary form.
- ▶ Tense Sign: In the active and middle, the tense sign is σ. In the passive, the tense sign is θ.
- ▶ Theme Vowel: The theme vowels are long, but they follow the pattern *o-e-e-o-e-o* (ω-η-η-ω-η-ω).
- ▶ Personal Endings: The aorist subjunctive uses the primary endings in all three voices. It should be noted, however, that the aorist passive subjunctive uses *active* endings.

The full paradigm of the first aorist subjunctive of the verb λυω follows. Note that the iota-subscript in certain forms reflects vowel contraction.

Active		λυω	Translation
Sing.	1st	λυ-σ-ω	I might loose.
	2nd	λυ-σ-η-ς	You might loose.
	3rd	λυ-σ-η	He/she/it might loose.
Pl.	1st	λυ-σ-ω-μεν	We might loose.
	2nd	λυ-σ-η-τε	You might loose.
	3rd	λυ-σ-ω-σι(ν)	They might loose.

Middle		λυω	Translation
Sing.	1st	λυ-σ-ω-μαι	I might loose for myself.
	2nd	λυ-σ-η	You might loose for yourself.
	3rd	λυ-σ-η-ται	He/she/it might loose for him/her/itself.
Pl.	1st	λυ-σ-ω-μεθα	We might loose for ourselves.
	2nd	λυ-σ-η-σθε	You might loose for yourselves.
	3rd	λυ-σ-ω-νται	They might loose for themselves.

Passive		λυω	Translation
Sing.	1st	λυ-θ-ω	I might be loosed.
	2nd	λυ-θ-η-ς	You might be loosed.
	3rd	λυ-θ-η	He/she/it might be loosed.
Pl.	1st	λυ-θ-ω-μεν	We might be loosed.
	2nd	λυ-θ-η-τε	You might be loosed.
	3rd	λυ-θ-ω-σι(ν)	They might be loosed.

24.5 Second Aorist Subjunctive

Some verbs follow a second aorist pattern. The form of the **second aorist active and middle subjunctive** may summarized by the following formula.

$$\text{Changed Stem} + \text{Theme Vowel} + \text{Personal Endings}$$
$$(\quad \text{ST*} \quad + \quad \text{V} \quad + \quad \text{PE} \quad)$$

- ▶ Stem: The second aorist stem is found by removing the augment and the personal ending from the third principle part of the verb.
- ▶ Theme Vowels: The theme vowels are long, but they follow the pattern *o-e-e-o-e-o* (ω-η-η-ω-η-ω).

▸ Personal Endings: The aorist subjunctive mood uses the primary endings in both the active and middle voices.

The full paradigm of the second aorist active and middle subjunctive of the verb βαλλω follows. Note that the iota-subscript in certain forms reflects vowel contraction.

Active	βαλλω (βαλ-)	Translation
Sing. 1st	βαλ-ω	I might throw.
2nd	βαλ-η-ς	You might throw.
3rd	βαλ-η	He/she/it might throw.
Pl. 1st	βαλ-ω-μεν	We might throw.
2nd	βαλ-η-τε	You might throw.
3rd	βαλ-ω-σι(ν)	They might throw.

Middle	βαλλω (βαλ-)	Translation
Sing. 1st	βαλ-ω-μαι	I might throw for myself.
2nd	βαλ-η	You might throw for yourself.
3rd	βαλ-η-ται	He/she/it might throw for him/her/itself.
Pl. 1st	βαλ-ω-μεθα	We might throw for ourselves.
2nd	βαλ-η-σθε	You might throw for yourselves.
3rd	βαλ-ω-νται	They might throw for themselves.

The **second aorist passive subjunctive** is built on the sixth principle part. The form may be summarized by the following formula.

Changed Stem + Tense Sign + Theme Vowel + Personal Endings
(ST* + [T] + V + PE)

▸ Stem: The stem of the second aorist passive subjunctive is found by removing the augment and the personal ending from the sixth principle part of the verb.
▸ Tense Sign: the tense sign θ might or might not be present. Its presence or absence must be verified by referring to the sixth principle part.

► Theme Vowels: The theme vowels are long, but they follow the pattern
  o-e-e-o-e-o (ω-η-η-ω-η-ω).

► Personal Endings: The aorist passive subjunctive uses the primary *active*
  endings.

The full paradigm of the second aorist passive subjunctive of the verb
βαλλω follows. Note that the iota-subscript in certain forms reflects vowel
contraction.

Passive		βαλλω (βαλ-)	Translation
Sing.	1st	βλη-θ-ω	I might be thrown.
	2nd	βλη-θ-η-ς	You might be thrown.
	3rd	βλη-θ-η	He/she/it might be thrown.
Pl.	1st	βλη-θ-ω-μεν	We might be thrown.
	2nd	βλη-θ-η-τε	You might be thrown.
	3rd	βλη-θ-ω-σι(ν)	They might be thrown.

24.6 Uses of the Subjunctive

Verbs in the subjunctive mood can occur either in independent (main)
or in dependent (subordinate) clauses. There are four primary **independent
clause uses**.

1. The *hortatory subjunctive* uses the first person plural subjunctive to urge
   the listener(s) to join the speaker in the action.

   Heb 4:15   κρατωμεν της ὁμολογιας . . .

   Let us hold fast the confession . . .

2. The *deliberative subjunctive* uses the subjunctive in a question to weigh
   a course of action.

   Matt 6:31   . . . λεγοντες, Τί <u>φαγωμεν</u>;

   . . . saying, "What might we eat?"

3. *Emphatic negation* uses οὐ μη + the aorist subjunctive to place special
   stress on a negative proposition.

   John 10:28 καὶ οὐ μη <u>ἀπολωνται</u> εἰς τον αἰωνα

   And they will <u>never</u> perish unto the age.

4. The *prohibitive subjunctive* uses μη + the second person aorist subjunctive to demand that the listener not begin an action.

Matt 6:31   μη οὖν <u>μεριμνησητε</u>...

Therefore, don't start being anxious . . .

Dependent clause uses of the subjunctive may be grouped under four headings. Two of those headings must be further sub-divided.

1. The *conditional subjunctive* introduces a condition with the conjunction ἐάν, then follows the conjunction with a verb in the subjunctive mood.

    John 8:36   ἐάν οὖν ὁ υἱος ὑμας <u>ἐλευθερωσῃ</u>...

    Therefore, if the Son frees you . . .

2. The subjunctive is frequently used with the conjunction ἱνα to state the expressed *purpose* or *result* of the action of the verb in the main clause.

    a. Positive purpose: ἱνα + subjunctive

        1 John 5:13   ταυτα ἐγραψα ὑμιν ἱνα <u>εἰδητε</u>...

        These things I wrote to you in order that you might know . . .

    b. Negative purpose: ἱνα μη + subjunctive

        1 John 2:1   ταυτα γραφω ὑμιν ἱνα μη <u>ἁμαρτητε</u>

        These things I am writing to you lest you (in order that you might not) sin.

    c. Result: ἱνα + subjunctive

        Rom 11:11   μη ἐπταισαν ἱνα <u>πεσωσιν</u>;

        They did not stumble so that they might fall, did they?

    d. Purpose-Result - Wallace argues that ἱνα + the subjunctive may also be used to indicate *both* the intention and of an action *and* its certain accomplishment (*Grammar*, 473).

        Phil 2:10   ...ἱνα ἐν τῳ ὀνοματι ᾽Ιησου παν γονυ <u>καμψῃ</u>

        . . . in order that at the name of Jesus every knee might bow

3. Some subordinate clauses use the subjunctive to state *indefinite* (general) cases related to the action of the verb in the main clause.

    a. Relative: ὅς ἀν + subjunctive

        Mark 9:37   ὅς ἀν ἐν των τοιουτων παιδιων <u>δεξηται</u>

        Whoever might receive one of such children . . .

b.   Temporal: ὅταν + subjunctive

Matt 6:5   ... καὶ ὅταν <u>προσευχησθε</u>

And whenever you (might) pray ...

4.   The subjunctive is sometimes used with ἵνα to introduce a *substantival* subordinate clause which functions as a noun. The clause may function as a subject, a predicate nominative, a direct object (the example below), or in apposition.

Matt 12:16   ἐπετιμησεν αὐτοις ἱνα μη φανερον αὐτον <u>ποιησωσιν</u>

He ordered them that they might not make him known.

24.7 Vocabulary

Verbs

461.	διέρχομαι	I am passing through	(43)
462.	κλαίω	I am weeping	(40)
463.	προσφέρω	I am bringing to, offering	(47)
464.	συνάγω	I am gathering together	(59)
465.	χαίρω	I am rejoicing	(74)

χαίρω, χαρήσομαι, ἐχάρην

Nouns and Pronoun

466.	ἡ ἐπαγγελία, -ας	promise	(52)
467.	ἡ θύρα, -ας	door	(39)
468.	ἡ τιμή, -ης	honor, price	(41)
469.	τό πάσχα	Passover	(29)
470.	τοιοῦτος, -αυτη, -ουτο	such [demonstrative pronoun]	(57)

Adjectives

471.	δεξιός, -α, -ον	right [as opposed to left]	(54)
472.	ἱκανός, -η, -ον	sufficient, able, considerable	(39)
473.	μέσος, -η, -ον	middle (Mesopotamia)	(58)
474.	ὀλίγος, -η, -ον	little, few (oligarchy)	(40)

475.	ὅμοιος, -α, -ον	like	(45)

Particles

476.	διότι	because, for [coord. conj.]	(23)
477.	οὖ	where	(24)
478.	πλείων, -ονος	larger, more	(58)
479.	ποῦ	to where/what place? whither?	(48)
480.	πῶς	how?	(103)

24.8 Form Identification - For each form, give the tense, voice, mood, person, number, dictionary form, and a translation. One example is given.

λυσωμαι   AMS1S   λυω   I might loose for myself

1. πιστευηται
2. βαλλωσι
3. βαλωσι
4. λελυμεθα
5. ἀκουσωνται *AMsub,*
6. θεραπευσηται
7. πιστευσητε
8. λυσῃς
9. θεραπευωμεν *Pres Ac 1 Plur*
10. πιστευσῃ
11. λυθητε *Aor Pass Subj*
12. γραψωνται
13. φαγωμεθα *A M Su 1 Pl*

14. γινωσκησθε
15. σωθητε
16. εἴπῃ *A A sub 3 S*
17. κηρυχθη
18. λαβωμαι
19. γινῃ
20. ἀγαπῶμεν *Ar*
21. ἀκουσθωσι *A Pass 3 plural*
22. προφητευωμαι
23. πινωμεν
24. ἀγαγωσι *Ar Act sub 3 plural*
25. ἐλθητε *Ar Pass*

24.9 Practice Exercises - Translate the following sentences. Parse all verbal forms.

1. οὗτος ἐστιν ὁ λογος ὃν ἠκουσατε ἀπ' ἀρχης, ἱνα ἀγαπῶμεν ἀλληλους. *this is the word which you heard from the beginning that we may love one another*

2. και ἐν τουτῳ γινωσκομεν ὅτι ἐγνωκαμεν αὐτον, ἐαν τας ἐντολας τηρῶμεν. *And this we know that we have known him if we have kept his commandments*

3. μετα τουτο λεγει τοις μαθηταις, ἐρχωμεθα εἰς την Ἰουδαιαν (Judea) παλιν. *After this he said to his disciples let us come into Judea again*

4. ἀμην λεγω ὑμιν, ὃς ἀν μη δεξηται την βασιλειαν του θεου ὡς τεκνον οὐ μη εἰσελθῃ εἰς αὐτην.

5. αὐτη δε ἐστιν ἡ ζωη, ἱνα γινωσκωσιν σε τον μονον θεον και ὃν ἀπεστειλας Ἰησουν Χριστον.

6. ἐαν εἰπωμεν ὅτι ἁμαρτιαν οὐκ ἐχομεν, ἡ ἀληθεια οὐκ ἐστιν ἐν ἡμιν.

7. ἐγω δε οὐ παρα ἀνθρωπου την μαρτυριαν λαμβανω ἀλλα ταυτα λεγω ἱνα ὑμεις σωθητε.

8. οὗτος ἐστιν ὁ ἀρτος ὁ ἐκ του οὐρανου καταβαινων ἱνα τις ἐξ αὐτου φαγῃ και μη ἀποθανῃ.

9. ἀλλ' ἱνα φανερωθῃ τῳ Ἰσραηλ (Israel) ἠλθον ἐγω ἐν ὑδατι βαπτιζων.

10. μη τις γεννηθῃ ἐξ ὑδατος και πνευματος οὐ δυναται εἰσελθειν εἰς την βασιλειαν του θεου.

11. ὁ μη γινωσκων ἁμαρτιαν ὑπερ ἡμων ἁμαρτιαν ἐγενετο ἱνα ἡμεις γενωμεθα δικαιοσυνη θεου ἐν αὐτῳ.

12. ὅταν Χριστος φανερωθῃ, και ὑμεις συν αὐτῳ φανερωθησεσθε ἐν δοξῃ.

13. ὁ ἀγγελος ἐφανη αὐτῳ λεγων, Ἰωσηφ (Joseph) υἱος Δαυιδ (David) μη φοβησθῃς παραλαβειν Μαριαν (Mary) την γυναικα σου.

14. τουτο δε γεγονεν ἱνα πληρωθῃ το *ῥηθεν ὑπο κυριου δια του προφητου.

*that which was spoken
→ from
lego

15. ὃς ἐαν δεξηται τεκνον ἐπι τῳ ὀνοματι μου ἐμε δεχεται.

16. ἀμην δε λεγω ὑμιν, ὁπου ἐαν κηρυχθῃ το εὐαγγελιον εἰς τον κοσμον ὃ ἐποιησεν αὐτη λαληθησεται.

17. ἐλεγεν γαρ αὐτη, ὁτι ἐαν ἁψωμαι των ἱματιων αὐτου σωθησομαι.

ἱΜΑΤΙΩΝ

18. μὴ δοκήσητε ὁτι ἠλθον λῦσαι τὸν νόμον ἢ τοὺς προφήτας· οὐκ ἠλθον λῦσαι ἀλλὰ πληρῶσαι

19. εἰπεν οὐν ὁ Ἰησους, ἀμην ἀμην λεγω ὑμιν, ἐαν μη φαγητε την σαρκα του υἱου του ἀνθρωπου και πιητε αὐτου το αἱμα, οὐκ ἐχετε ζωην ἐν ἑαυτοις.

20. εἰδομεν δε ὁτι οὐ δικαιουται ἀνθρωπος ἐξ ἐργων νομου ἀλλα δια πιστεως Ἰησου Χριστου, και ἡμεις εἰς Χριστον ἐπιστευσαμεν, ἱνα δικαιωθωμεν ἐκ πιστεως Χριστου και οὐκ ἐξ ἐργων νομου.

Μη + pres. impv : "stop ——"

Μη + aor subj : "do not start...
begin..."

GRAMMAR GRABBER: Imperative Mood

εἶπεν δὲ ὁ κύριος ἐν νυκτὶ δι᾽ ὁράματος τῷ Παύλῳ,
Μὴ φοβοῦ, ἀλλὰ λάλει καὶ μὴ σιωπήσῃς, διότι ἐγώ
εἰμι μετὰ σοῦ καὶ οὐδεὶς ἐπιθήσεταί σοι τοῦ κακῶσαί
σε, διότι λαός ἐστί μοι πολὺς ἐν τῇ πόλει ταύτῃ.
(Acts 18:9-10)

Now the Lord said to Paul at night through a vision, "Stop being
afraid, but keep on speaking and do not become silent, for I am with
you and no one will seize you to harm you, for many people in this
city are mine."

The imperative mood expresses commands or prohibitions. An
interesting feature of its use is the interaction with the kind of action
indicated by the tense of the verb. Look at the way the Lord addresses Paul
in Corinth.

A present tense prohibition may not only forbid a repeated action, but,
given the context, it may ask that an action already in progress be stopped.
So here, the Lord is not prohibiting the repeated action of being afraid, but
calling for Paul to turn away from his fear (Μὴ φοβοῦ, a present prohibition).

An aorist tense prohibition may not only forbid a simple action, but
forbid a starting of a contemplated action. Paul is not to "become silent" (μὴ
σιωπήσῃς, a prohibition [expressed with the aorist subjunctive]). The Lord
clearly commands Paul to "keep on speaking," and lets him know that he
is not to let fear so control him that he abandons his witness.

Note the strong promise attached. The Lord is with him; He will protect
him. There are many men and women to be drawn into the people of God
from among the Corinthians.

Chapter 25

OPTATIVE AND IMPERATIVE

The two remaining moods in which Greek verbs can occur are the Optative and the Imperative. The optative is rare, occurring only 67 times in the Greek New Testament. It will, therefore, be discussed only briefly. The imperative is much more frequent and will be explained at greater length.

25.1 The Optative Mood

The optative mood is the mood of more doubtful assertion. The speaker asserts that the action is *possible but doubtful*. English does not have a separate optative mood. The optative mood may occur in the present, future, aorist, or perfect tenses. The primary emphasis of tense is on the *kind* (not time) of action. Present tense, therefore, indicates *progressive* action; future and aorist indicate *summary* action; perfect indicates *completed-stative* action.

There is no augment in the aorist tense because there is no time of action in the optative. The optative uses (variant) primary endings in the active voice and secondary endings in the middle and passive voices. The key characteristic of the optative is the presence of an ι in the theme vowel. There are three primary uses of the optative.

1. The *voluntative optative* expresses a wish (basic use).

   1 Pet 1:2   χαρις ὑμιν και εἰρηνη <u>πληθυνθειη</u>

   Grace and peace be multiplied to you.

2. The *potential optative* expresses perplexity or possibility.

   Luke 3:15   ... διαλογιζομενων ... μηποτε αὐτος <u>εἰη</u> ὁ Χριστος

   ... wondering ... whether he might be the Christ.

3. The *conditional optative* expresses a future condition which is not likely to be fulfilled.

   1 Pet 3:14   ἀλλ᾽ εἰ και <u>πασχοιτε</u> δια δικαιοσυνην ...

   But even if you might suffer because of righteousness...

[handwritten note: 4th class condition]

25.2 The Imperative Mood

The imperative mood is the mood of volition. The speaker asserts that the action is *potential, but dependent on the volitional response of the person*

[handwritten note: negative : Μή / οὐκ]

addressed. In English, the imperative is used only in the second person singular or plural (e.g., Hit the ball!).

In Greek, the imperative mood occurs in the present, aorist, and perfect tenses, but the perfect tense imperative is so rare (0.2% according to Boyer) that it will not be addressed. The general time orientation is futuristic (i.e, subsequent to the command). The primary emphasis of tense is on the *kind* (not time) of action. The present tense, therefore, indicates *progressive* action, and the aorist tense indicates *summary* action.

There is no augment in the aorist tense because there is no time of action in the imperative. The imperative occurs in second and third persons only; there is no form for first person imperative (although its function is filled by the first person plural subjunctive). The basic imperative endings are summarized in the following chart.

Active	Singular	1st	not applicable
		2nd	--
		3rd	τω
	Plural	1st	not applicable
		2nd	τε
		3rd	τωσαν
Middle and Passive	Singular	1st	not applicable
		2nd	σο
		3rd	σθω
	Plural	1st	not applicable
		2nd	σθε
		3rd	σθωσαν

The similarities to the indicative endings should be noted (second person plural active, second person singular middle/passive, and second person plural middle/passive) as should the fact that the imperative does not appear in the first person singular or plural. The hortatory subjunctive serves to fill the role of the first person plural imperative. Several variant endings occur in the aorist imperative and will be dealt with below.

The third person imperative has no counterpart in English. It has long been common practice to translate those forms using "Let..." That practice, however, tends to give the impression that the speaker/writer is asking *permission* for something to happen. Although one of the uses of this mood is the imperative of permission, that particular use is rare (See below. Boyer classifies 2% of imperatives as expressing permission.) It is preferable to translate the third person singular imperative as "He/she/it *must* . . ." and the third person plural imperative as "They *must* . . ." That approach is reflected in the paradigms which follow.

25.3 Present Imperative

The basic idea of the present imperative is that of *progressive* action. There are several ways to reflect this tense idea in translation. One is to use the phrase "keep on . . ." Another is to insert the helping word "be . . ." before the verb. In either case, the verb in the imperative should end in "–ing." The form of the **present imperative** may be summarized by the following formula.

$$\text{Stem + Theme Vowel + Imperative Endings}$$
$$(\ \text{ST} + \quad \text{V} \quad + \quad \text{ImvE} \quad)$$

- ▸ Stem: The stem is found by removing the -ω from the dictionary form of the verb.
- ▸ Theme Vowel: The theme vowel is always ε, although in second person singular middle/passive it contracts with the ending.
- ▸ Imperative Endings: The imperative endings are those found in the chart above.

The full paradigm of the present imperative of the verb λυω follows. As is true in other moods and modes, the middle and passive imperative forms are identical. A decision on the appropriate translation of such forms which do "double duty" will be based on contextual clues.

Active		λυω			Translation
Sing.	1st				
	2nd	λυ	ε	--	(You) Be loosing!
	3rd	λυ	ε	τω	He/she/it must be loosing!
Pl.	1st				
	2nd	λυ	ε	τε	(You) Be loosing!
	3rd	λυ	ε	τωσαν	They must be loosing!

Middle			λυω		Translation
Sing.	1st				
	2nd	λυ	(ε +	σο) = ου	(You) Be loosing for yourself!
	3rd	λυ	ε	σθω	He/she/it must be loosing for him/her/itself!
Pl.	1st				
	2nd	λυ	ε	σθε	(You) Be loosing for yourselves!
	3rd	λυ	ε	σθωσαν	They must be loosing for themselves!

Passive			λυω		Translation
Sing.	1st				
	2nd	λυ	(ε +	σο) = ου	(You) Be being loosed!
	3rd	λυ	ε	σθω	He/she/it must be being loosed!
Pl.	1st				
	2nd	λυ	ε	σθε	(You) Be being loosed!
	3rd	λυ	ε	σθωσαν	They must be being loosed!

25.4 First Aorist Imperative

The basic idea of the aorist imperative is that of *summary* action. No helping words are necessary in the translation. The aorist active and middle voices are formed on the third principle part, and the aorist passive voice is built on the sixth principle part. As was true in the indicative and subjunctive moods, some verbs follow the first aorist pattern; others follow the second aorist pattern. The form of the **first aorist imperative** may be summarized by the following formula.

Stem + Tense Sign + Theme Vowel + Imperative Endings
(ST + S + V + ImvE)

▶ Stem: The stem of first aorist verbs is found by removing the -ω from the end of the dictionary form of the verb.

▶ Tense Sign: The tense sign is σ in the active and middle. In the passive it is θ.

▶ Theme Vowel: The theme vowel is α in the active and middle (except in the second person singular active) and η in the passive.

► Imperative Endings: The imperative endings are those found in the chart above (with certain exceptions). Remember that the aorist passive uses *active* endings.

The full paradigm of the first aorist imperative of the verb λυω follows. Note that when the sixth principle part of the verb lacks the θ tense sign (e.g., ἐγραφην), the aorist passive second person singular ending will be θι; otherwise it is τι.

Active		λυω				Translation
Sing.	1st					
	2nd	λυ	σ	<u>ο</u>	<u>ν</u>	(You) Loose!
	3rd	λυ	σ	α	τω	He/she/it must loose!
Pl.	1st					
	2nd	λυ	σ	α	τε	(You) Loose!
	3rd	λυ	σ	α	τωσαν	They must loose!

Middle		λυω				Translation
Sing.	1st					
	2nd	λυ	σ	<u>αι</u>	–	(You) Loose for yourself!
	3rd	λυ	σ	α	σθω	He/she/it must loose for him/her/itself.
Pl.	1st					
	2nd	λυ	σ	α	σθε	(You) Loose for yourselves!
	3rd	λυ	σ	α	σθωσαν	They must loose for themselves!

Passive		λυω				Translation
Sing.	1st					
	2nd	λυ	θ	η	<u>τι</u>	(You) Be loosed!
	3rd	λυ	θ	η	τω	He/she/it must be loosed!
Pl.	1st					
	2nd	λυ	θ	η	τε	(You) Be loosed!
	3rd	λυ	θ	η	τωσαν	They must be loosed!

25.5 Second Aorist Imperative

Some verbs, of course, follow a second aorist pattern. The form of the **second aorist active and middle imperative** may be summarized by the following formula.

Changed Stem + Theme Vowel + Imperative Endings
(ST*   +   V   +   ImvE   )

▶ Stem: The second aorist stem is found from by removing the augment and person endings from the third principle part of the verb.
▶ Theme Vowel: The theme vowel is always ε, although in the second person singular middle it contracts with the ending.
▶ Imperative Endings: The imperative mood uses the endings found in the chart above.
▶

The paradigm of the second aorist active and middle imperative of the verb βαλλω follows.

Active		βαλλω (βαλ-)			Translation
Sing.	1st				
	2nd	βαλ	ε	--	(You) Throw!
	3rd	βαλ	ε	τω	He/she/it must throw!
Pl.	1st				
	2nd	βαλ	ε	τε	(You) Throw!
	3rd	βαλ	ε	τωσαν	They must throw!

Middle		βαλλω (βαλ-)			Translation
Sing.	1st				
	2nd	βαλ	(ε +	σο) = ου	(You) Throw for yourself!
	3rd	βαλ	ε	σθω	He/she/it must throw for him/her/itself!
Pl.	1st				
	2nd	βαλ	ε	σθε	(You) Throw for yourselves!
	3rd	βαλ	ε	σθωσαν	They must throw for themselves!

The **second aorist passive imperative** is similar in form to the first aorist passive. The stem and the presence (or absence) of the tense sign must be verified from the sixth principle part. The aorist passive of the verb βαλλω follows.

Passive		βαλλω (βαλ-)	Translation
Sing.	1st		
	2nd	βλη θ η τι	(You) Be thrown!
	3rd	βλη θ η τω	He/she/it must be thrown!
Pl.	1st		
	2nd	βλη θ η τε	(You) Be thrown!
	3rd	βλη θ η τωσαν	They must be thrown!

25.6 Uses of the Imperative

There are four primary uses of the imperative: command, prohibition, request and permission. The statistics cited in the following discussion are derived from J. L. Boyer, "A Classification of Imperatives: A Statistical Study," *Grace Theological Journal* 8 (1987): 35-54.

The basic use of the imperative is to give a **command** demanding that the addressee undertake an action. (Boyer classifies 1169 uses as command.)

    a.   With the *present tense* the command demands that an action be undertaken continually or repeatedly.

        John 5:8   ... και περιπατει

                    ... and continue walking.

    b.   With the *aorist tense* the command demands that the action be undertaken immediately.

        John 5:8   αρον τον κραββατον σου ...

                    Take up your bed ...

The imperative of **prohibition** demands that the addressee refrain from an action. (Boyer classifies 188 uses as prohibition.)

    a.   The use of μη + the *present imperative* in a prohibition demands that an action in progress be stopped or forbids a repeated action.

        Phil 4:6   μηδεν μεριμνατε ...

                    Stop being anxious ...

    b.   The use of μη + the *aorist subjunctive* in a prohibition demands that an action being contemplated not be started or forbids a simple action.

        Matt 6:31   μη ουν μεριμνησητε ...

                    Therefore, don't start being anxious ...

The imperative of **request** (or "entreaty") has the force of an urgent request from a subordinate to a superior. (Boyer classifies 188 uses as request.)

Luke 17:5   προσθες ἡμιν πιστιν
Increase our faith.

The imperative of **permission** gives consent from a superior for an action desired or contemplated by a subordinate. (Boyer classifies 27 uses as permission.)

Matt 26:45   καθευδετε το λοιπον και ἀναπαυεσθε
Sleep on now and refresh yourselves.

25.7 Vocabulary

Verbs

481.	γαμέω	I am marrying	(28)
482.	ἐλεέω	I am having/showing mercy	(29)
483.	ἐνδύω	I am putting on	(27)
484.	ἑρμηνεύω	I am translating (hermeneutics)	(3)
485.	ἰσχύω	I am being strong, able	(28)
486.	κεῖμαι	I am lying	(24)
487.	ὀφείλω	I am owing, ought	(35)
488.	περισσεύω	I am abounding, being rich	(39)
489.	πράσσω	I am doing, performing (praxis)	(39)
490.	συνέρχομαι	I am coming together	(30)
491.	ὑποστρέφω	I am returning	(35)
492.	ὑποτάσσω	I am putting in subjection	(38)

Adjectives, Nouns

493.	ἀληθινός, -η, -ον	true	(28)
494.	ἡ θυσία, -ας	sacrifice	(28)
495.	ποῖος, -ά, ον	what sort of? what?	(33)
496.	ἡ φυλή, -ης	tribe (phylum)	(31)

Adverbs, Conjunctions

497.	ἄρτι	now, just now	(36)
498.	ὁμοίως	likewise	(30)
499.	εἴτε (... εἴτε)	whether (... or)	(65)
500.	πλήν	however, but, only [coord. conj.]	(31)

25.8 Form Identification - For each form, give the TVMPN, dictionary form, and a translation. One example is given.

ἐχέτω   PAImv3S   ἔχω   He/she/it must be having

1. πιστευετωσαν *PAI 3P*
2. βαλλου *PMPI*
3. βαλου *2 AMI2S*
4. κελευσασθω
5. βληθητι
6. μη ερχεσθε
7. ἀγαγε *AX*
8. γινου *PMPI2S*
9. λεγετωσαν *PAI3P*
10. μη πιπτετε *PAI*
11. θεραπευθητι
12. ἀκουσθητω
13. γραψον

14. ἀποκτεινατε
15. στραφηθι
16. σταυρωθητωσαν *API*
17. ἐλθε
18. ερχου *PMP PMPI*
19. ποιησατω *AAI 3S*
20. σωσον
21. λαβετε *AAI 2S*
22. μη ἁμαρτανετε *PAI 2P*
23. ἀκουετω
24. λυσασθε
25. δικαιωθητι

25.9 Practice Exercises - Translate the following sentences. Parse all verbal forms.

1. ἀλλα ἐνδυσασθε τον κυριον Ἰησουν Χριστον.
But putting on for yourselves the master Jesus Christ

2. και ἐλεγεν, ὁς ἐχει ὠτα ἀκουειν ἀκουετω.
And he was saying, he who has ears to hear let him hear

3. ἀλλα ὑποτασσεσθωσαν αἱ γυναικες, καθως και ὁ νομος λεγει.
But they must subject themselves wives just as and the law
speak → And may wives be subjecting just as the law says

4. ὡς οὐν παρελαβετε τον Χριστον Ἰησουν τον κυριον, ἐν αὐτῳ περιπατειτε.

5. και ἀποκριθεις ειπεν αὐτοις, ἀπαγγειλατε Ἰωαννῃ (John) ἁ ειδετε και ἠκουσατε.
And answering he said to them proclaim to John the things you saw and heard

6. *Jesus said to him, rise, take up your mattress and walk*

λεγει αυτω ο Ἰησους, ἐγειρε ἀρον τον κραβαττον (mattress) σου και περιπατει.

7. *But Jesus after he heard answered to him don't*

ὁ δε Ἰησους ἀκουσας ἀπεκριθη αὐτω, μη φοβου, μονον πιστευσον και σωθησεται. *stop fearing only believe a he will be saved*

8. τω Ἰησου ἠκολουθησαν δυο (two) τυφλοι κραζοντες και λεγοντες, ἐλεησον ἡμας, υἱος Δαυιδ (David).

9. δια τουτο λεγω ὑμιν, ὅσα προσευχεσθε και αἰτεῖσθε, πιστευετε ὅτι ἐλαβετε, και ἐσται ὑμιν.

10. καθως ἠγαπησεν με ὁ πατηρ, κἀγω ὑμας ἠγαπησα· μεινατε ἐν τη ἀγαπη τη ἐμη.

11. *And they said believe the lord Jesus and*
οἱ δε εἰπαν, πιστευσον ἐπι τον κυριον Ἰησουν και σωθηση σὺ και ὁ οἰκος σου. *you + your house will be saved*

12. *road nation your house depart + city*
εἰς ὁδον ἐθνων μη ἀπελθητε και εἰς πολιν Σαμαριτων (Samaritans) μη εἰσελθητε.

13. *But* ἀλλα ὑπαγετε εἰπατε τοις μαθηταις αὐτου και τω Πετρου ὅτι ἐρχομαι προ ὑμων εἰς Γαλιλαιαν (Galilee).

14. ἐτοιμαζετω δε ἀνθρωπος ἑαυτον και οὑτως ἐκ του ἀρτου ἐσθιετω και ἐκ του ποτηριου πινετω.

15. *the work your believe in order to make known that I*
τοις ἐργοις πιστευετε ἱνα γνωτε και γινωσκητε ὅτι ἐν ἐμοι πατηρ κἀγω ἐν τω πατρι. *am in the father + I am knowing the father*

16. *not rejoice the spirit Put on for yourself*
μη χαιρετε ὅτι τα πνευματα ὑμιν ὑποτασσεται· χαιρετε δε ὅτι τα ὀνοματα ὑμων ἐγγεγραπται ἐν τοις οὐρανοις.

17. ὁ λεγω ὑμιν ἐν τη σκοτια εἰπατε ἐν τω φωτι, και ὁ εἰς το οὐς ἀκουετε κηρυξατε ἐπι των δωματων (housetops).

18. και ἐλεγεν ὁ Ἰησους ὅτι πεπληρωται ὁ καιρος και ἐστιν ἐγγυς ἡ βασιλεια του θεου· μετανοειτε και πιστευετε ἐν τω εὐαγγελιω.

19. μη ἀγαπᾶτε τὸν κοσμον μηδε τὰ ἐν τω κοσμω· ἐάν
τίς ἀγαπᾷ τον κοσμον, οὐκ ἐστιν ἡ ἀγαπη του
πατρος ἐν αὐτω.

20. τοτε ὁ Ἰησους εἰπεν τοῖς μαθηταις αὐτου, εἰ τις
θελει ὀπισω μου ἐλθειν, ἀρνησασθω ἑαυτον και
ἀρατω τον σταυρον αὐτου και ἀκολουθειτω μοι.

GRAMMAR GRABBER: The Adjective πᾶς

ἀσπάσασθε Φιλόλογον καὶ ᾿Ιουλίαν, Νηρέα καὶ τὴν
ἀδελφὴν αὐτοῦ, καὶ ᾿Ολυμπᾶν, καὶ τοὺς σὺν αὐτοῖς
πάντας ἁγίους. (Rom 16.15)

Greet Philologus and Julia, Nereus and his sister, and Olympa, and
all the saints with them.

᾿Ενορκίζω ὑμᾶς τὸν κύριον ἀναγνωσθῆναι τὴν
ἐπιστολὴν πᾶσιν τοῖς ἀδελφοῖς. (1 Thess 5.27)

I adjure you by the Lord that the letter be read to every one of the
brothers.

The frequently used third declension adjective, πᾶς ("all, every, the
whole"), varies in its focus depending on whether it is in the attributive or
predicate position. In the attributive position, it presents a plural or
collective noun as a whole, without reference to its individual parts, οἱ
παντες ἁγιοι ("all the saints"). In the predicate position the individual
parts are in focus, παντες οἱ ἁγιοι ("every one of the saints"). Look at
the way Paul gives instructions at the conclusion of two letters and see if you
can detect the difference in focus.

At the conclusion of Romans, Paul commands that certain people be
greeted: Philologus, Julia, Nereus, and his sister, and Olympa. He then
includes an omnibus greeting, "to all the saints with them." That phrase
treats the remaining group of believers as a whole. At the end of 1
Thessalonians, he charges the body of believers to make sure the letter is
read to "every one of the brothers." In so doing he seeks to make certain that
every person in the group hears the contents of the letter. What a difference
the placement of article and adjective and noun makes!

Chapter 26

THIRD DECLENSION ADJECTIVES

Most adjectives follow the pattern of first and second declension nouns. There are, however, a few important adjectives which—in part—follow the pattern of third declension nouns. After the so-called third declension adjectives are discussed, several additional adjectives which will be introduced briefly.

26.1 πᾶς, πᾶσα, πᾶν

The most frequently occurring third declension adjective is πᾶς, πᾶσα, πᾶν, meaning "all," or "every" (1244 times). Its cognate ἅπας, ἅπασα, ἅπαν occurs an additional 34 times. The masculine and neuter follow the pattern of third declension consonant stem nouns; the feminine follows the pattern of first declension alpha-impure nouns. The full paradigm is set out below.

		Masculine	Feminine	Neuter
Sing.	Nom.	πας	πασα	παν
	Gen.	παντος	πασης	παντος
	Dat.	παντι	παση	παντι
	Acc.	παντα	πασαν	παν
Pl.	Nom.	παντες	πασαι	παντα
	Gen.	παντων	πασων	παντων
	Dat.	πασι	πασαις	πασι
	Acc.	παντας	πασας	παντα

πᾶς can be used in any of four ways. The various constructions are similar to those of other adjectives.

1. In the *attributive* position, πᾶς is usually translated as "whole."
   η πασα ἐκκλησια = "the whole church"
2. In the *predicate* position, πᾶς is usually translated as "all."
   πασα η ἐκκλησια = "all the church"
3. As a *substantive* (standing alone) πᾶς is usually translated "every" in the singular and "all" in the plural. It is sometimes helpful to supply a gloss which specifies the referent more precisely.

πᾶς   =   "every (one/thing)"
παντες   =   "all (people/things)"

4. When used with an anarthrous noun (a noun which does not have a definite article) πᾶς is usually translated as "every"in the singular and "all" in the plural.

πασα ἐκκλησια   =   "every church"
πασαι ἐκκλησιαι   =   "all churches"

26.2 ἀληθής, ἀληθές

The adjective ἀληθής, ἀληθές, meaning "true," is a two termination adjective which occurs 26 times in the New Testament. It follows the pattern of third declension vowel stem nouns. The full paradigm is set out below.

true

		Masculine/Feminine	Neuter
Sing.	Nom.	ἀληθής	ἀληθές
	Gen.	ἀληθοῦς	ἀληθοῦς
	Dat.	ἀληθεῖ	ἀληθεῖ
	Acc.	ἀληθῆ	ἀληθές
Pl.	Nom.	ἀληθεῖς	ἀληθῆ
	Gen.	ἀληθῶν	ἀληθῶν
	Dat.	ἀληθέσι(ν)	ἀληθέσι(ν)
	Acc.	ἀληθεῖς	ἀληθῆ

26.3 εἷς, οὐδείς, μηδείς

Although technically a numeral, εἷς, meaning "one," declines like a third declension adjective in the masculine and neuter. The feminine follows the alpha-pure pattern. It occurs 344 times in the New Testament. Its cognates οὐδείς and μηδείς ("no one") occur 234 and 90 times respectively.

one

	Masculine	Feminine	Neuter
Nom.	εἷς	μία	ἔν
Gen.	ἑνός	μιᾶς	ἑνός
Dat.	ἑνί	μιᾷ	ἑνί
Acc.	ἑνά	μίαν	ἔν

26.4 πολύς, πολλή, πολύ

The irregular adjective πολύς, πολλή, πολύ, meaning "much" or "many," occurs 416 times in the New Testament. It is "irregular" in that it uses two stems: πολυ- in the masculine and neuter; πολλο- in the feminine. The endings are standard first and second declension endings with the exception of the **masculine nominative and accusative singular** and the **neuter nominative and accusative singular**. You will want to take particular note of these four forms; their endings are most closely related to the third declension.

mnch/many

		Masculine	Feminine	Neuter
Sing.	Nom.	πολύς	πολλή	πολύ
	Gen.	πολλοῦ	πολλῆς	πολλοῦ
	Dat.	πολλῷ	πολλῇ	πολλῷ
	Acc.	πολύν	πολλήν	πολύ
Pl.	Nom.	πολλοί	πολλαί	πολλά
	Gen.	πολλῶν	πολλῶν	πολλῶν
	Dat.	πολλοῖς	πολλαῖς	πολλοῖς
	Acc.	πολλούς	πολλάς	πολλά

26.5 μέγας, μεγάλη, μέγα

The irregular adjective **μέγας, μεγάλη, μέγα**, meaning "great," occurs 243 times in the New Testament. It is "irregular" in that it also uses two stems: **μεγα**- in the masculine and neuter; **μεγαλ**- in the feminine. The endings are standard first and second declension endings with the exception of the **masculine nominative and accusative singular** and the **neuter nominative and accusative singular**. You will want to take particular note of these four forms; their endings are most closely related to the third declension.

great

		Masculine	Feminine	Neuter
Sing.	Nom.	μέγας	μεγάλη	μέγα
	Gen.	μεγάλου	μεγάλης	μεγάλου
	Dat.	μεγάλω	μεγάλη	μεγάλω
	Acc.	μέγαν	μεγάλην	μέγα
Pl.	Nom.	μεγάλοι	μεγάλαι	μεγάλα
	Gen.	μεγάλων	μεγάλων	μεγάλων
	Dat.	μεγάλοις	μεγάλαις	μεγάλοις
	Acc.	μεγάλους	μεγάλας	μεγάλα

26.6 Vocabulary

Adjectives

| 501. | ἀληθής, ἀληθές | true | (26) |

502.	ἅπας, ἅπασα, ἅπαν	each, every, all, whole	(34)
503.	μέγας, μεγάλη, μέγα	great, large (megaphone)	(243)
504.	μείζων, μεῖζον	greater, larger	
505.	μηδείς, μηδεμία, μηδέν	no one, none, nothing	(90)
506.	οὐδείς, οὐδεμία, οὐδέν	no one, none, nothing	(234)
507.	πᾶς, πᾶσα, πᾶν	each, every, all, whole	(1244)
508.	πολύς, πολλή, πολύ	much, many (poly-)	(416)

Numerals

509.	εἷς, μία, ἕν	one	(344)
510.	δύο	two	(135)
511.	τρεῖς, τρία	three	(68)
512.	τέσσαρες, τέσσαρα	four	(41)
513.	πέντε	five	(38)
514.	δέκα	ten	(25)
515.	δώδεκα	twelve	(75)

Particles

516.	γε	indeed, at least, really, even	(25)
517.	ἰδού, ἰδέ	Look! See! Behold!	(229)
518.	μήποτε	lest, otherwise	(25)
519.	ναί	truly, yes	(33)
520.	οὐαί	Woe!	(46)

26.7 Form Identification - For each form give the gender, case, number, dictionary form, and a translation. One example is given.

πασῃ	FDS	πας	to/for every (one)

1. ἕνα
2. πολυν
3. ἀληθη
4. μεγα
5. πολλαι
6. παν
7. μεγαλη
8. πολλῳ
9. παντα
10. ἀληθεις
11. μεγαλων
12. μιας
13. παντες
14. πολλοις
15. παντων
16. πολυ

17. ἄπασα

18. ἕν

19. μηδεις

20. μεγαλοι

26.8 Practice Exercises - Translate the following sentences. Parse all verbal forms.

1. αὑτη ἐστιν ἡ μεγαλη και πρωτη ἐντολη.
is   great   + first   commandment

2. ἀσπαζονται ὑμας αἱ ἐκκλησιαι πασαι του Χριστου.
greeting you   church   each   of Christ

3. εἰς ὑπερ παντων ἀπεθανεν, ἀρα παντες ἀπεθανον.
one for   of all   died   then all   died

4. μεγαλη σου ἡ πιστις· γενηθητω σοι ὡς θελεις.
great you   faith   done made you   Want   below

5. και οἰδας ὁτι ἡ μαρτυρια ἡμων ἀληθης ἐστιν.
+ knows both   or   testimony your truth   is are

6. οὑτος μεγας κληθησεται ἐν τῃ βασιλειᾳ των οὐρανων.
this great   called   kingdom   of heavens

7. παντες γαρ ὑμεις υἱοι φωτος ἐστε και υἱοι ἡμερας.
all for you son light   + son Day

8. χαιρετε, ὁτι ὁ μισθος ὑμων πολυς ἐν τοις οὐρανοις.
rejoice be   reward your Many   to/for heavens

9. οὐδεις γαρ ἡμων ἑαυτῳ ζῃ και οὐδεις ἑαυτῳ ἀποθνῃσκει.
noone/none for our himself lives + None   dying

10. και ἠκολουθησαν αὐτῳ ὀχλοι πολλοι και ἐθεραπευσεν αὐτους ἐκει.
+ followed   crowd Many + healed   them there

11. οἰδαμεν δε ὁτι τοις ἀγαπωσιν τον θεον παντα ἐνεργει εἰς ἀγαθον.
Knowing be   love   God all working

12. παλιν ἐντολην καινην γραφω ὑμιν, ὁ ἐστιν ἀληθες ἐν αὐτῳ και ἐν ὑμιν.
all commandment new write you   truth   you

13. νυνι δε μενει πιστις, ἐλπις, ἀγαπη, τα τρια ταυτα· μειζων δε τουτων ἡ ἀγαπη.
Now abiding faith hope love three this greater for this

14. και γαρ ἐν ἑνι πνευματι ἡμεις παντες εἰς ἑν σωμα ἐβαπτισθημεν εἰτε δουλοι εἰτε ἐλευθεροι.
+ For   spirit all   baptized slave   free

15. ἐν γαρ ἑνι σωματι πολλα μελη ἐχομεν, τα δε μελη παντα οὐ ἐχει την αὐτην πραξιν (function).
for body Many have   all

GRAMMAR GRABBER: δίδωμι

οἱ πατέρες ἡμῶν τὸ μάννα ἔφαγον ἐν τῇ ἐρήμῳ,
καθώς ἐστιν γεγραμμένον, Ἄρτον ἐκ τοῦ οὐρανοῦ
ἔδωκεν αὐτοῖς φαγεῖν. εἶπεν οὖν αὐτοῖς ὁ Ἰησοῦς,
Ἀμὴν ἀμὴν λέγω ὑμῖν, οὐ Μωϋσῆς δέδωκεν ὑμῖν τὸν
ἄρτον ἐκ τοῦ οὐρανοῦ, ἀλλ᾽ ὁ πατήρ μου δίδωσιν
ὑμῖν τὸν ἄρτον ἐκ τοῦ οὐρανοῦ τὸν ἀληθινόν· ὁ γὰρ
ἄρτος τοῦ θεοῦ ἐστιν ὁ καταβαίνων ἐκ τοῦ οὐρανοῦ
καὶ ζωὴν διδοὺς τῷ κόσμῳ. Εἶπον οὖν πρὸς αὐτόν,
Κύριε, πάντοτε δὸς ἡμῖν τὸν ἄρτον τοῦτον.
(John 6:31-34)

Look at the five underlined verbs in John 6:31-34. Can you parse any of them? ἔδωκεν looks like a strange aorist, or maybe a perfect. δέδωκεν looks more like a normal perfect. δίδωσιν and διδοὺς have a kind of reduplication we have not met before. δὸς defies analysis. Could it be a participle?

Welcome to the world of –μι verbs, a necessary set of paradigms for a small set of frequently occurring verbs! In the next chapters you will learn the –μι verb conjugation patterns. Paying close attention to the paradigms provided and committing key forms to memory will repay dividends in personal translation proficiency. Now for some parsing. All five forms come from the verb δίδωμι, "I am giving."

ἔδωκεν	AAI3s
δέδωκεν	PfAI3s
δίδωσιν	PAI3s
διδοὺς	PAPtc MNS
δὸς	AAImv2s

How would you translate the passage?

Chapter 27

διδωμι

So far, all the verbs discussed have been "thematic" verbs. That is, they are characterized by *theme vowels* which precede the personal endings. There is, however, a group of verbs which are "a-thematic" in that they do not have theme vowels. The dictionary form of these verbs ends in –μι rather than –ω and reflects an earlier stage in the development of the Greek language. In the Greek New Testament the most common –μι verbs are compounds of three paradigmatic verbs, διδωμι, τιθημι, and ἱστημι. After a brief introduction to the special characteristics of these verbs, διδωμι (the most common, with 616 occurrences including compounds) will be discussed in some detail.

27.1 Special Characteristics of –μι Verbs

The *present* tense of each of the paradigmatic verbs is characterized by *iota* reduplication. In the case of διδωμι and τιθημι, this reduplication is similar to that seen in the perfect tense of –ω, but ἱστημι reduplicates by using a rough breathing mark.

$$\text{δι δω μι}$$
$$\text{τι θη μι}$$
$$\text{ἱ στη μι}$$

From the discussion of reduplication above, the stem of the verbs may be readily seen. In fact, the verbal stem of each of these verbs alternates between two forms:

give διδωμι	=	δω– / δο–
put/place τιθημι	=	θη– / θε–
stand/set ἱστημι	=	στη– / στα–

The personal endings in the present tense differ somewhat from those of –ω verbs and reflect the endings which were used in the classical period.

Singular	1st	μι	Plural	1st	μεν
	2nd	ς		2nd	τε
	3rd	σι		3rd	σι

27.2 Principal Parts of διδωμι

As may be seen from a listing of its principle parts, διδωμι differs from –ω verbs primarily in the first and third principle parts. In fact, the (first) aorist active and middle differ from what might be expected only in that they have a Κ rather than a σ as the tense sign.

PAI1S	FAI1S	AAI1S	PfAI1S	PfM/PI1S	API1S
διδωμι	δώσω	ἔδωκα	δέδωκα	δέδομαι	ἐδόθην

27.3 Present Tense of διδωμι

The present active and middle/passive indicative forms as well as the infinitive and basic participle forms are set out in the following chart.

Present

		Active	Middle & Passive
Singular	1st	δίδω-μι	δίδο-μαι
	2nd	δίδω-ς	δίδο-σαι
	3rd	δίδω-σι	δίδο-ται
Plural	1st	δίδο-μεν	δίδο-μεθα
	2nd	δίδο-τε	δίδο-σθε
	3rd	δίδο-ασι	δίδο-νται
Infinitive		δίδο-ναι	δίδο-σθαι
Participle	MNS	δίδους	δίδο-μενος
	FNS	δίδουσα	δίδο-μενη
	NNS	δίδον	δίδο-μενον

27.4 Imperfect Tense of διδωμι

The imperfect tense is also built on the first principle part. The active and middle/passive indicative forms are set out in the following chart.

Imperfect

		Active	Middle & Passive
Singular	1st	ἐ-δίδου-ν	ἐ-δίδο-μην
	2nd	ἐ-δίδου-ς	ἐ-δίδο-σο
	3rd	ἐ-δίδου	ἐ-δίδο-το
Plural	1st	ἐ-δίδο-μεν	ἐ-δίδο-μεθα
	2nd	ἐ-δίδο-τε	ἐ-δίδο-σθε
	3rd	ἐ-δίδο-σαν	ἐ-δίδο-ντο

27.5 Aorist Tense of διδωμι

The aorist active, middle, and passive indicative forms as well as the infinitive and the basic participle forms are set out in the following chart.

Aorist

		Active	Middle	Passive
Singular	1st	ἐ-δωκα	ἐ-δο-μην	ἐ-δοθη-ν
	2nd	ἐ-δωκα-ς	ἐ-δου	ἐ-δοθη-ς
	3rd	ἐ-δωκε	ἐ-δο-το	ἐ-δοθη
Plural	1st	ἐ-δωκα-μεν	ἐ-δο-μεθα	ἐ-δοθη-μεν
	2nd	ἐ-δωκα-τε	ἐ-δο-σθε	ἐ-δοθη-τε
	3rd	ἐ-δωκα-ν	ἐ-δο-ντο	ἐ-δοθη-σαν
Infinitive		δου-ναι	δο-σθαι	δοθη-ναι
Participle	MNS	δους	δο-μενος	δοθεις
	FNS	δουσα	δο-μενη	δοθεισα
	NNS	δον	δο-μενον	δοθεν

27.6 Vocabulary

Compounds of δίδωμι

521.	ἀποδίδωμι	I am giving back, repaying	(48)
522.	παραδίδωμι	I am betraying, handing over	(119)

Other Important −μι Verbs

523.	ἀφίημι	I am forgiving, permitting	(143)
524.	δεικνύω, δείκνυμι	I am showing	(33)
525.	ὀμνύω, ὄμνυμι	I am swearing, taking an oath	(26)
526.	πάρειμι	I am being present	(24)
527.	πίμπλημι	I am filling	(24)
528.	φημί	I am saying	(66)

Thematic Verbs

529.	ἀγιάζω	I am sanctifying	(28)
530.	ἀγοράζω	I am buying	(30)
531.	ἀδικέω	I am doing wrong, treating unjustly	(28)
532.	ἀποκαλύπτω	I am revealing (apocalypse)	(26)
533.	βαστάζω	I am bearing, carrying	(27)

534.	γνωρίζω	I am making known	(25)
535.	δουλεύω	I am being enslaved	(25)
536.	ἐγγίζω	I am coming/drawing near	(42)
537.	ἐλπίζω	I am hoping	(31)
538.	θαυμάζω	I am being amazed	(43)
539.	καθαρίζω	I am cleansing (catharsis)	(31)
540.	κάθημαι	I am sitting	(91)

27.7 Form Identification - For each form give the parsing (tense, voice, mood, person, number), the dictionary form, and a translation.

1. δωσω
2. δεδοται
3. δίδοασι
4. διδωσιν
5. δεδωκεν
6. διδους
7. ἐδωκατε
8. ἐδίδοσο
9. ἀποδωσουσιν
10. ἀποδουναι

11. ἀπεδωκας
12. ἀποδον
13. ἀποδοθηναι
14. ἀποδιδοντες
15. παραδιδοσθαι
16. παραδοθεις
17. παρεδιδου
18. παραδους
19. παρεδωκα
20. παρεδοθη

27.8 Practice Exercises - Translate the following sentences. Parse all verbal forms.

1. αἰτεῖτε και δοθησεται ὑμιν, ζητεῖτε και εὑρησετε.

2. κατα την δοθεισαν αὐτῳ σοφιαν ἐγραψεν ἡμιν.

3. ἐγω γαρ παρελαβον ἀπο κυριου, ὅ και παρεδωκα ὑμιν.

4. οὐ γαρ ἐδωκεν ἡμιν ὁ θεος πνευμα φοβου ἀλλα δυναμεως και ἀγαπης.

5. ἰδοντες δε οἱ ὀχλοι ἐδοξασαν τον θεον τον δοντα ἐξουσιαν τοις ἀνθρωποις.

6. ὑμιν δεδοται γνωναι τα μυστηρια της βασιλειας των οὐρανων ἐκεινοις δὲ οὐ δεδοται

you given know Mysteries Kingdom of the heavens them given

7. ἐγραψα δε ὑμιν ἀπο μερους δια την χαριν την δοθεισαν μοι ὑπο του θεου.

wrote + you in part through grace given me under by of God

8. εἰπεν αὐτοις ὁ Ἰησους μελλει ὁ υἱος του ἀνθρωπου παραδιδοσθαι εἰς χειρας ἀνθρωπων.

said them Jesus going the son of man betrayed delivered hands of men

9. αὐτον ἀποδωσει μου ὁ κυριος ἐν ἐκεινη τη ἡμερα κατα τα ἐργα αὐτου.

reward my lord that day According work his

10. γνωριζομεν δε ὑμιν την χαριν του θεου την δεδομενην ἐν ταις ἐκκλησιαις της Μακεδονιας (Macedonians).

Known + you grace of God that given churches

11. κἀγω την δοξαν ἣν δεδωκας μοι δεδωκα αὐτοις, ἱνα ὦσιν ἐν καθως ἡμεις ἕν.

+ the glory given my given that be one just as we one

12. παντα μοι παρεδοθη ὑπο του πατρος μου, και οὐδεις γινωσκει τον υἱον εἰ μη (except) ὁ πατρος.

All my handed the father + none the son the father

13. Ἰησους ὁ κυριος ἡμων παρεδοθη δια τας ἁμαρτιας ἡμων καὶ ἠγερθη δια την δικαιοσυνην ἡμων.

Jesus lord our handed through sinners righteousness

14. οἰδατε ὁτι μετα δυο ἡμερας το πασχα γινεται, και ὁ υἱος του ἀνθρωπου παραδιδοται εἰς το σταυρωθηναι.

Know be/that two day suffer + the son of man betraying

15. ὁ υἱος του ἀνθρωπου οὐκ ἠλθεν διακονηθηναι ἀλλα διακονησαι και δουναι την ψυχην αὐτου λυτρον (ransom) ἀντι πολλων.

the son of man not to be serve but Served and many

16. οἱ ἀνδρες ἀγαπατωσαν τας γυναικας, καθως και ὁ Χριστος ἠγαπησεν την ἐκκλησιαν και ἑαυτον παρεδωκεν ὑπερ αὐτης.

+ christ

17. ἐν τουτω γινωσκομεν ὁτι ἐν αὐτω μενομεν και αὐτος ἐν ἡμιν, ὁτι ἐκ του πνευματος αὐτου δεδωκεν ἡμιν.

this Know that abiding + with that from spirit of he

18. τοτε παραδωσουσιν ὑμας εἰς θλιψιν και ἀποκτενοῦσιν ὑμας, και ἐσεσθε μισουμενοι ὑπο παντων των ἐθνων δια το ὀνομα μου.

GRAMMAR GRABBER: τίθημι

μείζονα ταύτης ἀγάπην οὐδεὶς ἔχει, ἵνα τις τὴν
ψυχὴν αὐτοῦ <u>θῇ</u> ὑπὲρ τῶν φίλων αὐτοῦ... οὐχ ὑμεῖς
με ἐξελέξασθε, ἀλλ᾽ ἐγὼ ἐξελεξάμην ὑμᾶς καὶ
<u>ἔθηκα</u> ὑμᾶς ἵνα ὑμεῖς ὑπάγητε καὶ καρπὸν φέρητε
καὶ ὁ καρπὸς ὑμῶν μένῃ. (John 15:13, 16)

No one has greater love than this, that someone should lay down
his life on behalf of his friends . . . You did not choose me, but I
chose you and appointed you that you should go and bear fruit and
your fruit should abide.

The introduction to –μι verbs in the last chapter has given you enough
orientation so that you are probably able to pick out instances of a new one
in the verses above. You can probably take a stab at their tense voice and
mood as well. That's right, θῇ in the verse 13 and ἔθηκα in verse 16 are
both from τίθημι ("I put, place"), the second important –μι verb.

Both forms are aorists. θῇ is aorist active subjunctive third person
singular. Jesus uses it as he declares the principle: "No one has greater love
than this, that someone *should lay down (place down)* his life on behalf of his
friends." ἔθηκα is aorist active indicative first singular and occurs in a
second declaration: "I *appointed (placed)* you that you should go and bear
fruit." Again, mastering this –μι verb and its cognates will aid you greatly
in achieving and maintaining proficiency in reading the Greek New
Testament.

Chapter 28
τιθημι

Although not occurring as frequently in the New Testament as διδωμι and its compounds, τιθημι (100 times) and its compounds (126 times) occur frequently enough to make them worth noting. The similarities to διδωμι are readily apparent.

28.1 Principal Parts of τιθημι

As may be seen from a listing of its principle parts, τίθημι differs from –ω verbs primarily in the first and third principle parts. In fact, the (first) aorist active and middle differ from what might be expected only in that they have a κ rather than a σ as the tense sign.

PAI1S	FAI1S	AAI1S	PfAI1S	PfM/PI1S	API1S
τίθημι	θήσω	ἔθηκα	τέθεικα	τέθειμαι	ἐτέθην

28.2 Present Tense of τιθημι

The present active and middle/passive indicative forms as well as the infinitive and basic participle forms are set out in the following chart.

Present		Active	Middle & Passive
Singular	1st	τίθη-μι	τίθε-μαι
	2nd	τίθη-ς	τίθε-σαι
	3rd	τίθη-σι	τίθε-ται
Plural	1st	τίθε-μεν	τίθε-μεθα
	2nd	τίθε-τε	τίθε-σθε
	3rd	τίθε-ασι	τίθε-νται
Infinitive		τίθε-ναι	τίθε-σθαι
Participle	MNS	τίθεις	τίθε-μενος
	FNS	τίθεισα	τίθε-μενη
	NNS	τίθεν	τίθε-μενον

28.3 Imperfect Tense of τίθημι

The imperfect tense is also built on the first principle part. The active and middle/passive indicative forms are set out in the following chart.

Imperfect		Active	Middle & Passive
Singular	1st	ἐ-τίθη-ν	ἐ-τίθε-μην
	2nd	ἐ-τίθει-ς	ἐ-τίθε-σο
	3rd	ἐ-τίθει	ἐ-τίθε-το
Plural	1st	ἐ-τίθε-μεν	ἐ-τίθε-μεθα
	2nd	ἐ-τίθε-τε	ἐ-τίθε-σθε
	3rd	ἐ-τίθε-σαν	ἐ-τίθε-ντο

28.4 Aorist Tense of τίθημι

The aorist active, middle, and passive indicative forms as well as the infinitive and the basic participle forms are set out in the following chart.

Aorist		Active	Middle	Passive
Singular	1st	ἐ-θηκα	ἐ-θε-μην	ἐ-τέθη-ν
	2nd	ἐ-θηκα-ς	ἐ-θου	ἐ-τέθη-ς
	3rd	ἐ-θηκε	ἐ-θε-το	ἐ-τέθη
Plural	1st	ἐ-θηκα-μεν	ἐ-θε-μεθα	ἐ-τέθη-μεν
	2nd	ἐ-θηκα-τε	ἐ-θε-σθε	ἐ-τέθη-τε
	3rd	ἐ-θηκα-ν	ἐ-θε-ντο	ἐ-τέθη-σαν
Infinitive		θει-ναι	θε-σθαι	τέθη-ναι
Participle	MNS	θεις	θε-μενος	τέθεις
	FNS	θεισα	θε-μενη	τέθεισα
	NNS	θεν	θε-μενον	τέθεν

28.5 Vocabulary

τίθημι *and Frequently Occurring Compounds*

541.	τίθημι	I am placing, putting	(100)
542.	ἐπιτίθημι	I am placing on/upon	(39)
543.	παρατίθημι	I am placing before	(19)

Masculine Nouns

544.	ὁ νοῦς, νοός	mind (noetic)	(24)
545.	ὁ ὀφθαλμός, -ου	eye (ophthalmology)	(100)
546.	ὁ παῖς, παιδός	child, servant (pedagogy)	(24)
547.	ὁ στρατιώτης, -ου	soldier	(26)

Feminine Nouns

548.	ἡ ἀδελφή, -ης	sister	(26)
549.	ἡ ἀδικία, -ας	unrighteousness	(25)
550.	ἡ ἀσθενεία, -ας	weakness	(24)
551.	ἡ ἑορτή, -ης	feast	(25)
552.	ἡ μάχαιρα, -ης	sword	(29)
553.	ἡ νεφέλη, -ης	cloud (nephelometer)	(25)
554.	ἡ παρουσία, -ας	coming, arrival, presence	(24)
555.	ἡ πορνεία, -ας	fornication (pornography)	(25)
556.	ἡ χήρα, -ας	widow	(26)
557.	ἡ χώρα, -ας	country, rural area	(28)

Adverbs and Conjunction

558.	ἐκεῖθεν	from there/that place, thence	(37)
559.	πόθεν	from where/ what place? whence?	(29)
560.	ὥσπερ	as, just as, even as [subordinate]	(36)

28.6 Form Identification - For each form give the parsing (tense, voice, mood, person, number), the dictionary form, and a translation.

1. τεθειται		10. ἐτιθην
2. τιθησιν		11. ἐτιθει
3. ἐθετο		12. τεθειμενος
4. ἐθηκας		13. ἐτιθεσο
5. θεις		14. θειναι
6. θησω		15. τεθησεται
7. τιθεασιν		16. ἐπεθηκα
8. τιθεντες		17. ἐπιτιθεασιν
9. ἐτεθη		18. ἐπιθησει

19. ἐπεθηκαν
20. ἐπιθεις
21. παρατιθεμαι
22. παρατιθησι

23. παραθειναι
24. παρεθετο
25. παρεθηκεν

28.7 Practice Exercises - Translate the following sentences. Parse all verbal forms.

1. τας χειρας ἐπιτιθεις ἐθεραπευεν αὐτους.

2. αἱ δε γὺναικες ἐθεωρουν ποῦ τεθειται.

3. πατηρ, εἰς χειρας σου παρατιθεμαι το πνευμα μου.

4. ἐγω τιθημι την ψυχην μου, ἱνα παλιν λαβω αὐτην.

5. θησω το πνευμα μου ἐπ' αὐτον, και κρισιν τοις ἐθνεσιν ἀπαγγελεῖ.

6. ὁ ποιμην (shepherd) ὁ καλος την ψυχην αὐτου τιθησιν ὑπερ των προβατων (sheep).

7. και νυν παρατιθεμαι ὑμας τω θεω και τω λογω της χαριτος αὐτου.

8. ἐγραψεν δε τιτλον (inscription) ὁ Πιλατος και ἐθηκεν ἐπι του σταυρου.

9. και ταὺτα εἰπων θεις τα γονατα (knees) αὐτου συν πασιν αὐτοις προσηυξατο.

10. θεμελιον (foundation) γαρ ἀλλον οὐδεις δυναται θειναι παρα τον κειμενον, ὃς ἐστιν Ἰησους Χριστος.

11. ὁ θεος ἐθετο τα μελη ἐν ἑκαστον αὐτων ἐν τω σωματι καθως ἠθελησεν.

12. λεγει αὐτοις ὁτι ἠραν τον κυριον μου, και οὐκ οἰδα που ἐθηκαν αὐτον.

13. τεθεικα σε εἰς φῶς ἐθνῶν, τοῦ εἶναι σε εἰς σωτηριαν ἑως ἐσχατου της γης.

14. ἐν τουτῳ ἐγνωκαμεν την ἀγαπην, ὁτι ἐκεινος ὑπερ ἡμων την ψυχην αὐτου ἐθηκεν.

15. τοτε προσηνεχθησαν αὐτῳ παιδια ἱνα τας χειρας ἐπιθῃ καὶ προσευξηται· οἱ δε μαθηται ἐπετιμησαν αὐτοις.

16. χαριν ἐχω τῳ Χριστῳ Ἰησου τῳ κυριῳ ἡμων, ὁτι πιστον με ἡγησατο θεμενος εἰς διακονιαν.

17. οὐκ ἐθετο ἡμας ὁ θεος εἰς ὀργην ἀλλα εἰς σωτηριαν δια του κυριου ἡμων Ἰησου Χριστου.

18. εἰπεν δε προς αὐτους, οὐχ ὑμων ἐστιν γνωναι χρονους ἠ καιρους οὑς ὁ πατηρ ἐθετο ἐν τῃ ἰδιᾳ ἐξουσιᾳ.

19. ἐαν τις ἐπιθῃ ἐπι τους λογους μου, ἐπιθησει ὁ θεος ἐπ᾽ αὐτον τας πληγας (plagues) τας γεγραμμενας ἐν τῳ βιβλιῳ τουτῳ.

20. ἐπ᾽ ἐσχατου των ἡμερων τουτων ἐλαλησεν ὁ θεος ἡμιν ἐν υἱῳ ὁν ἐθηκεν κληρονομον (heir) παντων δι᾽ οὑ και ἐποιησεν τους αἰωνας.

1. he placed his hands on them + healed them
2. And the wines beheld where he placed it.
3. father to your hands I commit my spirit.
4. I place my life that I may recieve it again
5. i will lay my spirit over him + he will proclaim judgement to the nations
6. A good shepard puts his soul/life on behalf of his sheep
7. And Now I entrust you to God + to his word of grace
8. + Pilate wrote the Inscription + placed it on the cross
9. And after saying this, he fell to his knees + prayed with all of them

GRAMMAR GRABBER: ἵστημι

Μαρία δὲ εἰστήκει πρὸς τῷ μνημείῳ ἔξω κλαίουσα. ὡς οὖν ἔκλαιεν, παρέκυψεν εἰς τὸ μνημεῖον καὶ θεωρεῖ δύο ἀγγέλους ἐν λευκοῖς καθεζομένους, ἕνα πρὸς τῇ κεφαλῇ καὶ ἕνα πρὸς τοῖς ποσίν, ὅπου ἔκειτο τὸ σῶμα τοῦ Ἰησοῦ. καὶ λέγουσιν αὐτῇ ἐκεῖνοι, Γύναι, τί κλαίεις; λέγει αὐτοῖς ὅτι Ἦραν τὸν κύριόν μου, καὶ οὐκ οἶδα ποῦ ἔθηκαν αὐτόν. ταῦτα εἰποῦσα ἐστράφη εἰς τὰ ὀπίσω, καὶ θεωρεῖ τὸν Ἰησοῦν ἑστῶτα, καὶ οὐκ ᾔδει ὅτι Ἰησοῦς ἐστιν. (John 20:11-14)

Now Mary stood outside the tomb weeping. Then as she was weeping, she looked into the tomb and saw two angels in white who were sitting, one at the head and one at the feet where the body of Jesus was lying. And they were saying to her, "Woman, why are you weeping?" She was saying to them, "They took my Lord, and I do not know where they put him." While she was saying these things she turned around and saw Jesus standing, and did not know that it was Jesus.

Our final –μι verb involves a reduplication which almost disappears. Can you find two instances of ἵστημι in the section above? Need a clue? Watch the breathing marks.

If you chose the verbs εἰστήκει and ἑστῶτα (20:14), you were right. They are pluperfect and perfect forms of ἵστημι ("I am standing, placing"). The reduplication has "shrunk" to a rough breathing mark. The same phenomenon occurs in the present (ἵστημι) and imperfect (ἵστην) tense forms. The meaning of the verb points to a common action, "standing," yet its form is so peculiar that careful attention must be paid to breathing marks and spelling so that their particular instances can be properly identified.

Chapter 29

ἱστημι

The various forms of ἱστημι (154 times) and its compounds (191 times) are second only to διδωμι in frequency of occurrence among –μι verbs. Four verbs account for more than 50% of the compound forms: ἀνιστημι (108), ἐφιστημι (21), καθιστημι (21), and παριστημι (41). ἱστημι differs from the other –μι verbs in two ways: it reduplicates by using a rough breathing mark, and it has both a first aorist form and a second aorist form.

29.1 Principal Parts of ἱστημι

As may be seen from a listing of its principle parts, ἱστημι differs from –ω verbs primarily in the first and third principle parts. One complication in the third principle part is that ἱστημι has *both* a first aorist form (transitive) *and* a second aorist form (intransitive). This distinction and its implications will be discussed below. At this point it is sufficient simply to note it.

PAI1S	FAI1S	AAI1S	PfAI1S	PfM/PI1S	API1S
ἱστημι	στήσω	ἔστησα	ἔστηκα	ἔσταμαι	ἐστάθην
		ἔστην			

29.2 Present Tense of ἱστημι

The present active and middle/passive indicative forms as well as the infinitive and basic participle forms are set out in the following chart.

		Active	Middle & Passive
Singular	1st	ἱστη-μι	ἱστα-μαι
	2nd	ἱστη-ς	ἱστα-σαι
	3rd	ἱστη-σι	ἱστα-ται
Plural	1st	ἱστα-μεν	ἱστα-μεθα
	2nd	ἱστα-τε	ἱστα-σθε
	3rd	ἱστα-σι	ἱστα-νται

Infinitive		ἵστα-ναι	ἵστα-σθαι
Participle	MNS	ἵστας	ἱστά-μενος
	FNS	ἵστασα	ἱστά-μενη
	NNS	ἵσταν	ἱστά-μενον

29.3 Imperfect Tense of ἵστημι

The imperfect tense is also built on the first principle part. The active and middle/passive indicative forms are set out in the following chart.

		Active	Middle & Passive
Singular	1st	ἵστη-ν	ἱστά-μην
	2nd	ἵστη-ς	ἱστά-σο
	3rd	ἵστη	ἱστά-το
Plural	1st	ἱστά-μεν	ἱστά-μεθα
	2nd	ἱστά-τε	ἱστά-σθε
	3rd	ἱστά-σαν	ἱστά-ντο

29.4 First Aorist Tense of ἵστημι

The active, middle, and passive indicative forms as well as the infinitive and the basic participle forms of the first aorist tense are set out in the following chart.

transitive

		Active	Middle	Passive
Singular	1st	ἐ-στησα	ἐ-στησα-μην	ἐ-στάθη-ν
	2nd	ἐ-στησα-ς	ἐ-στησω	ἐ-στάθη-ς
	3rd	ἐ-στησε	ἐ-στησα-το	ἐ-στάθη
Plural	1st	ἐ-στησα-μεν	ἐ-στησα-μεθα	ἐ-στάθη-μεν
	2nd	ἐ-στησα-τε	ἐ-στησα-σθε	ἐ-στάθη-τε
	3rd	ἐ-στησα-ν	ἐ-στησα-ντο	ἐ-στάθη-σαν
Infinitive		στησαι	στησα-σθαι	στάθη-ναι
Participle	MNS	στησας	στησα-μενος	στάθεις
	FNS	στησασα	στησα-μενη	στάθεισα
	NNS	στησαν	στησα-μενον	στάθεν

29.5 Second Aorist Tense

The second aorist tense occurs only in the active voice. The indicative, infinitive, and participle forms are set out in the following chart.

intransitive

		Active
Singular	1st	ἐ-στη-ν
	2nd	ἐ-στη-ς
	3rd	ἐ-στη
Plural	1st	ἐ-στη-μεν
	2nd	ἐ-στη-τε
	3rd	ἐ-στη-σαν
Infinitive		στη-ναι
Participle	MNS	στας
	FNS	στασα
	NNS	σταν

29.6 The Transitive and Intransitive Meanings of ἵστημι

As mentioned above, ἵστημι can have either a transitive (takes a direct object) or an intransitive (does not take a direct object) meaning. When ἵστημι is used transitively, it has the meaning "I place, put, set, cause to stand." When it is used intransitively, it has the meaning "I stand." The difference may be seen in the following English sentences.

Transitive:	I am placing the vase on the wall.
Intransitive:	I am standing on the wall.

In the first sentence, the subject ("I") is performing an act ("placing," i.e., "causing to stand") which is *transferred* to a direct object ("the vase"). In the second sentence, the subject ("I") is performing an act ("am standing") which is not transferred to a direct object.

This transitive/intransitive distinction is seen clearly in the aorist tense, where the first aorist (ἔστησα) carries the transitive meaning ("I placed," i.e., "caused to stand") and the second aorist (ἔστην) carries the intransitive meaning ("I stood"). The other tenses of ἵστημι, however, are also used to make the same distinction. In general, the present, imperfect, future, and first aorist tenses are used transitively, while the second aorist, perfect and pluperfect tenses are used intransitively. Basic translations of the first person singular form of each tense in the active voice are:

Transitive	PAI1S	ἵστημι	I am causing to stand.
	IAI1S	ἵστην	I was causing to stand.
	FAI1S	στήσω	I shall cause to stand.
	1AAI1S	ἔστησα	I caused to stand.

Intransitive	2AAI1S	ἔστην	I stood.
	PfAI1S	ἔστηκα	I stand, am standing.
	PlpfAI1S	εἱστήκειν	I have stood.

29.7 Vocabulary

ἵστημι and Frequently Occurring Compounds

561.	ἵστημι	I am standing, causing to stand	(154)
562.	ἀνίστημι	I am raising, rising	(108)
563.	ἐφίστημι	I am standing over, coming upon	(21)
564.	καθίστημι	I am setting, constituting	(21)
565.	παρίστημι	I am being present, standing by	(41)

Adjectives

566.	ἐκλεκτός, -η, -ον	chosen, elect (eclectic)	(22)
567.	ἐλευθερός, -α, -ον	free	(23)
568.	καθαρός, -α, -ον	clean (catharsis)	(27)
569.	πλούσιος, -α, -ον	rich (plutocrat)	(28)
570.	πνευματικός, -η, -ον	spiritual (pneumatic)	(26)

Thematic Verbs

571.	καθίζω	I am sitting, seating (cathedral)	(46)
572.	καταργέω	I am abolishing	(27)
573.	κατηγορέω	I am accusing	(23)
574.	καταλείπω	I am leaving	(24)
575.	κελεύω	I am commanding	(25)
576.	λυπέω	I am grieving	(26)
577.	περιβάλλω	I am putting around, clothing	(23)
578.	προσέχω	I am giving heed to, attending to	(24)
579.	σκανδαλίζω	I am causing to stumble (scandal)	(29)
580.	τελέω	I am finishing, fulfilling	(28)

29.8 Form Identification - For each form give the parsing (tense, voice, mood, person, number), the dictionary form, and a translation.

1. σταθησεται

2. ἐστησεν

3, ἐστη

4. ἐστησαν

5. σταθεντες

6. ἑσταναι

7. ἑστηκατε

8. σταθηναι

9. ἐσταθη

10. ἑστηκασιν

11. στας

12. εἱστηκεισαν

13. ἀνεστησαν

14. ἀναστηθι

15. ἀναστησω

16. ἀναστας

17. ἀνεστη

18. καταστησω

19. κατεσταθησαν

20. καθισταται

21. καθιστησιν

22. παρεστηκεν

23. παραστησομεθα

24. παρισταται

25. παρεστησατε

29.9 Practice Exercises - Translate the following sentences. Parse all verbal forms.

1. και ἀναστας ἠκολουθησεν αὐτῳ.

2. και ἐστησαν δυο, Ἰωσηφ (Joseph) και Ματθιαν (Matthias).

3. οἱ νεκροι ἐν Χριστῳ ἀναστησονται πρωτον.

4. και ἀναστ...
και ἀνασταντες ἐξεβαλον αὐτον ἐξω της πολεως.

5. καλεσαμενος παιδιον ἐστησεν αὐτο ἐν μεσῳ αὐτων.
   transitive

6. και ἐπι βασιλεων σταθησεσθε ἑνεκεν ἐμου εἰς μαρτυριαν αὐτοις.

7. και τινες των παρεστηκοτων ἀκουσαντες ἐλεγον, ἰδε Ἠλιαν (Elijah) φωνει.

8. εἱστηκει δε και ᾿Ιουδας (Judas) ὁ παραδιδους αὐτον μετ᾿ αὐτων.

9. και ἰδου τρεῖς ἀνδρες ἐπεστησαν ἐπι την οἰκιαν ἐν ᾗ ἠμεν.

10. ἠλθεν ἡ ἡμερα ἡ μεγαλη της ὀργης αὐτων, και τίς δυναται σταθηναι;

11. οὐτως γεγραπται παθειν τον Χριστον και ἀναστηναι ἐκ νεκρων τη τριτη ἡμερᾳ.

12. ταυτα δε αὐτων λαλουντων αὐτος ἐστη ἐν μεσῳ αὐτων και λεγει αὐτοις, εἰρηνη ὑμιν.

13. ὁ ἐγειρας τον κυριον ᾿Ιησουν και ἡμας συν ᾿Ιησου ἐγερεῖ και παραστησει συν ὑμιν.

14. τῳ ἰδιῳ κυριῳ στηκει ἢ πιπτει· σταθησεται δε, δυναται γαρ ὁ κυριος στηναι αὐτον.

15. εἱστηκεισαν δε παρα τῳ σταυρῳ του ᾿Ιησου ἡ μητηρ και ἡ ἀδελφη της μητρος αὐτου.

16. ἐγω εἰμι Γαβριηλ (Gabriel) ὁ παρεστηκως ἐνωπιον του θεου και ἀπεσταλην λαλησαι προς σε και εὐαγγελισασθαι σοι ταυτα.

17. ἐτι αὐτου λαλοῦντος τοις ὀχλοις ἰδου ἡ μητηρ και οἱ ἀδελφοι αὐτου ἐστηκασι ἐξω ζητοῦντες αὐτῳ λαλησαι.

18. ὡσπερ γαρ παρεστησατε τα μελη ὑμων δουλα τη ἀκαθαρσια (uncleanness) οὐτως νυν παραστησατε τα μελη ὑμων δουλα τη δικαιοσυνη.

19. ἐδιδασκεν γαρ τους μαθητας αὐτου και ἐλεγεν αὐτοις ὁτι ὁ υἱος του ἀνθρωπου παραδιδοται εἰς χειρας ἀνθρωπων και μετα τρεῖς ἡμερας ἀναστησεται.

20. τουτο γαρ ἐστιν το θελημα του πατρος μου, ἰνα πας ὁ θεωρῶν τον υἱον και πιστευων εἰς αὐτον ἐχῃ ζωην αἰωνιον, και ἀναστησω αὐτον ἐγω ἐν τη ἐσχατη ἡμερᾳ.

Chapter 30

HOW TO KEEP YOUR GREEK FRESH

Congratulations! You have now been exposed to all of the basic vocabulary, forms, and concepts you need in order to move to the next level in your study of New Testament Greek. You have, no doubt, invested dozens of hours and hundreds of dollars to reach this point. The question which now begins to haunt the hearts and minds of most students is: "If I don't use it, will I lose it?" The answer to that question is both "no" and "yes."

Our brains are amazing instruments. Apart from physical impairment, no information which we put into our brains is ever lost. Our ability to retrieve the information, however, can be seriously hampered by neglect. No, the information is never lost, but, yes, its usefulness might well be.

The solution, of course, is to rephrase the above question as a positive principle — "If you use it, you won't lose it." — and, then, to put the principle into practice. Everyone recognizes the validity of the principle. The difficult part is putting it into practice. This chapter is intended as a means of helping you enhance your retrieval system so that the investment you have made in becoming introduced to Greek pays long-term dividends.

30.1 Basic Points to Remember

Certain points are "givens" in the process of learning a language, whether the goal is proficiency in reading or in speaking.

1. *Languages are always being relearned.* Sometimes that relearning is a matter of recall; sometimes it is a matter of correction; sometimes it is a matter or refinement. In every instance, forgiving yourself is an essential aspect of the task. Relearning is the nature of the subject matter.

2. *Language learning is a skill, not a commodity.* It is not enough simply to be able to reproduce a paradigm from memory; you must be able to apply the information from that paradigm to specific situations. Nor is it enough to say that you have successfully completed a quiz on a given chapter; you must be able to recall and use the content of that chapter in practical ways.

3. *Systematic review is essential in language learning.* All review is helpful, but establishing a systematic plan enhances its value. The plan, however, is not the goal; it is a means to reach the goal. If you find that your initial plan is not working, revise it and keep moving. The plan is your tool; you are not its slave.

4. *Frequency of exposure is crucial in developing language proficiency.* Reviewing for fifteen minutes a day on each of five days is more productive in the long run than reviewing for seventy-five minutes on a single day. Your plan for review should build in repeated exposure to the text, preferably on a daily basis.

5. *There is no substitute for time and experience.* What distinguishes the Greek teacher from his/her students? Time and experience. Once upon a time every Greek student had to learn the alphabet and the paradigms for second declension nouns. It is those students who persevere in using what they have learned who, in time, gain the experience they need to become proficient in working with the text of the Greek New Testament.

30.2 A Plan of Attack

In order for Greek to be a usable tool in ministry on a regular basis, you must pay attention to both the "forest" and the "trees." That is, you must be *comfortable* in viewing the text in context, and you must be *careful* in handling the details of a given passage. The best way to increase your comfort level with the text is to handle it as often and as extensively as possible. The best way to ensure that you are taking proper care with a passage you are planning to preach or teach is to spend time translating it and analyzing its syntax. Many individuals, therefore, find a two-pronged plan of attack helpful.

Developing a **reading program** is the best way to increase your comfort level with the Greek New Testament. There is absolutely no substitute for exposure to the Greek text on a regular basis. Because fifteen minutes a day on each of five days is more productive in the long run than seventy-five minutes on a single day, you might want to set that pattern as your standard. The time spent is more important than the amount of text covered. Nevertheless, your goal should be to move quickly through the text, grasping its basic meaning in context. You should not let yourself be stopped by features in the text which "stump" you. Your goal is to gain familiarity with the text and comfort in handling it. As you read, it is a good practice to record the parsing of each verb you encounter and the meaning of any unfamiliar vocabulary words. The list of those items will give you a head start when you return to the passage at a later date. Suggestions for developing a reading program are given in the section which follows.

Doing a **finished translation** of a passage you are planning to preach or teach is the best way to give proper attention to the nuances of language present in it. Thinking intentionally about the aspect, voice, and mood of verbs, the use of participles and infinitives, the meaning of words, the logical and syntactical relationship between phrases and clauses, and other details of the passage will help you understand more accurately the message the author is seeking to communicate. In certain literary genres (Paul's letters, for example) it is also helpful to develop a graphical representation of the passage's syntax in conjunction with your translation. Such a representation may take the form of sentence diagrams, a mechanical layout, or any other method which helps you "see" the passage's main idea(s). Because this process can become lengthy, you should aim at a total of two hours to complete it. Then "fit the task to the time" and work as efficiently as possible. Suggestions for working toward your finished translation are given below.

30.3 Developing a Reading Program

There are any number of approaches to developing a program for reading through the Greek New Testament. You could, for example, simply begin with Matthew's Gospel and continue in canonical order through to Revelation. Alternately, you could organize the various books in order of length, beginning with the shortest. You might, however, be most comfortable organizing the books on the basis of translation difficulty. In so doing, you would be able to reinforce the basics which you have learned by reading John's writings before encountering the intricacies of books such as Acts and Hebrews. Such a program also has the benefit of increasing your confidence level as you move forward. The following listing is a suggested order for the latter approach.

1. 1-3 John	12. Galatians
2. Gospel of John	13. Romans
3. Revelation	14. James
4. 1-2 Thessalonians	15. Luke
5. Philippians	16. 1-2 Timothy
6. Ephesians	17. Jude
7. Colossians & Philemon	18. 2 Corinthians
8. Mark	19. 1-2 Peter
9. Matthew	20. Acts
10. Titus	21. Hebrews
11. 1 Corinthians	

Once you have established the basic order in which you will be doing your reading, you will need to set goals for your *pattern* and your *pace*. For example, fifteen minutes a day, five days a week is a good pattern; five lines of text per session is a reasonable pace. If you were to read five lines of text in each fifteen minute session (proceeding by sentence units) five days a week, you would read through the book of Philippians (200 lines) in eight weeks.

Essential to your task is a reader's lexicon of the New Testament. Perhaps the most useful such work is Sakae Kubo's *A Reader's Greek-English Lexicon of the New Testament*. Kubo's lexicon is organized by book, chapter, and verse and provides every word used fifty times or less in the New Testament (301 words). It also gathers "special vocabulary" in a comprehensive list at the beginning of each book. Since you have learned all of the vocabulary words which occur *twenty-five* times or more (514) plus a number of additional words (66), Kubo's listings should enable you to move efficiently through any passage in the New Testament.

You will also want to record for future reference the parsing of any verbal forms and the meaning of any unfamiliar vocabulary words. To this end it is helpful to use a reading/translation worksheet which enables you to record your findings as well as add to them later. A partial example is included below. Although some students prefer to work with pencil and paper, you can also create an electronic format which lets you work directly at your computer.

Reading/Translation Worksheet	
Passage: Phil 1:3-5	
Translation	Parsing
1:3	εὐχαριστω = PAI1S εὐχαριστέω ἡ μνεια = remembrance
1:4	ἡ δεησις = entreaty, prayer ποιουμενος = PAPtcMNS ποιέω
1:5	ἡ κοινωνια = partnership, fellowship

30.4 Arriving at a Finished Translation

Chapter 5 introduced a recommended procedure for translating passages in the New Testament. It involved building your translation sentence by sentence and consisted of four steps:

1. Use punctuation to identify the extent of each sentence.
2. Identify any subordinate conjunctions and/or relative pronouns, and isolate the subordinate clauses which they introduce.
3. Construct a translation of the main clause(s) by identifying, parsing, and translating the verb(s); identifying any expressed subject; identifying any direct object; and arranging these items in "standard" English word order (subject–verb–object–"other stuff").
4. Construct a translation of any subordinate clause(s) within the sentence using the same process as in step 3, and connect the subordinate clause(s) to the main clause(s) in a sequence which conveys the author's intended meaning.

If you have been using that procedure consistently, it should now be so ingrained as to have become nearly unconscious. As you begin to build your finished translation, you can use the worksheet on which you recorded preliminary parsings and unfamiliar vocabulary words during your initial reading of the passage to record that translation and additional details related to it. A partial example is provided below.

Reading/Translation Worksheet	
Passage: __Phil 1:3-5__	
Translation	Parsing
1:3 I am thanking my God at every remembrance of you,	εὐχαριστω = PAI1S εὐχαριστέω ἡ μνεια = remembrance ἐπι + dative = time; "at, during, at the time of" (*BAGD*, 287)
1:4 always in every prayer of mine on behalf of all of you, making entreaty with joy	ἡ δεησις = entreaty, prayer ποιουμενος = PAPtcMNS ποιέω
1:5 because of your fellowship in the gospel from the first day until now,	ἡ κοινωνια = partnership, fellowship ἐπι + dative = cause; "because of" (*BAGD*, 287)

At this point, it will be helpful to highlight some of the "clues" which help you arrive at a finished translation of the passage you are planning to preach or teach. Those clues include context, syntax, word meaning, and word inflection. As you move to the next level in your study of Greek, you will have the opportunity to learn more about how to put each of them to good use.

Context is "king." It is the matrix within which all the other clues exist. Words, for example, have meaning only in context. Without a context, a word is simply a collection of letters which points to a list of possible dictionary definitions. For this reason, it is best to work with the text in paragraph length segments. Although the paragraph structure set out in the Greek New Testament has been determined by the editors rather than by the original authors, that structure is generally a good starting point for segmenting the text.

Syntax deals with the structure of sentences and the relationships between individual sentences. A consideration of the syntax within a given paragraph will take into account the punctuation which the editors have provided, the connectors (conjunctions and prepositions) which the author has used to develop his argument, and the word order within the sentences. As was true in regard to paragraph structure, the punctuation of the Greek New Testament has been determined by the editors. There may well be times when you disagree with their decisions, but in general, the punctuation they have provided should be observed.

Word meaning, of course, plays an important role in translating. All words have a range of possible meanings, and arriving at a finished translation of a passage involves determining which element in that range of meaning is appropriate in a given context. In addition to the dictionary in the back of your Greek New Testament, it will be helpful to have ready access to a Greek-based concordance and a good lexicon. Recommendations for both resources are listed in the section which follows.

Because Greek is a highly inflected language, *word inflection* plays a key role in determining an author's intended meaning. The kind of action (aspect) indicated by a present tense verb, for example, is quite different from that indicated by an aorist tense verb. Similarly, a noun or pronoun in the accusative most likely has a different relationship to the other words in its sentence than a noun or pronoun in the genitive case does. All of the paradigms and forms which you have memorized to this point in your studies give you an important key to unlocking the meaning of a text.

30.5 Building Your Greek Reference Library

A **basic library** for the study of New Testament Greek will include a copy of the Greek New Testament, one or more lexicons, an introductory grammar, and a Greek-based concordance. If you own the book you are currently reading, you already possess an introductory grammar, and you have probably already purchased a copy of the Greek New Testament. What remains, therefore, are the lexicons and the concordance.

For pursuing your reading program, it is difficult to improve on Sakae Kubo's *Reader's Greek-English Lexicon of the New Testament*. If you are serious about finished translation, you will want to consider Walter Bauer's *Greek-English Lexicon of the New Testament and Other Early Christian Literature* (*BAGD*), which is currently in its third English edition, translated, revised, and augmented by W. F. Arndt, F. W. Gingrich, and F. W. Danker. *The Exhaustive Concordance to the Greek New Testament*, edited by John R Kohlenberger, Edward W. Goodrick, and James A. Swanson, is a good option to complete your basic library.

As you move into the next level in your study of the Greek New Testament, you will want to add to your basic library so that it becomes an **expanded library**. To the resources you already own, you will want to add one or more intermediate grammars, a word study dictionary, a volume on textual criticism, and a synopsis of the gospels.

For years the standard intermediate grammar has been *A Manual Grammar of the New Testament*, by H. E. Dana and J. R. Mantey (1927). Daniel Wallace's text, *Greek Grammar Beyond the Basics* (1996), is a more recent entry into the field which has gained a good following..

The two leading word study dictionaries are *The Theological Dictionary of the New Testament* (*TDNT*), edited by Gerhard Kittel, and *The New International Dictionary of New Testament Theology* (*DNTT*), edited by Colin Brown. *TDNT* consists of nine volumes plus an index; *DNTT* consists of three volumes plus an index. Although *TDNT* has more extensive discussions, *DNTT* is easier to use and is generally more up to date.

Bruce Metzger's *Textual Commentary on the Greek New Testament* provides both an introduction to the field of textual criticism and a summary discussion of the issues surrounding each of the textual variants included in the United Bible Society's Greek New Testament. For comparing parallel passages in the Gospels, Kurt Aland's *Synopsis of the Four Gospels* is a valuable resource. It is a Greek-English work which includes the text of the Greek New Testament on the left-hand page and the text of a literal English translation on the facing page.

30.6 What Do I Do With All of This Stuff Now?

The whole point of learning New Testament Greek is to able to put it into practice to communicate the message of Scripture accurately. The subject of exegesis belongs properly to another book. It might be useful, however, to understand the basic elements involved in moving from text to sermon or lesson plan. There are five steps in the process: survey, analysis, synthesis, application, and sermon/lesson development.

In the **survey** step you seek to become familiar with the key issues which the passage raises. Those issues might be text critical, historical, literary, and/or theological. It is often helpful in this step to create a "shopping list" of items you will want to investigate as you study the passage.

The **analysis** step examines items which are important for understanding the author's intended message. The basic areas you will want to consider are historical, literary, and theological. Under the *historical* area you will want to review the circumstances surrounding the writing of the book and passage you are studying as well as any historical-cultural-religious details which are not readily understood by your audience. Under the *literary* area you will want to think about the general and immediate context of your passage, whether or not the passage represents a special literary type (e.g., parable, poetry), the grammatical and rhetorical features present in the passage, and any important or difficult words which are present. It is in the literary area that you will find your knowledge of Greek to be particularly helpful. In the *theological* area you will want to compare your passage with parallel and/or contrasting passages, think about the way in which your passage contributes to the overall teaching of Scripture, and resolve any apparent theological difficulties which might be present.

The **synthesis** step seeks to "put the pieces together" in order to create a coherent interpretation of the passage. In this step you will want to state the basic message of the passage in a single sentence, develop an outline which represents the structure of the passage, and review the passage's place in the book, the progress of redemption, and the progress of revelation. This step is also a good place to consider the way in which the basic message of the passage relates to contemporary thinking and attitudes.

The **application** step is where "the rubber meets the road." What commands, promises, and principles in your passage can be lived out by the men and women who hear its message? What specific steps might be needed to implement the changes which should result from this passage?

Finally, the **sermon/lesson development** step "packages" the results of your exegetical work in such a way that it communicates the truth of the passage as well as persuading your audience to take the decisive step of obedience. At this point in the process, exegesis dovetails with homiletics and pedagogy. Both of those topics, however, go far beyond the scope of this introductory Greek text.

Appendix A: Noun Paradigms

Definite Article

		M	F	N
S	N	ὁ	ἡ	το
	G	του	της	του
	D	τῳ	τῃ	τῳ
	A	τον	την	το

		M	F	N
P	N	οἱ	αἱ	τα
	G	των	των	των
	D	τοις	ταις	τοις
	A	τους	τας	τα

First and Second Declension Noun Endings

		1st Declension				2nd Declension	
		Alpha-Pure	Alpha-Impure	Eta	Masculine	M/F	N
S	N	α	α	η	ης	ος	ον
	G	ας	ης	ης	ου	ου	ου
	D	ᾳ	ῃ	ῃ	ῃ	ῳ	ῳ
	A	αν	αν	ην	ην	ον	ον
P	N	αι				οι	α
	G	ων				ων	ων
	D	αις				οις	οις
	A	ας				ους	α

Third Declension Nouns Endings

		Consonant Stem		Vowel Stem	
		M/F	N	M/F	N
S	N	Memorize	—	ς	—
	G	ος	ος	ως	ος
	D	ι	ι	ι	ι
	A	α/ν	—	α/ν	—
P	N	ες	α	ες	α
	G	ων	ων	ων	ων
	D	σι	σι	σι	σι
	A	ας	α	ες	α

Representative First and Second Declension Nouns

		1st Declension				2nd Declension	
		ὡρα	δοξα	ἀρχη	μαθητης	λογος	ἐργον
S	N	ὡρα	δοξα	ἀρχη	μαθητης	λογος	ἐργον
	G	ὡρας	δοξης	ἀρχης	μαθητου	λογου	ἐργου
	D	ὡρᾳ	δοξῃ	ἀρχῃ	μαθητῃ	λογῳ	ἐργῳ
	A	ὡραν	δοξαν	ἀρχην	μαθητην	λογον	ἐργον
P	N	ὡραι	δοξαι	ἀρχαι	μαθηται	λογοι	ἐργα
	G	ὡρων	δοξων	ἀρχων	μαθητων	λογων	ἐργων
	D	ὡραις	δοξαις	ἀρχαις	μαθηταις	λογοις	ἐργοις
	A	ὡρας	δοξας	ἀρχας	μαθητας	λογους	ἐργα

Representative Third Declension Nouns - Consonant Stems

		ἀρχων	ἐλπις	σωμα
S	N	ἀρχων	ἐλπις	σωμα
	G	ἀνχοντος	ἐλπιδος	σωματος
	D	ἀρχοντι	ἐλπιδι	σωματι
	A	ἀρχοντα	ἐλπιδα	σωμα
P	N	ἀρχοντες	ἐλπιδες	σωματα
	G	ἀρχονων	ἐλπιδων	σωματων
	D	ἀρχουσι	ἐλπισι	σωμασι
	A	ἀρχοντας	ἐλπιδας	σωματα

Representative Third Declension Nouns - Vowel Stems

		ἱερευς	πολις	γενος
S	N	ἱερευς	πολις	γενος
	G	ἱερεως	πολεως	γενους
	D	ἱερει	πολει	γενει
	A	ἱερεα	πολιν	γενος
P	N	ἱερεις	πολεις	γενη
	G	ἱερεων	πολεων	γενων
	D	ἱερευσι	πολεσι	γενεσι
	A	ἱερεις	πολεις	γενη

Personal Pronouns

		1st Person	2nd Person	3rd Person M	3rd Person F	3rd Person N
S	N	ἐγω	συ	αὐτος	αὐτη	αὐτο
	G	ἐμου (μου)	σου	αὐτου	αὐτης	αὐτου
	D	ἐμοι (μοι)	σοι	αὐτῳ	αὐτη	αὐτῳ
	A	ἐμε (με)	σε	αὐτον	αὐτην	αὐτο
P	N	ἡμεις	ὑμεις	αὐτοι	αὐται	αὐτα
	G	ἡμων	ὑμων	αὐτων	αὐτων	αὐτων
	D	ἡμιν	ὑμιν	αὐτοις	αὐταις	αὐτοις
	A	ἡμας	ὑμας	αὐτους	αὐτας	αὐτα

Near Demonstrative Pronoun

		M	F	N
S	N	οὑτος	αὑτη	τουτο
	G	τουτου	ταυτης	τουτου
	D	τουτῳ	ταυτη	τουτῳ
	A	τουτον	ταυτην	τουτο
P	N	οὑτοι	αὑται	ταυτα
	G	τουτων	τουτων	τουτων
	D	τουτοις	ταυταις	τουτοις
	A	τουτους	ταυτας	ταυτα

Far Demonstrative Pronoun

		M	F	N
S	N	ἐκεινος	ἐκεινη	ἐκεινο
	G	ἐκεινου	ἐκεινη	ἐκεινου
	D	ἐκεινῳ	ἐκεινης	ἐκεινῳ
	A	ἐκεινον	ἐκεινην	ἐκεινο
P	N	ἐκεινοι	ἐκειναι	ἐκεινα
	G	ἐκεινων	ἐκεινων	ἐκεινων
	D	ἐκεινοις	ἐκειναις	ἐκεινοις
	A	ἐκεινους	ἐκεινας	ἐκεινα

Relative and Interrogative Pronouns

		Relative			Interrogative		
		M	F	N	M	F	N
S	N	ὅς	ἥ	ὅ	τίς	τίς	τί
	G	οὗ	ἧς	οὗ	τίνος	τίνος	τίνος
	D	ᾧ	ᾗ	ᾧ	τίνι	τίνι	τίνι
	A	ὅν	ἥν	ὅ	τίνα	τίνα	τί
P	N	οἵ	αἵ	ἅ	τίνες	τίνες	τίνα
	G	ὧν	ὧν	ὧν	τίνων	τίνων	τίνων
	D	οἷς	αἷς	οἷς	τίσι	τίσι	τίσι
	A	οὕς	ἅς	ἅ	τίνας	τίνας	τίνα

Reflexive Pronouns - First and Second Persons

		First Person		Second Person	
		Masculine	Feminine	Masculine	Feminine
S	N	—	—	—	—
	G	ἐμαυτ - ου	ἐμαυτ - ης	σεαυτ - ου	σεαυτ - ης
	D	ἐμαυτ - ῳ	ἐμαυτ - ῃ	σεαυτ - ῳ	σεαυτ - ῃ
	A	ἐμαυτ - ον	ἐμαυτ - ην	σεαυτ - ον	σεαυτ - ην
P	N	—	—	—	—
	G	ἐαυτ - ων	ἐαυτ - ων	ἐαυτ - ων	ἐαυτ - ων
	D	ἐαυτ - οις	ἐαυτ - αις	ἐαυτ - οις	ἐαυτ - αις
	A	ἐαυτ - ους	ἐαυτ - ας	ἐαυτ - ους	ἐαυτ - ας

Reflexive Pronoun - Third Person

		Masculine	Feminine	Neuter
S	N	—	—	—
	G	ἐαυτ - ου	ἐαυτ - ης	ἐαυτ - ου
	D	ἐαυτ - ῳ	ἐαυτ - ῃ	ἐαυτ - ῳ
	A	ἐαυτ - ον	ἐαυτ - ην	ἐαυτ - ον
P	N		—	
	G		ἐαυτ - ων	
	D		ἐαυτ - αις	
	A		ἐαυτ - ας	

Representative First and Second Declension Adjective - Consonant Stem

		M	F	N
S	N	ἀγαθός	ἀγαθή	ἀγαθόν
	G	ἀγαθοῦ	ἀγαθῆς	ἀγαθοῦ
	D	ἀγαθῷ	ἀγαθῇ	ἀγαθῷ
	A	ἀγαθόν	ἀγαθήν	ἀγαθόν
P	N	ἀγαθοί	ἀγαθαί	ἀγαθά
	G	ἀγαθῶν	ἀγαθῶν	ἀγαθῶν
	D	ἀγαθοῖς	ἀγαθαῖς	ἀγαθοῖς
	A	ἀγαθούς	ἀγαθάς	ἀγαθά

Representative First and Second Declension Adjective - ε, ι, ρ Stem

		M	F	N
S	N	ἅγιος	ἁγία	ἅγιον
	G	ἁγίου	ἁγίας	ἁγίου
	D	ἁγίῳ	ἁγίᾳ	ἁγίῳ
	A	ἅγιον	ἁγίαν	ἅγιον
P	N	ἅγιοι	ἅγιαι	ἅγια
	G	ἁγίων	ἁγίων	ἁγίων
	D	ἁγίοις	ἁγίαις	ἁγίοις
	A	ἁγίους	ἁγίας	ἅγια

First and Third Declension Adjective πας

		Masculine	Feminine	Neuter
S	N	πας	πασα	παν
	G	παντος	πασης	παντος
	D	παντι	πασῃ	παντι
	A	παντα	πασαν	παν
P	N	παντες	πασαι	παντα
	G	παντων	πασων	παντων
	D	πασι	πασαις	πασι
	A	παντας	πασας	παντα

Third Declension Adjective ἀληθής

		Masculine/Feminine	Neuter
S	N	ἀληθής	ἀληθές
	G	ἀληθοῦς	ἀληθοῦς
	D	ἀληθεῖ	ἀληθεῖ
	A	ἀληθῆ	ἀληθές
P	N	ἀληθεῖς	ἀληθῆ
	G	ἀληθῶν	ἀληθῶν
	D	ἀληθέσι(ν)	ἀληθέσι(ν)
	A	ἀληθεῖς	ἀληθῆ

Irregular Adjective πολύς

		Masculine	Feminine	Neuter
S	N	πολύς	πολλή	πολύ
	G	πολλοῦ	πολλῆς	πολλοῦ
	D	πολλῷ	πολλῇ	πολλῷ
	A	πολύν	πολλήν	πολύ
P	N	πολλοί	πολλαί	πολλά
	G	πολλῶν	πολλῶν	πολλῶν
	D	πολλοῖς	πολλαῖς	πολλοῖς
	A	πολλούς	πολλάς	πολλά

Irregular Adjective μέγας

		Masculine	Feminine	Neuter
S	N	μέγας	μεγάλη	μέγα
	G	μεγάλου	μεγάλης	μεγάλου
	D	μεγάλῳ	μεγάλῃ	μεγάλῳ
	A	μέγαν	μεγάλην	μέγα
P	N	μεγάλοι	μεγάλαι	μεγάλα
	G	μεγάλων	μεγάλων	μεγάλων
	D	μεγάλοις	μεγάλαις	μεγάλοις
	A	μεγάλους	μεγάλας	μεγάλα

can use on exam

Appendix B: Verb Paradigms ✗ ἐ

for exam

The Verb εἰμί

		PAI.	PAS	PAImv	PAInf	FDI	IAI
S	1	εἰμί	ὦ	—	εἶναι	ἔσομαι	ἤμην
	2	εἶ	ᾖς	ἴσθι		ἔσῃ	ἦς
	3	ἐστί(ν)	ᾖ	ἔστω		ἔσται	ἦν
P	1	ἐσμέν	ὦμεν	—		ἐσόμεθα	ἦμεν
	2	ἐστέ	ἦτε	ἐστέ		ἔσεσθε	ἦτε
	3	εἰσί(ν)	ὦσι(ν)	ἔστωσαν		ἔσονται	ἦσαν

Thematic Verb Endings

			Indicative		Subjunctive	Imperative
			Present Future Perfect	Imperfect Aorist Pluperfect	Present Aorist	Present Aorist
Act	S	1	—	ν/–	—	
		2	ς	ς	ς	–/ον/τι/θι
		3	—	—	—	τω
	P	1	μεν	μεν	μεν	
		2	τε	τε	τε	τε
		3	σι	ν/σαν	σι	τωσαν
Mid & Pas	S	1	μαι	μην	μαι	
		2	σαι	σο	σαι	σο
		3	ται	το	ται	σθω
	P	1	μεθα	μεθα	μεθα	
		2	σθε	σθε	σθε	σθε
		3	νται	ντο	νται	σθωσαν

Present, Future, and Perfect Indicative of λυω

			Present	Future	Perfect
Act	S	1	λυω	λυσω	λελυκα
		2	λυεις	λυσεις	λελυκας
		3	λυει	λυσει	λελυκε
	P	1	λυομεν	λυσομεν	λελυκαμεν
		2	λυετε	λυσετε	λελυκατε
		3	λυουσι(ν)	λυσουσι(ν)	λελυκασι(ν)
Mid	S	1	λυομαι	λυσομαι	λελυμαι
		2	λυη	λυση	λελυσαι
		3	λυεται	λυσεται	λελυται
	P	1	λυομεθα	λυσομεθα	λελυμεθα
		2	λυεσθε	λυσεσθε	λελυσθε
		3	λυονται	λυσονται	λελυνται
Pas	S	1	λυομαι	λυθησομαι	λελυμαι
		2	λυη	λυθηση	λελυσαι
		3	λυεται	λυθησεται	λελυται
	P	1	λυομεθα	λυθησομεθα	λελυμεθα
		2	λυεσθε	λυθησεσθε	λελυσθε
		3	λυονται	λυθησνται	λελυνται

Present Indicative of Representative Contract Verbs

Act	S	1	ἀγαπῶ	ποιῶ	σταυρῶ
		2	ἀγαπᾷς	ποιεῖς	σταυροῖς
		3	ἀγαπᾷ	ποιεῖ	σταυροῖ
	P	1	ἀγαπῶμεν	ποιοῦμεν	σταυροῦμεν
		2	ἀγαπᾶτε	ποιεῖτε	σταυροῦτε
		3	ἀγαπῶσι(ν)	ποιοῦσι(ν)	σταυροῦσι(ν)
Mid & Pas	S	1	ἀγαπῶμαι	ποιοῦμαι	σταυροῦμαι
		2	ἀγαπᾷ	ποιῇ	σταυροῖ
		3	ἀγαπᾶται	ποιεῖται	σταυροῦται
	P	1	ἀγαπώμεθα	ποιούμεθα	σταυρούμεθα
		2	ἀγαπᾶθε	ποιεῖσθε	σταυροῦσθε
		3	ἀγαπῶνται	ποιοῦνται	σταυροῦνται

Imperfect, Aorist, and Pluperfect Indicative of λυω

			Imperfect	1st Aorist	Pluperfect
Act	S	1	ἔλυον	ἔλυσα	ἐλελύκειν
		2	ἔλυες	ἔλυσας	ἐλελύκεις
		3	ἔλυε(ν)	ἔλυσε(ν)	ἐλελύκει
	P	1	ἐλύομεν	ἐλύσαμεν	ἐλελύκειμεν
		2	ἐλύετε	ἐλύσατε	ἐλελύκειτε
		3	ἔλυον	ἔλυσαν	ἐλελύκεισαν
Mid	S	1	ἐλυόμην	ἐλυσάμην	ἐλελύμην
		2	ἐλύου	ἐλύσω	ἐλέλυσο
		3	ἐλύετο	ἐλύσατο	ἐλέλυτο
	P	1	ἐλυόμεθα	ἐλυσάμεθα	ἐλελύμεθα
		2	ἐλύεσθε	ἐλύσασθε	ἐλέλυσθε
		3	ἐλύοντο	ἐλύσαντο	ἐλέλυντο
Pas	S	1	ἐλυόμην	ἐλύθην	ἐλελύμην
		2	ἐλύου	ἐλύθης	ἐλέλυσο
		3	ἐλύετο	ἐλύθη	ἐλέλυτο
	P	1	ἐλυόμεθα	ἐλύθημεν	ἐλελύμεθα
		2	ἐλύεσθε	ἐλύθητε	ἐλέλυσθε
		3	ἐλύοντο	ἐλύθησαν	ἐλέλυντο

Imperfect Indicative of Representative Contract Verbs

Act	S	1	ἠγάπων	ἐποίουν	ἐσταύρουν
		2	ἠγάπας	ἐποίεις	ἐσταύρους
		3	ἤγπα	ἐποίει	ἐσταύρου
	P	1	ἠγαπῶμεν	ἐποιοῦμεν	ἐσταυροῦμεν
		2	ἠγαπᾶτε	ἐποιεῖτε	ἐσταυροῦτε
		3	ἠγάπων	ἐποίουν	ἐσταύρουν
Mid & Pas	S	1	ἠγαπώμην	ἐποιούμην	ἐσταυρούμην
		2	ἠγαπῶ	ἐποιοῦ	ἐσταυροῦ
		3	ἠγαπᾶτο	ἐποιεῖτο	ἐσταυροῦτο
	P	1	ἠγαπώμεθα	ἐποιούμεθα	ἐσταυρούμεθα
		2	ἠγαπᾶθε	ἐποιεῖσθε	ἐσταυροῦσθε
		3	ἠγαπῶντο	ἐποιοῦντο	ἐσταυροῦντο

Participle Endings

		Active			Middle/Passive		
		M	F	N	M	F	N
S	N	ν/ς	α	α	ν	ος	η	ον
	G	ος	ης	ας	ος	ου	ης	ου
	D	ι	η	ᾳ	ι	ῳ	η	ῳ
	A	α	αν	αν	ν	ον	ην	ον
P	N	ες	αι	αι	α	οι	αι	α
	G	ων	ων	ων	ων	ων	ων	ων
	D	σι	αις	αις	σι	οις	αις	οις
	A	ας	ας	ας	α	ους	ας	α

Present Participle of λυω

			M	F	N
Act	S	N	λυων	λυουσα	λυον
		G	λυοντος	λυουσης	λυοντος
		D	λυοντι	λυουση	λυοντι
		A	λυοντα	λυουσαν	λυον
	P	N	λυοντες	λυουσαι	λυοντα
		G	λυοντων	λυουσων	λυοντων
		D	λυουσι	λυουσαις	λυουσι
		A	λυοντας	λυουσας	λυοντα
Mid & Pas	S	N	λυομενος	λυομενη	λυομενον
		G	λυομενου	λυομενης	λυομενου
		D	λυομενῳ	λυομενη	λυομενῳ
		A	λυομενον	λυομενην	λυομενον
	P	N	λυομενοι	λυομεναι	λυομενα
		G	λυομενων	λυομενων	λυομενων
		D	λυομενοις	λυομεναις	λυομενοις
		A	λυομενους	λυομενας	λυομενα

Present Participle Contractions - Alpha Contract Verbs

			M	F	N
Act	S	N	–ῶν	–ῶσα	–ῶν
		G	–ῶντος	–ώσης	–ῶντος
Mid &	P	N	–ώμενος	–ωμένη	–ώμενον
Pas		G	–ωμενου	–ωμενης	–ωμενου

Present Participle Contractions - Epsilon Contract Verbs

			M	F	N
Act	S	N	–ῶν	–οῦσα	–οῦν
		G	–οῦντος	–οῦσης	–οῦντος
Mid &	P	N	–ούμενος	–ουμένη	–ούμενον
Pas		G	–ουμενου	–ουμενης	–ουμενου

Present Participle Contractions - Omicron Contract Verbs

			M	F	N
Act	S	N	–ῶν	–οῦσα	–οῦν
		G	–οῦντος	–οῦσης	–οῦντος
Mid &	P	N	–ούμενος	–ουμένη	–ούμενον
Pas		G	–ουμενου	–ουμενης	–ουμενου

Present Active Participle of εἰμι

		M	F	N
S	N	ὤν	οὖσα	ὄν
	G	ὄντος	οὔσης	ὄντος
	D	ὄντι	οὔσῃ	ὄντι
	A	ὄντα	οὖσαν	ὄν
P	N	ὄντες	οὖσαι	ὄντα
	G	ὄντων	οὐσῶν	ὄντων
	D	οὖσι(ν)	οὔσαις	οὖσι
	A	ὄντας	οὔσας	ὄντα

Aorist Participle of λυω

			Masculine	Feminine	Neuter
Act	S	N	λυσας	λυσασα	λυσαν
		G	λυσαντος	λυσασης	λυσαντος
		D	λυσαντι	λυσαση	λυσαντι
		A	λυσαντα	λυσασαν	λυσαν
	P	N	λυσαντες	λυσασαι	λυσαντα
		G	λυσαντων	λυσασων	λυσαντων
		D	λυσασι	λυσασαις	λυσασι
		A	λυσαντας	λυσασας	λυσαντα
Mid	S	N	λυσαμενος	λυσαμενη	λυσαμενον
		G	λυσαμενου	λυσαμενης	λυσαμενου
		D	λυσαμενω	λυσαμενη	λυσαμενω
		A	λυσαμενον	λυσαμενην	λυσαμενον
	P	N	λυσαμενοι	λυσαμεναι	λυσαμενα
		G	λυσαμενων	λυσαμενων	λυσαμενων
		D	λυσαμενοις	λυσαμεναις	λυσαμενοις
		A	λυσαμενους	λυσαμενας	λυσαμενα
Pas	S	N	λυθεις	λυθεισα	λυθεν
		G	λυθεντος	λυθεισης	λυθεντος
		D	λυθεντι	λυθειση	λυθεντι
		A	λυθεντα	λυθεισαν	λυθεν
	P	N	λυθεντες	λυθεισαι	λυθεντα
		G	λυθεντων	λυθεισων	λυθεντων
		D	λυθεισι	λυθεισαις	λυθεισι
		A	λυθεντας	λυθεισας	λυθεντα

Perfect Participle of λυω

			M	F	N
Act	S	N	λελυκως	λελυκυια	λελυκος
		G	λελυκοτος	λελυκυιας	λελυκοτος
		D	λελυκοτι	λελυκυιᾳ	λελυκοτι
		A	λελυκοτα	λελυκυιαν	λελυκος
	P	N	λελυκοτες	λελυκυιαι	λελυκοτα
		G	λελυκοτων	λελυκυιων	λελυκοτων
		D	λελυκοσι	λελυκυιαις	λελυκοσι
		A	λελυκοτας	λελυκυιας	λελυκοτα
Mid & Pas	S	N	λελυμενος	λελυμενη	λελυμενον
		G	λελυμενου	λελυμενης	λελυμενου
		D	λελυμενῳ	λελυμενῃ	λελυμενῳ
		A	λελυμενον	λελυμενην	λελυμενον
	P	N	λελυμενοι	λελυμεναι	λελυμενα
		G	λελυμενων	λελυμενων	λελυμενων
		D	λελυμενοις	λελυμεναις	λελυμενοις
		A	λελυμενους	λελυμενας	λελυμενα

Infinitives of λυω   "+o . . . "

	Present	1st Aorist	Perfect
Active	λυειν	λυσαι	λελυκεναι
Middle	λυεσθαι	λυσασθαι	λελυσθαι
Passive	λυεσθαι	λυθηναι	λελυσθαι

Present Infinitives of Representative Contract Verbs

	Alpha Contract	Epsilon Contract	Omicron Contract
Active	ἀγαπᾶν	ποιεῖν	σταυροῦν
Middle	ἀγαπᾶσθαι	ποιεῖσθαι	σταυροῦσθαι
Passive	ἀγαπᾶσθαι	ποιεῖσθαι	σταυροῦσθαι

Subjunctive and Imperative Moods of λυω

			Subjunctive		Imperative	
			Present	Aorist	Present	Aorist
Act	S	1	λυω	λυσω	—	—
		2	λυης	λυσης	λυε	λυσον
		3	λυη	λυση	λυετω	λυσατω
	P	1	λυωμεν	λυσωμεν	—	—
		2	λυητε	λυσητε	λυετε	λυσατε
		3	λυωσι(ν)	λυσωσι(ν)	λυετωσαν	λυσατωσαν
Mid	S	1	λυωμαι	λυσωμαι	—	—
		2	λυη	λυση	λυου	λυσαι
		3	λυηται	λυσηται	λυεσθω	λυσασθω
	P	1	λυωμεθα	λυσωμεθα	—	—
		2	λυησθε	λυσησθε	λυεσθε	λυσασθε
		3	λυωνται	λυσωνται	λυεσθωσαν	λυσασθωσαν
Pas	S	1	λυωμαι	λυθω	—	—
		2	λυη	λυθης	λυου	λυθητι
		3	λυηται	λυθη	λυεσθω	λυθητω
	P	1	λυωμεθα	λυθωμεν	—	—
		2	λυησθε	λυθητε	λυεσθε	λυθητε
		3	λυωνται	λυθωσι(ν)	λυεσθωσαν	λυθητωσαν

"I might be ...ing

" " for myself

Present Subjunctive of Representative Contract Verbs

Act	S	1	ἀγαπῶ	ποιῶ	σταυρῶ
		2	ἀγαπᾷς	ποιῇς	σταυροῖς
		3	ἀγαπᾷ	ποιῇ	σταυροῖ
	P	1	ἀγαπῶμεν	ποιῶμεν	σταυρῶμεν
		2	ἀγαπᾶτε	ποιῆτε	σταυρῶτε
		3	ἀγαπῶσι(ν)	ποιῶσι(ν)	σταυρῶσι(ν)
Mid & Pas	S	1	ἀγαπῶμαι	ποιῶμαι	σταυρῶμαι
		2	ἀγαπᾷ	ποιῇ	σταυροῖ
		3	ἀγαπᾶται	ποιῆται	σταυρῶται
	P	1	ἀγαπωμεθα	ποιώμεθα	σταυρώμεθα
		2	ἀγαπᾶθε	ποιῆσθε	σταυρῶσθε
		3	ἀγαπῶνται	ποιῶνται	σταυρῶνται

" " ...ed

Present Imperative of Representative Contract Verbs "must be …ing"

Act	S	2	ἀγάπα	ποίει	σταύρου
		3	ἀγαπάτω	ποιείτω	σταυρούτω
	P	2	ἀγαπᾶτε	ποιείτε	σταυροῦτε
		3	ἀγαπάτωσαν	ποιείτωσαν	σταυρούτωσαν
Mid & Pas	S	2	ἀγαπῶ	ποιοῦ	σταυροῦ
		3	ἀγαπάσθω	ποιείσθω	σταυρούσθω
	P	2	ἀγαπᾶσθε	ποιεῖσθε	σταυροῦσθε
		3	ἀγαπάσθωσαν	ποιείσθωσαν	σταυρούσθωσαν

Second Aorist Forms of βαλλω

			Active	Middle	Passive
Indic	S	1	ἐβαλον	ἐβαλομην	ἐβληθην
		2	ἐβαλες	ἐβαλου	ἐβληθης
		3	ἐβαλε	ἐβαλετο	ἐβληθη
	P	1	ἐβαλομεν	ἐβαλομεθα	ἐβληθημεν
		2	ἐβαλετε	ἐβαλεσθε	ἐβληθητε
		3	ἐβαλον	ἐβαλοντο	ἐβληθην
Subj	S	1	βαλω	βαλωμαι	βληθω
		2	βαλης	βαλη	βληθης
		3	βαλη	βαληται	βληθη
	P	1	βαλωμεν	βαλωμεθα	βληθωμεν
		2	βαλητε	βαλησθε	βληθητε
		3	βαλωσι(ν)	βαλωνται	βληθωσι(ν)
Imv	S	2	βαλε	βαλου	βληθητι
		3	βαλετω	βαλεσθω	βληθητω
	P	2	βαλετε	βαλεσθε	βληθητε
		3	βαλετωσαν	βαλεσθωσαν	βληθητωσαν
Infinitive			βαλειν	βαλεσθαι	βληθηναι
Ptc	MNS		βαλων	βαλομενος	βληθεις
	FNS		βαλουσα	βαλομενη	βληθεισα
	NNS		βαλον	βαλομενον	βληθεν

Present Indicative Forms of Representative –μι Verbs

			δίδωμι	τίθημι	ἵστημι
Act	S	1	δίδωμι	τίθημι	ἵστημι
		2	δίδως	τίθης	ἵστης
		3	δίδωσι	τίθησι	ἵστησι
	P	1	δίδομεν	τίθεμεν	ἵσταμεν
		2	δίδοτε	τίθετε	ἵστατε
		3	δίδοασι	τίθεασι	ἵστασι
Mid	S	1	δίδομαι	τίθεμαι	ἵσταμαι
&		2	δίδοσαι	τίθεσαι	ἵστασαι
Pas		3	δίδοται	τίθεται	ἵσταται
	P	1	δίδομεθα	τίθεμεθα	ἵσταμεθα
		2	δίδοσθε	τίθεσθε	ἵστασθε
		3	δίδονται	τίθενται	ἵστανται

Present Infinitive Forms of Representative –μι Verbs

	δίδωμι	τίθημι	ἵστημι
Active	δίδοναι	τίθεναι	ἱστάναι
Middle/Passive	δίδοσθαι	τίθεσθαι	ἵστασθαι

Present Participle Forms of Representative –μι Verbs

		δίδωμι	τίθημι	ἵστημι
Act	MNS	δίδους	τίθεις	ἱστάς
	FNS	δίδουσα	τίθεισα	ἵστασα
	NNS	δίδον	τίθεν	ἱστάν
Mid	MNS	δίδομενος	τίθεμενος	ἱστάμενος
&	FNS	δίδομενη	τίθεμενη	ἱσταμενη
Pas	NNS	δίδομενον	τίθεμενον	ἱσταμενον

Present Subjunctive of Representative –μι Verbs

			δίδωμι	τίθημι	ἵστημι
Act	S	1	διδῶ	τιθῶ	ἱστῶ
		2	διδῷς	τιθῇς	ἱστῇς
		3	διδῷ	τιθῇ	ἱστῇ
	P	1	διδῶμεν	τιθῶμεν	ἱστῶμεν
		2	διδῶτε	τιθῆτε	ἱστῆτε
		3	διδῶσι(ν)	τιθῶσι(ν)	ἱστῶσι(ν)
Mid	S	1	διδῶμαι	τιθῶμαι	ἱστῶμαι
&		2	διδῷ	τιθῇ	ἵστῃ
Pas		3	διδῶται	τιθῆται	ἱστῆται
	P	1	διδώμεθα	τιθώμεθα	ἱστώμεθα
		2	διδῶσθε	τιθῆσθε	ἱστῆσθε
		3	διδῶνται	τιθῶνται	ἱστῶνται

Present Imperative of Representative –μι Verbs

			δίδωμι	τίθημι	ἵστημι
Act	S	2	δίδου	τίθει	ἵστη
		3	διδότω	τιθέτω	ἱστάτω
	P	2	δίδοτε	τίθετε	ἵστατε
		3	διδότωσαν	τιθέτωσαν	ἱστάτωσαν
Mid	S	2	δίδοσο	τίθεσο	ἵστασο
&		3	διδόσθω	τιθέσθω	ἱστάσθω
Pas	P	2	δίδοσθε	τίθεσθε	ἵστασθε
		3	διδόσθωσαν	τιθέσθωσαν	ἱστάσθωσαν

Aorist Indicative Forms of Representative –μι Verbs

			δίδωμι	τίθημι	ἵστημι	
					1st Aor.	2nd Aor.
Act	S	1	ἔδωκα	ἔθηκα	ἔστησα	ἔστην
		2	ἔδωκας	ἔθηκας	ἔστησας	ἔστης
		3	ἔδωκε(ν)	ἔθηκε(ν)	ἔστησε(ν)	ἔστη
	P	1	ἐδώκαμεν	ἐθήκαμεν	ἐστήσαμεν	ἔστημεν
		2	ἐδώκατε	ἐθήκατε	ἐστήσατε	ἔστητε
		3	ἔδωκαν	ἔθηκαν	ἔστησαν	ἔστησαν
Mid	S	1	ἐδόμην	ἐθέμην	ἐστησάμην	
		2	ἔδου	ἔθου	ἐστήσω	
		3	ἔδοτο	ἔθετο	ἐστήσατο	
	P	1	ἐδόμεθα	ἐθέμεθα	ἐστησάμεθα	
		2	ἔδοσθε	ἔθεσθε	ἐστήσασθε	
		3	ἔδοντο	ἔθεντο	ἐστήσαντο	
Pas	S	1	ἐδόθην	ἐτέθην	ἐστάθην	
		2	ἐδόθης	ἐτέθης	ἐστάθης	
		3	ἐδόθη	ἐτέθη	ἐστάθη	
	P	1	ἐδόθημεν	ἐτέθημεν	ἐστάθημεν	
		2	ἐδόθητε	ἐτέθητε	ἐστάθητε	
		3	ἐδόθησαν	ἐτέθησαν	ἐστάθησαν	

Aorist Infinitive Forms of Representative –μι Verbs

	δίδωμι	τίθημι	ἵστημι	
			1st Aor.	2nd Aor.
Active	δοῦναι	θεῖναι	στῆσαι	στῆναι
Middle	δόσθαι	θέσθαι	στησάσθαι	
Passiv	δοθηναι	τέθηναι	στάθηναι	

Aorist Participle Forms of Representative –μι Verbs

		δίδωμι	τίθημι	ἵστημι	
				1st Aor.	2nd Aor.
Act	MNS	δούς	θείς	στησάς	στάς
	FNS	δοῦσα	θεῖσα	στησάσα	στᾶσα
	NNS	δόν	θέν	στησάν	στάν
Mid	MNS	δόμενος	θέμενος	στησάμενος	
	FNS	δομένη	θεμένη	στησαμένη	
	NNS	δόμενον	θέμενον	στησάμενον	
Pas	MNS	δοθεις	τέθεις	στάθεις	
	FNS	δοθεισα	τέθεισα	στάθεισα	
	NNS	δοθεν	τέθεν	στάθεν	

Aorist Imperative of Representative –μι Verbs

			δίδωμι	τίθημι	ἵστημι
Active	Sing	2	δός	θές	στῆθι
		3	δότω	θέτω	στήτω
	Pl	2	δότε	θέτε	στήτε
		3	δότωσαν	θέτωσαν	στήτωσαν
Middle	Sing	2	δοῦ	θοῦ	
		3	δόσθω	θέσθω	
	Pl	2	δόσθε	θέσθε	
		3	δόσθωσαν	θέσθωσαν	
Passive	Sing	2	δόθητι	τέθητι	στάθητι
		3	δοθήτω	τεθήτω	σταθήτω
	Pl	2	δόθητε	τέθητε	στάθητε
		3	δοθήτωσαν	τεθήτωσαν	σταθήτωσαν

Aorist Subjunctive of Representative –μι Verbs

			δίδωμι	τίθημι	ἵστημι
Act	S	1	δῶ	θῶ	στῶ
		2	δῷς	θῇς	στῇς
		3	δῷ	θῇ	στῇ
	P	1	δῶμεν	θῶμεν	στῶμεν
		2	δῶτε	θῆτε	στῆτε
		3	δῶσι(ν)	θῶσι(ν)	στῶσι(ν)
Mid	S	1	δῶμαι	θῶμαι	
		2	δῷ	θῇ	
		3	δῶται	θῆται	
	P	1	δώμεθα	θώμεθα	
		2	δῶσθε	θῆσθε	
		3	δῶνται	θῶνται	
Pas	S	1	δοθῶ	τεθῶ	σταθῶ
		2	δοθῇς	τεθῇς	σταθῇς
		3	δοθῇ	τεθῇ	σταθῇ
	P	1	δοθῶμεν	τεθῶμεν	σταθῶμεν
		2	δοθῆτε	τεθῆτε	σταθῆτε
		3	δοθῶσι(ν)	τεθῶσι(ν)	σταθῶσι(ν)

Appendix C: Principal Parts of Irregular Verbs

PAI1S	FAI1S	AAI1S	PfAI1S	PfM/PI1S	API1S
ἄγω	ἄξω	ἤγαγον	(ἦχα)	ἦγμαι	ἤχθην
αἴρω	ἀρῶ	ἦρα	ἦρκα	ἦρμαι	ἤρθην
ἀκούω	ἀκούσω	ἤκουσα	ἀκήκοα	-----	ἠκούσθην
ἁμαρτάνω	ἁμαρτήσω	ἥμαρτον	ἡμάρτηκα	-----	-----
ἀνοίγω	ἀνοίξω	ἤνοιξα	ἀνέῳγα	ἀνέῳγμαι	ἀνεῴχθην
ἀποκτείνω	ἀποκτενῶ	ἀπέκτεινα	-----	-----	ἀπεκτάνθην
ἀπόλλυμι	ἀπολέσω	ἀπώλεσα	ἀπόλωλα	-----	-----
ἀποστέλλω	ἀποστελῶ	ἀπέστειλα	ἀπέσταλκα	ἀπέσταλμαι	ἀπεστάλην
ἀφίημι	ἀφήσω	ἀφῆκα	ἀφεῖκα	ἀφέωμαι	ἀφέθην
βαίνω	βήσομαι	ἔβην	βέβηκα	-----	ἐβηθην
βάλλω	βαλῶ	ἔβαλον	βέβληκα	βέβλημαι	ἐβλήθην
γίνομαι	γενήσομαι	ἐγενόμην	γέγονα	γεγένημαι	ἐγενήθην
γινώσκω	γνώσομαι	ἔγνων	ἔγνωκα	ἔγνωσμαι	ἐγνώσθην
γράφω	γράψω	ἔγραψα	γέγραφα	γέγραμμαι	ἐγράφην
δείκνυμι	δείξω	ἔδειξα	-----	δέδειγμαι	ἐδείχθην
δέχομαι	δέξομαι	ἐδεξάμην	-----	δέδεγμαι	ἐδέχθην
δίδωμι	δώσω	ἔδωκα	δέδωκα	δέδομαι	ἐδόθην
διώκω	διώξω	ἐδίωξα	-----	δεδίωγμαι	ἐδιώχθην
δύναμαι	δυνήσομαι	ἠδυνάμην	-----	-----	ἠδυνήθην
ἐγγίζω	ἐγγιῶ	ἤγγισα	ἤγγικα	-----	-----
ἐγείρω	ἐγερῶ	ἤγειρα	ἐγήγερκα	ἐγήγερμαι	ἠγέρθην
εἰμί	ἔσομαι	ἤμην	-----	-----	-----
ἐλπίζω	ἐλπιῶ	ἤλπισα	ἤλπικα	-----	-----
ἐργάζομαι	-----	ἠργασάμην	-----	εἴργασμαι	εἴργασθην
ἔρχομαι	ἐλεύσομαι	ἦλθον	ἐλήλυθα	-----	-----

αι	ἔφαγον	-----		-----	-----
	εὐηγγελισάμην	-----	εὐηγγέλισμαι	εὐηγγελίσθην
εὑρήσω	εὗρον	εὕρηκα	-----	εὑρέθην
-χω	ἕξω	ἔσχον	ἔσχηκα	-----	-----
θέλω	θελήσω	ἠθέλησα	-----	-----	-----
θνῄσκω	θανοῦμαι	ἔθανον	τέθνηκα	-----	-----
ἵστημι	στήσω	ἔστησα	ἕστηκα	ἕσταμαι	ἐστάθην
	ἔστην				
καλέω	καλέσω	ἐκάλεσα	κέκληκα	κέκλημαι	ἐκλήθην
κρίνω	κρινῶ	ἔκρινα	κέκρικα	κέκριμαι	ἐκρίθην
λαμβάνω	λήμψομαι	ἔλαβον	εἴληφα	εἴλημμαι	ἐλήμφθην
λέγω	ἐρῶ	εἶπον	εἴρηκα	εἴρημαι	ἐρρέθην
λείπω	λείψω	ἔλιπον	λελοιπα	λέλειμμαι	ἐλείφθην
μένω	μενῶ	ἔμεινα	μεμένηκα	-----	-----
ὁράω	ὄψομαι	εἶδον	ἔωρακα	ἔωραμαι	ὤφθην
πάσχω	πείσομαι	ἔπαθον	πέπονθα	-----	-----
πείθω	πείσω	ἔπεισα	πέποιθα	πέπεισμαι	ἐπείσθην
πίνω	πίομαι	ἔπιον	πέπωκα	-----	------
πίπτω	πεσοῦμαι	ἔπεσον	πέπτωκα	-----	-----
στρέφω	στρέψω	ἔστρεψα	-----	-----	ἐστράφην
σῴζω	σώσω	ἔσωσα	σέσωκα	σέσωσμαι	ἐσώθην
τελέω	(τελέσω)	ἐτέλεσα	τετέλεκα	τετέλεσμαι	ἐτελέσθην
τίθημι	θήσω	ἔθηκα	τέθεικα	τέθειμαι	ἐτέθην
φαίνω	φανοῦμαι	ἔφανα	-----	-----	ἐφάνην
φέρω	οἴσω	ἤνεγκα	ἐνήνοχα	-----	ἠνέχθην
φθείρω	φθερῶ	ἔφθειρα	-----	ἔφθαρμαι	ἐφθάρην

Appendix D: Flow Charts

FLOW CHART FOR PARSING VERBS IN THE INDICATIVE MOOD

Begin Here

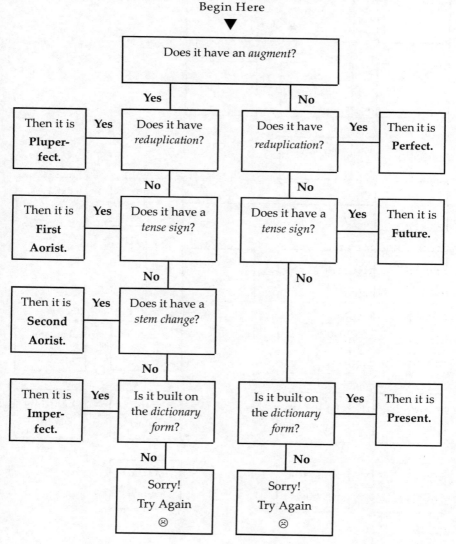

FLOW CHART FOR PARSING THEMATIC VERBS
(ANY MOOD OR MODE)

Begin Here

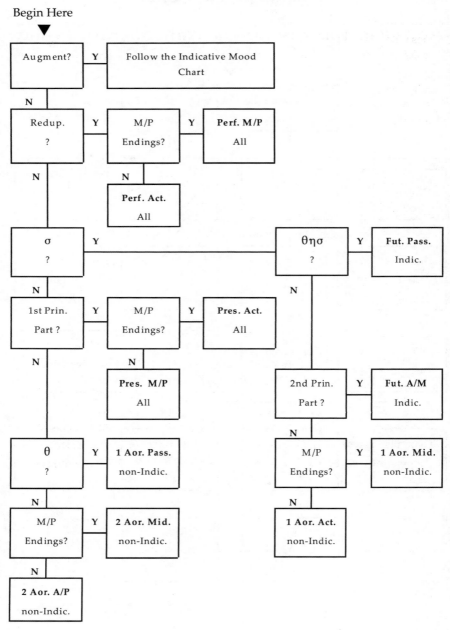

FLOW CHART FOR ANALYZING THE USE OF PARTICIPLES

Begin Here
▼

| Does it have a *definite article*? | **Yes** → | Does it have a *noun the same gender, case, and number* which it could be modifying? | **No** → | Then it is **Substantival.** |

No ↓

| Does it have a *noun the same gender, case, and number* which it could be modifying? | **Yes** → | Then it is **Adjectival.** |

(from "Does it have a *definite article*?" — No → "Does it have a *noun the same gender, case, and number* which it could be modifying?")

No ↓

| Is it in the *nominative* case? | **Yes** → | Is there a *verb* which it could be modifying? | **Yes** → | Then it is **Adverbial.** |

No ↓ (under "Is it in the *nominative* case?")

It *might* be an **Absolute** construction.

No ↓ (under "Is there a *verb* which it could be modifying?")

Then it is **Verbal**

(under "Then it is **Adverbial.**")

Is it manner, means, time, cause, condition, concession, purpose, or attendant circumstance?

FLOW CHART FOR ANALYZING THE USE OF INFINITIVES

Begin Here

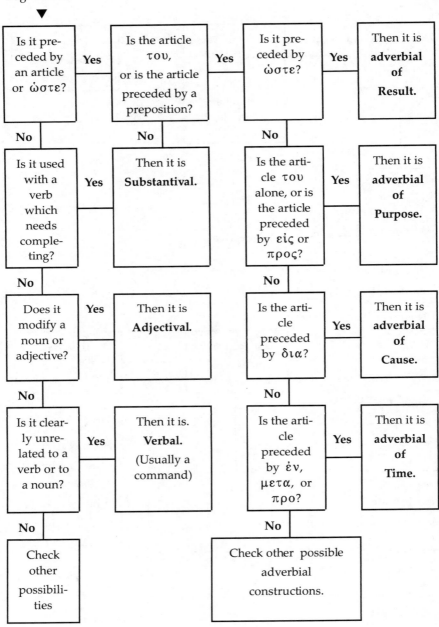

Appendix E: Greek-English Vocabulary

ἀγαθός, -η, -ον good

ἀγαπάω I am loving

ἀγάπη, -ης, ἡ love

ἀγαπητός, -η, -ον beloved

ἄγγελος, -ου, ὁ angel, messenger

ἁγιάζω I am sanctifying

ἅγιος, -α, -ον holy

ἀγοράζω I am buying

ἀγρός, -ου, ὁ field

ἄγω I am leading

ἀδελφή, -ης, ἡ sister

ἀδελφός, -ου, ὁ brother

ἀδικέω I am doing wrong/evil, treating unjustly

ἀδικία, -ας, ἡ unrighteousness

ἀδύνατος, -ον impossible

αἷμα, -ατος, τό blood

αἴρω I am taking, taking up, taking away

αἰτέω I am asking

αἰώνιος, -ον eternal

αἰών, αἰῶνος, ὁ age

ἀκάθαρτος, -ον unclean

ἀκοή, -ης, ἡ hearing, report

ἀκολουθέω I am following [dative direct object]

ἀκούω I am hearing, listening to

ἀλήθεια, -ας, ἡ truth

ἀληθής, ἀληθές true

ἀληθινός, -η, -ον true

ἀλλά but

ἀλλήλων one another

ἄλλος, -η, -ον other, another of the same kind

ἁμαρτάνω I am sinning

ἁμαρτία, -ας, ἡ sin

ἁμαρτωλός, -ου, ὁ sinner

ἄν -ever

ἀνά (with acc.) up, again

ἀναβαίνω I going up, ascending

ἀναβλέπω I am looking up, regaining sight

ἀναγινώσκω I am reading

ἀνάστασις, -εως, ἡ resurrection

ἄνεμος, -ου, ὁ wind

ἀνήρ, ἀνδρός, ὁ man, husband

ἄνθρωπος, -ου, ὁ man

ἀνίστημι I am raising, rising

ἀνοίγω I am opening

ἀντί (with gen.) instead of, in place of, because of

ἄξιος, -α, ον worthy

ἀπαγγέλλω I am announcing, reporting

ἅπας, ἅπασα, ἅπαν each, every, all, whole

ἀπέρχομαι I am departing

ἄπιστος, -ον unbelieving, faithless

ἀπο (with gen.) from, away from, by means of, of

ἀποδίδωμι I am giving back, repaying

ἀποθνήσκω I am dying

ἀποκαλύπτω I am revealing

ἀποκρίνομαι I am answering [dative direct object]

ἀποκτείνω I am killing

ἀπόλλυμι I am destroying

ἀπολύω I am releasing, setting free

ἀπόστολος, -ου, ὁ apostle

ἀποστέλλω I am sending out

ἅπτομαι I am touching

ἄρα therefore

ἀρνέομαι I am denying

ἀρνίον, -ου, τό lamb

ἄρτι now, just now

ἄρτος, -ου, ὁ bread

ἀρχή, -ης, ἡ beginning

ἀρχιερεύς, -εως, ὁ high priest, chief priest

ἄρχομαι I am beginning

ἄρχω I am ruling [genitive direct object]

ἄρχων, -οντος, ὁ ruler

ἀσθενεία, -ας, ἡ weakness

ἀσθενέω I am being weak, sick

ἀσπάζομαι I am greeting

αὐτός, -η, -ο he, she, it, self, same

ἀφίημι I am forgiving, dismissing, permitting

ἄχρι (with gen.) until, up to

βάλλω I am throwing

βαπτίζω I am baptizing

βασιλεία, -ας, ἡ kingdom, reign

βασιλεύς, -εως, ὁ king

βαστάζω I am bearing, carrying

βιβλίον, -ου, τό book

βίβλος, -ου, ἡ book

βλασφημέω I am blaspheming, reviling

βλέπω I am seeing, looking

βοάω I am shouting, crying out

βούλομαι I am wishing

γαμέω I am marrying

γάρ for

γε indeed, at least, really, even

γενεά, -ας, ἡ generation

γεννάω I am begetting, giving birth

γένος, -ους, τό family, race, kind

γῆ, γῆς, ἡ earth, land, ground

γίνομαι *I am, am becoming, am existing*

γινώσκω *I am knowing*

γλῶσσα, -ης, ἡ *tongue, language*

γνωρίζω *I am making known*

γνῶσις, -εως, ἡ *knowledge*

γράμμα, -ατος, τό *letter*

γραμματεύς, -εως. ὁ *scribe, teacher of the law*

γραφή, -ης, ἡ *writing, Scripture*

γράφω *I am writing*

γυνή, γυναικός, ἡ *woman, wife*

δαιμόνιον, -ου, τό *demon*

δέ *and, but, now*

δεῖ *it is necessary*

δεικνύω, δείκνυμι *I am showing*

δέκα *ten*

δένδρον, -ου, το *tree*

δεξιός, -α, -ον *right [as opposed to left]*

δεύτερος, -α, -ον *second*

δέχομαι *I am receiving*

διά *(with gen.) through, by means of; (with acc.) because of, on account of*

διάβολος, -ου, ὁ *slanderer, devil*

διαθήκη, -ης, ἡ *covenant*

διακονέω *I am serving, ministering*

διακονία, -ας, ἡ *ministry, service*

διάκονος, -ου, ὁ *servant, minister*

διαλογίζομαι *I am discussing, reasoning*

διδάσκαλος, -ου, ὁ *teacher*

διδάσκω *I am teaching*

διδαχή, -ης, ἡ *teaching*

δίδωμι *I am giving*

δίκαιος, -α, -ον *righteous, just*

δικαιόω *I am justifying, declaring righteous*

δικαιοσύνη, -ης, ἡ *righteousness*

διό *therefore*

διώκω *I am pursuing, persecuting*

διέρχομαι *I am passing through*

διότι *because, for*

δοκέω *I am thinking, supposing*

δόξα, -ης, ἡ *glory*

δοξάζω *I am glorifying*

δουλεύω *I am being enslaved*

δοῦλος, -ου, ὁ *slave, servant*

δουλόω *I am enslaving*

δύναμαι *I can, am able*

δύναμις, -εως, ἡ *power*

δυνατός, -η, -ον *powerful, possible*

δύο *two*

δώδεκα *twelve*

δῶρον, -οῦ, τό *gift*

ἐάν *if*

ἐάν μη *except, unless*

ἑαυτοῦ, -ης *himself, herself, itself*

ἐγγίξω I am approaching, coming near

ἐγγύς near

ἐγείρω I am raising

ἐγώ I

ἔθνος, -ους, τό nation, Gentile

εἰ if

εἰμί I am

εἰρήνη, -ης, ἡ peace

εἰς (with acc.) into, in, to

εἷς, μία, ἕν one

εἰσέρχομαι I am entering

ἐκ (with gen.) out of, from, by means of, by reason of

ἕκαστος, -η -ον each, every

ἐκβάλλω I am casting out, throwing out

ἐκεῖ there, in that place

ἐκεῖθεν from there/that place, thence

ἐκεῖνος, -η, -ο that

ἐκκλησία, -ας, ἡ church

ἐκλεκτός, -η, -ον chosen, elect

ἐκπορεύομαι I am coming out, going out

ἐλευθερός, -α, -ον free

ἐλεέω I am having/showing mercy

ἔλεος, -ους, τό mercy

ἐλευθερόω I am setting free

ἐλπίζω I am hoping

ἐλπίς, -ιδος, ἡ hope

ἐμαυτοῦ, -ης myself

ἐμός, -η, -ον my, mine

ἔμπροσθεν (with gen.) before, in front of

ἐν (with dat.) in, with, among, by means of

ἐνδύω I am putting on

ἕνεκα, ἕνεκεν (with gen.) because of, for the sake of

ἐνεργέω I am working, operating, being effective

ἐντέλλομαι I am commanding

ἐντολή, -ης, ἡ commandment

ἐνώπιον (with gen.) before

ἐξέρχομαι I am coming/going out

ἔξεστι(ν) it is lawful

ἐξουσία, -ας, ἡ authority

ἔξω outside

ἑορτή, -ης, ἡ feast

ἐπαγγελία, -ας, ἡ promise

ἐπεί since, because

ἐπερωτάω I am asking, asking for

ἐπί (with gen., dat., acc.) upon, on

ἐπιγινώσκω I am coming to know, recognize

ἐπιθυμία, -ας, ἡ desire, lust

ἐπικαλέω I am calling upon

ἐπιλαμβάνομαι I am seizing, taking hold of

ἐπιστολή, -ης, ἡ letter, epistle

ἐπιστρέφω I am returning, turning back

ἐπιτίθημι I am placing on/upon

ἐπιτιμάω I am rebuking

ἐπτά seven

ἐργάζομαι I am working

ἔργον, -ου, τό work

ἔρημος, -ου, ἡ wilderness

ἑρμηνεύω I am translating

ἔρχομαι I am coming, going

ἐρωτάω I am asking, requesting

ἐσθίω I am eating

ἔσχατος, -η, -ον last

ἕτερος, -α, -ον different, other of a
    different kind

ἔτι yet, still

ἑτοιμάζω I am preparing

ἔτος, -ους, τό year

εὐαγγελίζομαι I am preaching the
    gospel/good news

εὐαγγέλιον, -ου, τό gospel

εὐδοκία, -ας, ἡ good will, pleasure,
    favor

εὐθύς, εὐθέως immediately, at once

εὐλογέω I am blessing

εὑρίσκω I am finding

εὐχαριστέω   I am giving thanks
    [dative direct object]

ἐφίστημι I am standing over, coming
    upon

ἐχθρός, -ου, ὁ enemy

ἔχω I am having

ἕως (with gen.) until, up to

ζάω I am living

ζητέω I am seeking

ζύμη, -ης, ἡ leaven

ζωή, -ης, ἡ life

ἤ or

ἡγέομαι I am considering, regarding,
    leading

ἤδη already

ἥκω I have come [perfect]

ἥλιος, -ου, ὁ sun

ἡμέρα, -ας, ἡ day

ἡμέτερος, -α, -ον our

θάλασσα, -ης, ἡ sea

θάνατος, -ου, ὁ death

θαυμάζω I am being amazed

θεάομαι I am beholding

θέλημα, -ατος, τό will

θέλω I am wishing

θεός, -οῦ, ὁ God, god

θεραπεύω I am healing

θεωρέω I am seeing, perceiving

θηρίον, -ου, τό wild beast

θλίψις, -εως, ἡ tribulation, affliction

θρόνος, -ου, ὁ throne

θυγάτηρ, θυγατρός, ἡ daughter

θύρα, -ας, ἡ door

θυσία, -ας, ἡ sacrifice

ἰάομαι *I am healing*

ἴδιος, -α, -ον *one's own*

ἰδού, ἰδέ *Look! See! Behold!*

ἱερεύς, -εως, ὁ *priest*

Ἰησοῦς, -ου, ὁ *Jesus*

ἱκανός, -η, -ον *sufficient, able, considerable*

ἱμάτιον, -ου, τό *cloak, garment*

ἵνα *in order that, so that, that*

ἱνα μη *lest, in order that not*

ἵστημι *I am standing, causing to stand*

ἰσχυρός, -α, -ον *strong*

ἰσχύω *I am being strong, able*

καί *and, also, even*

καθαρίζω *I am cleansing*

καθαρός, -α, -ον *clean*

κάθημαι *I am sitting*

καθίζω *I am sitting, seating*

καθίστημι *I am setting, constituting*

καθώς *as, just as*

καινός, -η, -ον *new*

καιρός, -ου, ὁ *time, occasion*

κακός, -η, -ον *bad*

καλέω *I am calling*

καλός, -η, -ον *good, beautiful*

καλῶς *rightly, well*

καρδία, -ας, ἡ *heart*

καρπός, -ου, ὁ *fruit*

κατά *(with gen.) against, down; (with acc.) according to*

καταβαίνω *I am coming down, descending*

καταλαμβάνω *I am attaining, laying hold of*

καταλείπω *I am leaving*

καταργέω *I am abolishing, bringing to nothing*

κατηγορέω *I am accusing, bringing charges against*

κατοικέω *I am dwelling, inhabiting*

καυχάομαι *I am boasting*

κεῖμαι *I am lying*

κελεύω *I am commanding*

κερδαίνω *I am gaining, profiting*

κεφαλή, -ης, ἡ *head*

κηρύσσω *I am preaching*

κλαίω *I am weeping*

κόσμος, -ου, ὁ *world*

κράζω *I am crying out, shouting*

κρατέω *I am grasping, taking hold of*

κρίμα, -ατος, τό *judgment*

κρίνω *I am judging*

κρίσις, -εως, ἡ *judgment*

κύριος, -ου, ὁ *lord, master*

κώμη, -ης, ἡ *village*

λαλέω *I am speaking*

λαμβάνω *I am taking, receiving*

λαός, -ου, ὁ *people*

λείπω *I am leaving*

λέγω *I am saying, speaking*

λίθος, -ου, ὁ *stone*

λογίζομαι *I am considering*

λόγος, -ου, ὁ *word, saying, message*

λοιπός, -η, -ον *rest, remaining*

λυπέω *I am grieving*

λύω *I am loosing, destroying*

μαθητής, -ου, ὁ *disciple*

μανθάνω *I am learning*

μαρτυρέω *I am bearing witness*

μαρτυρία, -ας, ἡ *witness, testimony*

μάρτυς, -υρος, ὁ *witness*

μακάριος, -α, -ον *blessed*

μᾶλλον *more, rather*

μάχαιρα, -ης, ἡ *sword*

μέγας, μεγάλη, μέγα *great, large*

μείζων, μεῖζον *greater, larger*

μέλος, -ους, τό *member*

μέλλω *I am about to*

μὲν . . . δέ *on the one hand . . . on the other hand*

μένω *I am staying, abiding*

μέρος, -ους, τό *part, piece, member*

μέσος, -η, -ον *middle*

Μεσσίας, -ου, ὁ *Messiah, Anointed One*

μετά *(with gen.) with; (with acc.) after*

μετανοέω *I am repenting*

μή *not*

μηδέ, μητέ *nor, and not, not even*

μηδείς, μηδεμία, μηδέν *no one, none, nothing*

μήποτε *lest, otherwise*

μήτηρ, μητρός, ἡ *mother*

μικρός, -α, -ον *small, little*

μιμνῄσκομαι *I am remembering*

μισέω *I am hating*

μισθός, -ου, ὁ *wages, hire, reward*

μνημεῖον, -ου, τό *tomb, monument*

μνημονεύω *I am remembering*

μόνος, -η, -ον *only, alone*

μυστήριον, -ου, τό *mystery*

ναί *truly, yes*

ναός, -ου, ὁ *temple, sanctuary*

νεκρός, -α, -ον *dead*

νεός, -α, -ον *new*

νεφέλη, -ης, ἡ *cloud*

νικάω *I am overcoming, conquering*

νοέω *I am understanding, perceiving*

νόμος, -ου, ὁ *law*

νοῦς, νοός, ὁ *mind*

νῦν *now*

νύξ, νυκτός, ἡ *night*

ὁδός, -ου, ἡ *road, way*

οἱ μὲν . . . οἱ δέ *some . . . others*

οἶδα *I am knowing*

οἰκία, -ας, ἡ *house*

οἰκοδομέω *I am building (up), edifying*

οἶκος, -ου, ὁ *house, household*

οἶνος, -ου, ὁ *wine*

ὀλίγος, -η, -ον *little, few*

ὅλος, -η, -ον *whole, all, complete*

ὀμνύω, ὄμνυμι *I am swearing, taking an oath*

ὅμοιος, -α, -ον *like*

ὁμοίως *likewise*

ὁμολογέω *I am confessing, declaring*

ὄνομα, -ατος, τό *name*

ὀπίσω *(with gen.) behind, after*

ὅπου *where*

ὅπως *that, in order that*

ὁράω *I am seeing*

ὀργή, -ης, ἡ *anger, wrath*

ὄρος, -ους, τό *mountain*

ὅς, ἥ, ὅ *who, which, that*

ὅσος, -η, -ον *as great as, as many as*

ὅστις, ἥτις, ὅ τι *who, whoever, which, whichever*

ὅταν *whenever*

ὅτε *when*

ὅτι *because, that*

οὖ *where*

οὐ, οὐκ, οὐχ, οὐχι *not*

οὐ μη *never*

οὐαί *Woe!*

οὐδέ, οὐτέ *and not, nor, not even*

οὐδὲ ... οὐδέ *neither ... nor*

οὐδείς, οὐδεμία, οὐδέν *no one, none, nothing*

οὐκέτι *no longer*

οὖν *therefore,*

οὔπω *not yet*

οὐρανός, -ου, ὁ *heaven*

οὖς, ὠτός, τό *ear*

οὗτος, αὕτη, τοῦτο *this*

οὕτως *thus, so, in this manner*

ὀφείλω *I am owing, ought*

ὀφθαλμός, -ου, ὁ *eye*

ὄχλος, -ου, ὁ *crowd*

παιδίον, -ου, τό *child*

παῖς, παιδός, ὁ *child, servant*

πάλιν *again*

πάντοτε *always*

παρά *(with gen.) from; (with dat.) with, in the presence of; (with acc.) beside, by*

παραβολή, -ης, ἡ *parable*

παραγγέλλω *I am commanding, charging*

παραγίνομαι *I am coming, arriving, appearing*

παραδίδωμι *I am betraying, handing over*

παρακαλέω *I am urging, exhorting, comforting*

παράκλησις, -εως, ἡ *encouragement, comfort*

παραλαμβάνω *I am accepting, receiving*

παρατίθημι *I am placing before*

πάρειμι *I am being present*

παρέρχομαι *I am passing, passing by*

παρίστημι *I am being present, standing by*

παρουσία, -ας, ἡ *coming, arrival, presence*

παρρησία, -ας, ἡ *boldness, confidence*

πᾶς, πᾶσα, πᾶν *each, every, all, whole*

πάσχα, τό *Passover*

πάσχω *I am suffering*

πατήρ, πατρός, ὁ *father*

πείθω *I am trusting in, persuading*

πειράζω *I am testing, tempting*

πέμπω *I am sending*

πέντε *five*

περί *(with gen.) about, concerning, with reference to; (with acc.) around*

περιβάλλω *I am putting around, clothing*

περιπατέω *I am walking*

περισσεύω *I am abounding, being rich*

περιστερά, -ας, ἡ *dove*

περιτομή, -ης, ἡ *circumcision*

Πέτρος, -ου, ὁ *Peter*

πίμπλημι *I am filling*

πίνω *I am drinking*

πίπτω *I am falling*

πιστεύω *I am believing, regarding as reliable*

πίστις, -εως, ἡ *faith*

πιστός, -η, -ον *faithful*

πλανάω *I am deceiving, leading astray*

πλείων, -ονος *larger, more*

πλῆθος, -ους, τό *multitude, crowd*

πλήν *however, but, only*

πληρόω *I am filling, fulfilling*

πλήρωμα, -ατος, τό *fulness*

πλοῖον, -ου, τό *boat*

πλούσιος, -α, -ον *rich*

πνεῦμα, -ατος, τό *Spirit, spirit*

πνευματικός, -η, -ον *spiritual*

πόθεν *from where / what place? whence?*

ποιέω *I am making, doing (poet)*

ποῖος, -α, ον *what sort of? what?*

πόλις, -εως, ἡ *city*

πολύς, πολλή, πολύ *much, many*

πονηρός, -α, -ον *evil*

πορεύομαι *I am coming, going*

πορνεία, -ας, ἡ *fornication*

πότε *when?*

ποτήριον, -ου, το *up*

ποῦ *to where/what place? whither?*

πούς, ποδός, ὁ *foot*

πράσσω *I am doing, performing*

πρεσβύτερος, -ου, ὁ *elder*

πρίν *before*

πρό *(with gen.) before*

πρόβατον, -ου, τό *sheep*

πρός *(with dat.) at, on, near; (with acc.) to, toward, with, for the purpose of*

προσέρχομαι *I am approaching*

προσευχή, -ης, ἡ *prayer*

προσεύχομαι *I am praying*

προσέχω *I am giving heed to, attending to*

προσκαλέομαι *I am summoning, calling to myself*

προσκυνέω *I am worshiping*

προσφέρω *I am bringing to, offering*

πρόσωπον, -ου, τό *face*

προφητεύω *I am prophesying*

προφήτης, -ου, ὁ *prophet*

πρῶτος, -η, -ον *first*

πτωχός, -η, -ον *poor*

πύρ, πυρός, τό *fire*

πῶς *how?*

ῥῆμα, -ατος, τό *word, saying*

σάββατον, -ου, τό *the Sabbath*

σάρξ, σαρκός, ἡ *flesh*

σεαυτοῦ, -ης *yourself*

σημεῖον, -ου, τό *sign*

σήμερον *today*

σκανδαλίζω *I am causing to stumble*

σκηνόω *I am living, dwelling [in a tent]*

σκοτία, -ας, ἡ *darkness*

σκότος, -ους, τό *darkness*

σός, σή, σόν *your [sing.]*

σοφία, -ας, ἡ *wisdom*

σοφός, -η, -ον *wise*

σπείρω *I am sowing*

σπέρμα, -ατος, τό *seed, descendant*

σταυρός, -ου, ὁ *cross*

σταυρόω *I am crucifying*

στόμα, -ατος, τό *mouth*

στρατιώτης, -ου, ὁ *soldier*

στρέφω *I am turning*

σύ *you [sing.]*

συκή, -ης, ἡ *fig tree*

σύν *(with dat.) with*

συνάγω *I am gathering together*

συναγωγή, -ης, ἡ *synagogue, assembly*

συνέδριον, -ου, τό *council*

συνείδησις, -εως, ἡ *conscience*

συνέρχομαι *I am coming together*

σώζω I am saving

συνίημι I am understanding, comprehending

σῶμα, -ατος, τό body

σωτήρ, σωτῆρος, ὁ savior

σωτηρία, -ας, ἡ salvation

τε and

τε ... καί both ... and

τέκνον, -ου, τό child

τελειόω I am perfecting, completing

τελέω I am finishing, fulfilling

τέλος, -ους, τό end

τελώνης, -ου, ὁ tax collector

τέσσαρες, τέσσαρα four

τηρέω I am keeping

τίθημι I am placing, putting

τιμάω I am honoring

ἡ τιμή, -ης honor, price

τίς, τί who? which? what? why?

τις, τι someone, anyone, one, a certain one

τοιοῦτος, -αυτη, -ουτο such

τόπος, -ου, ὁ place

τότε then

τρεῖς, τρία three

τρίτος, -η, -ον third

τύπος, -ου, ὁ mark, type, example

τυφλός, -ου, ὁ blind man

ὕδωρ, ὕδατος, τό water

υἱός, -οῦ, ὁ son

ὑμέτερος, -α, -ον your [pl.]

ὑπάγω I am departing, going away

ὑπάρχω I am, exist

ὑπέρ (with gen.) for; (with acc.) above, over

ὑπό (with gen.) by; (with acc.) under

ὑποκριτής, -ου, ὁ hypocrite

ὑπομονή, -ης, ἡ endurance, steadfastness

ὑποστρέφω I am returning

ὑποτάσσω I am putting in subjection

φαίνω I am shining

φανερόω I am making manifest

φέρω I am bringing, bearing

φεύγω I am bringing, bearing

φεύγω I am fleeing (fugitive)

φημί I am saying

φιλέω I am loving

φίλος, -ου, ὁ friend

φιλός, -η, -ον friendly

φοβέομαι I am fearing

φόβος, -ου, ὁ fear

φρονέω I am thinking, having in mind

φυλακή, -ης, ἡ guard, prison, watch

φυλή, -ης, ἡ tribe

φωνή, -ης, ἡ voice

φωνέω *I am calling*

φωτίζω *I am giving light to*

φῶς, φωτός, τό *light*

χαίρω *I am rejoicing*

χαρά, -ας, ἡ *joy*

χαρίζομαι *I am giving freely, grant-*
    ing

χάρις, -ιτος, ἡ *grace, favor*

χείρ, χειρός, ἡ *hand*

χήρα, -ας, ἡ *widow*

χορτάζω *I am feeding, satisfying*

χρεία, -ας, ἡ *need*

Χριστός, -ου, ὁ *Christ*

χρόνος, -ου, ὁ *time*

χώρα, -ας, ἡ *country, rural area*

χωρίς + **gen**. *without, apart from*

ψεύδομαι *I am lying*

ψυχή, -ης, ἡ *life, soul*

ὧδε *here, in this place*

ὥρα, -ας, ἡ *hour*

ὡς *as, like, about*

ὥσπερ *as, just as, even as*

ὥστε *so that*

Appendix F: Translation Helps

These helps are basic, and you might find that you will have to supply helping words (e.g., with a noun in the dative case) or think through the translation of a verb when it occurs in a tense other than one with which you are familiar. If a form occurs more than once, it is listed only in the verse where it first occurs. When there is no "gloss" at the right margin, you are working with a word which you have already met in the vocabulary lists.

Although proper names which you have not learned have been supplied in the practice exercises, they are not supplied in the translation helps. You should, in most instances, be able to sound out the name (e.g., Φαρισαιοι = Pharisees). When you are not able to sound out the name, use the dictionary in the back of your Greek New Testament.

Be certain to parse every verb which you encounter (Tense, Voice, Mood, Person, Number, Dictionary form). If the verb has already been parsed for you in the helps, it would be wise to include it in your list anyway so that you become accustomed to listing and parsing every verb in a given text.

Remember that Greek uses inflection to indicate such items as the subject and the direct object. It is not always possible simply to translate word for word. You might need to analyze the pieces of a sentence before you can translate it into "normal" English. It is wise to get into the habit of following a regular procedure for translating passages in the New Testament:

1. Use punctuation (period, raised dot, question mark) to identify the extent of the sentence. A sentence is often longer than one verse of Scripture.

2. Identify any subordinate conjunctions and/or relative pronouns; they always mark the beginning of subordinate clauses. Isolate any subordinate clauses within the sentence.

3. Construct a translation of the main clause by (a) identifying, parsing, and translating the main verb(s), (b) identifying any expressed subject (noun in the nominative), (c) identifying any direct object (noun in accusative), (d) arranging these items in "standard" English word order (subject–verb–object).

4. Construct a translation of any subordinate clauses within the sentence by following the same process as in step 3.

Translation Helps for John 1:1-34
(For use with Chapters 5-10)

1:1	ἦν	past tense; 3S; εἰμί	
1:2	οὗτος	pronoun; MNS; οὗτος	"this one"
1:3	πάντα	adjective; NNPl; πᾶς	"all things"
	αὐτοῦ	pronoun; MGS; αὐτός	"him"
	ἐγένετο	past tense; 3S; γίνομαι	
	χωρὶς	preposition with genitive case	"apart from"
	ἕν	numeral; NAS; εἷς	"one thing"
	ὅ	pronoun; NNS; ὅς	"which"
	γέγονεν	perfect tense; 3S; γίνομαι	"has . . ."
1:4	αὐτῷ	pronoun; MDS; αὐτός	"him"
	φῶς	noun; MNS; φῶς	"light"
1:5	κατέλαβεν	past tense; 3S; καταλαμβάνω	
	αὐτὸ	pronoun; NAS; αὐτός	"it"
1:6	ἀπεσταλμένος	participle; MNS; ἀποστέλλω	"who was sent"
	ὄνομα	noun; NNS; ὄνομα	"name"
1:7	ἦλθεν	past tense; 3S; ἔρχομαι	
	μαρτυρήσῃ	simple action; 3S; μαρτυρεω	"might . . ."
	φωτός	noun; NGS; φῶς	"light"
	πάντες	adjective; MNPl; πᾶς	"all (men)"
	πιστεύσωσιν	simple action; 3Pl; πιστευω	"might . . ."
1:8	ἐκεῖνος	pronoun; MNS; ἐκεῖνος	"that one"
1:9	ἀληθινόν	adjective; NNS; ἀληθινός	"true"
	ὅ	pronoun; NNS	"which"
	πάντα	adjective; MAS; πᾶς	"every"
	ἐρχόμενον	participle; NNS; ἔρχομαι	"which is coming"

| 1:10 | αὐτὸν | pronoun; 3S; αὐτός | "him" |
| | ἔγνω | past tense; 3S; γινώσκω | |

1:11	ἴδια	adjective; NAPl; ἴδιος	"his own things"
	ἴδιοι	adjective; MNPl; ἴδιος	"his own (men)"
	παρέλαβον	past tense; 3Pl; παραλαμβάνω	

1:12	ὅσοι	pronoun; MNPl; ὅσος	"as many as"
	ἔλαβον	past tense; 3Pl; λαμβάνω	
	ἔδωκεν	past tense; 3S; δίδωμι	
	αὐτοις	pronoun; MDPl; αὐτός	"them"
	γενέσθαι	infinitive; γίνομαι	"to . . ."
	πιστεύουσιν	participle; MDPl; πιστεύω	"those believing"

1:13	οἳ	pronoun; MNPl; ὅς	"who"
	αἱμάτων	noun; MGPl; αἷμα	"blood(s)"
	θελήματος	noun; NGS; θέλημα	"will"
	σαρκὸς	noun; FGS; σάρξ	"flesh"
	ἀνδρὸς	noun; MGS; ἀνήρ	"of man"
	ἐγεννήθησαν	past tense; 3Pl; γεννάω (passive voice)	

1:14	ἐγένετο	past tense; 3S; γίνομαι	
	σὰρξ	noun; FNS; σάρξ	"flesh"
	ἐσκήνωσεν	past tense; 3S; σκήνοω	
	ἐθεασάμεθα	past tense; 1Pl; θεάομαι	
	μονογενοῦς	adjective; NGS; μονογενής	"only, unique"
	πατρός	noun; MGS; πατήρ	"father"
	πλήρης	adjective; MNS; πλήρης	"full"
	χάριτος	noun; FGS; χάρις	"grace"

1:15	κέκραγεν	perfect tense; 3S; κράζω	"has . . ."
	λέγων	participle; MNS; λέγω	"saying"
	οὗτος	pronoun; MNS; οὗτος	"this one"
	ἦν	past tense; 3S; εἰμί	
	ὃν	pronoun; MAS; ὅς	"whom"
	εἶπον	past tense; 1S; λέγω	
	ὀπίσω	preposition with genitive case	"behind"
	ἐρχόμενος	participle; MNS; ἔρχομαι	"who is coming"

	ἐμπροσθέν	preposition with genitive case	"before"
	γέγονεν	perfect tense; 3S; γίνομαι	"has . . ."
	πρῶτός	preposition with genitive case	"before"

1:16	πληρώματος	noun; NGS; πλήρωμα	"fulness"
	πάντες	adjective; MNPl; πᾶς	"all"
	χάριν	noun; FAS; χάρις	"grace"

1:17	ἐδόθη	aorist tense; 3S; δίδωμι (passive voice)	
	ἐγένετο	aorist tense; 3S; γίνομαι	

1:18	οὐδεὶς	pronoun; MNS; οὐδείς	"no one"
	ἑώρακεν	perfect tense; 3S; ὁράω	"has . . ."
	πώποτε	adverb	"at any time"
	ὢν	participle; MNS; εἰμί	"who is"
	κόλπον	noun; MAS; κόλπος	"bosom"
	ἐκεῖνος	pronoun; MNS; ἐκεῖνος	"that one"
	ἐξηγήσατο	aorist tense; 3S; ἐξηγέομαι	"he explained"

1:19	αὕτη	pronoun; FNS; οὗτος	"this"
	ἀπέστειλαν	AAI3Pl; ἀποστέλλω	
	ἱερεῖς	noun; MAPl; ἱερευς	"priest"
	ἐρωτήσωσιν	simple action; 3Pl; ἐρωτάω	"might . . ."
	τίς	pronoun; MNS; τίς	"who?"

1:20	ὡμολόγησεν	AAI3S; ὁμολογέω	
	ἠρνήσατο	AAI3S; ἀρνέομαι	

1:21	ἠρώτησαν	AAI3Pl; ἐρωτάω	
	τί	pronoun; NNS; τίς	"what?"
	ἀπεκρίθη	past tense; 3S; ἀποκρίνομαι	

1:22	ἀπόκρισιν	noun; ἀπόκρισις	"answer"
	δῶμεν	simple action; 1Pl; δίδωμι	"might . . ."
	πέμψασιν	participle; MDPl; πέμπω	"the ones who sent"
	σεαυτοῦ	pronoun; GS; σεαυτοῦ	"yourself"

1:23	ἔφη	AAI3S; φημί	"he said"
	βοῶντος	participle; MGS; βοάω	"one crying"
	εὐθύνατε	imperative; 2Pl; εὐθύνω	"make straight!"

| 1:24 | ἀπεσταλμένοι | participle; MNPl; ἀποστέλλω | "the ones who had been sent" |

| 1:25 | ἠρώτησαν | AAI3Pl; ἐρωτάω | |
| | τί | pronoun; τίς | "why?" |

1:26	ἀπεκρίθη	past tense; 3S; ἀποκρίνομαι	
	λέγων	participle; MNS; λέγω	"saying"
	μέσος	preposition with genitive case	"in the midst"
	ἔστηκεν	perfect tense; 3S; ἵστημι	"he stands"
	ὃν	pronoun; MAS'; ὅς	"whom"

1:27	ἐρχόμενος	participle; MNS; ἔρχομαι	"who is coming"
	οὗ	pronoun; MGS; ὅς'	"for whom"
	ἄξιος	adjective; MNS; ἄξιος	"worthy"
	λύσω	simple active; 1S; λύω	"might . . ."
	ἱμάντα	noun; MAS; ἱμάς	"strap"
	ὑποδήματος	noun; NGS; ὑπόδημα	"sandal"

1:28	ταῦτα	pronoun; NNPl; οὗτος	"these things"
	ἐγένετο	aorist tense; 3S; γίνομαι	
	πέραν	preposition with genitive case	"beyond"
	ὅπου	adverbial relative of place	"where"
	βαπτίζων	participle; MNS; βαπτίζω	"baptizing"

1:29	ἐπαύριον	adverb	"next day"
	ἴδε	imperative; 2S; ὁράω	
	ἀμνὸς	noun; MNS; ἀμνός	"lamb"
	αἴρων	participle; MNS; αἴρω	"who is . . ."

1:30	οὗτος	pronoun; MNS; οὗτος	"this one
	ἔρχεται	present tense; 3S; ἔρχομαι	
	ὃς	pronoun; MNS; ὅς	"who"
	γέγονεν	perfect tense; 3S; γίνομαι	

πρῶτός   preposition with genitive case   "before

1:31 κἀγὼ   καί + ἐγώ
ᾔδειν   pluperfect tense; 1S; οἶδα
φανερωθῇ   simple passive; 3S; φανερόω   "might be . . ."
τοῦτο   pronoun; NAS; οὗτος   "this"
βαπτίζων   participle; MNS; βαπτίζω   "baptizing"

1:32 λέγων   participle; MNS; λέγω   "saying"
τεθέαμαι   perfect tense; 1S; θεάομαι
καταβαῖνον   participle; NNS; καταβαίνω   "which is . . ."
ἔμεινεν   AAI3S; μένω

1:33 πέμψας   participle; MNS; πέμπω   "the one who . . ."
βαπτίζειν   infinitive; βαπτίζω   "to be . . ."
ἐκεῖνός   pronoun; MNS; ἐκεῖνος   "that one"
ὃν ἂν   pronoun; MNS; ὅς ἄν   "whomever"
ἴδῃς   simple active; 2S; ὁράω   "might . . ."
μένον   participle; MAS; μένω   "abiding"
οὗτός   pronoun; MNS; οὗτος   "this one"
ἁγίῳ   adjective; NDS; ἅγιος   "holy"

1:34 μεμαρτύρηκα   perfect; μαρτυρέω

Translation Helps for Mark 8:11-30
(For use with Chapters 11-15)

8:11 ἐξῆλθον   ἐξερχομαι;   "I am departing"
ἤρξαντο   aorist tense; 3Pl; ἀρχομαι   "I am beginning"
συζητεῖν   infinitive; συζητεω   "to be questioning"
ζητοῦντες   participle; MNPl; ζητεω   "seeking"
πειράζοντες   participle; MNPl; πειραζω   "testing"

8:12 ἀναστενάξας   participle; MNS; ἀναστεναζω   "he groaned and . . ."
τί   pronoun   "Why . . .?"
αὕτη   pronoun; FNS; οὗτος   "this"
δοθήσεται   future passive; 3S; διδωμι

| ταύτῃ | pronoun; FDS; οὖτος | "this" |

8:13

ἀφεὶς	participle; MNS; ἀφιημι	"and leaving"
πάλιν	adverb	"again"
ἐμβὰς	participle; MNS; ἐμβαινω	"he got in and"
το πέραν	NAS	"the other side"

8:14

ἐπελάθοντο	AAI3Pl; ἐπιλανθάνομαι	"I am forgetting"
λαβεῖν	infinitive; λαμβάνω	"to . . ."
εἰ μὴ	idiomatic	"except"
ἕνα	number; MAS; εἰς	"one"
ἑαυτῶν	pronoun; MGPl; ἑαυτοῦ	"themselves"

8:15

| διεστέλλετο | impf; 3S; διαστέλλομαι | "I am commanding" |
| λέγων | participle; MNS; λέγω | "and was . . ." |

8:16

| διελογιζοντο | impf; 3Pl; διαλογίζομαι | |
| ἀλλήλους | pronoun; MAPl; ἀλλήλων | "one another" |

8:17

γνοὺς	participle; MNS; γινώσκω	"when he . . ."
τί	pronoun	"why?"
οὔπω	adverb	"not yet"
συνίετε	present tense; συνίημι	
πεπωρωμένην	participle; FAS; πωρόω	"made stubborn"

8:18

| ἔχοντες | participle; MNPl; ἔχω | ". . . ing" |
| μνημονεύετε | μνημονεύω | "I am remembering" |

8:19

πεντε	number	"five"
ἔκλασα	κλάω	"I am breaking"
πεντακισχιλίους	adjective; MAPl	"5,000"
πόσους	interrogative; MAPl; πόσος	"how many?"
κοφίνους	noun; κόφινος	"basket"
κλασμάτων	noun; κλάσμα	"fragment"
πλήρεις	adjective; MAPl; πλήρης	"full"
δώδεκα	number; δώδεκα	"twelve"

8:20	ἑπτά	number; ἑπτά	"seven"
	τετρακισχίλιοι	adjective; MNPl	"4,000"
	πόσων	interrogative; MGPl; πόσος	"how many?"
	σπυρίδων	noun; σπυρίς	"basket"
	πληρώματα	noun; πλήρωμα	"fullness"
8:21	οὔπω	adverb	"not yet"
	συνίετε	present tense; συνίημι	
8:22	τυφλον	noun; τυφλος	"blind man"
	ἅψηται	aorist deponent; 3S; ἅπτομαι	"might ..."
8:23	ἐπιλαβόμενος	participle; MNS; ἐπιλαμβάνομαι	"and took hold of"
	ἐξήνεγκεν	ἐκφέρω	"I am bringing out"
	ἔξω	adverb	"outside"
	πτύσας	participle; MNS; πτυω	"and spat"
	ὄμματα	noun; ὄμμα	"eye"
	ἐπιθεὶς	participle; MNS; ἐπιτίθημι	"and put upon"
	ἐπηρώτα	ἐπερωτάω	"I am asking"
	τι	pronoun; NAS; τις	"anything"
8:24	ἀναβλέψας	participle; MNS; ἀναβλέπω	"he looked up and ..."
	περιπατοῦντες	participle; MNPl; περιπατέω	"walking"
8:25	εἶτα	adverb	"then"
	ἐπέθηκεν	AAI3S; ἐπιτίθημι	"I am putting upon"
	ὀφθαλμούς	noun; ὀφθαλμός	"eye"
	διέβλεψεν	διαβλέπω	"I am looking intently"
	ἀποκατέστη	API3S; ἀποκαθίστημι	"I am restoring"
	ἐνέβλεπεν	ἐμβλέπω	"I am looking at"
	τηλαυγῶς	adverb	"clearly"
	ἅπαντα	adjective; NAPl; ἅπας	"all things"
8:26	λέγων	participle; MNS; λέγω	"saying"
	εἰσελθῃς	εἰσέρχομαι	
		(translate as a simple command)	

8:27 ἐπηρώτα   ἐπερωταω
λέγων   participle; MNS; λεγω   "saying"
τίνα   pronoun; MAS; τίς   "whom"
εἶναι   infinitive; εἰμι   "to ..."

8:28 οἱ δὲ   idiomatic   "and they"
λέγοντες   participle; MNPl; λεγω   "saying"
ἄλλοι   pronoun; MNPl; ἄλλος   "other, another"
εἷς   number; MNS; εἷς   "one"

8:29 ἀποκριθεὶς   participle; MNS; ἀποκρίνομαι
(translate as simple past tense)

8:30 μηδενὶ   pronoun; MDS; μηδείς   "no one"
λέγωσιν   present tense; 3Pl; λέγω   "might be ..."

Translation Helps for Mark 8:31-9:1
(For use with Chapters 21-23)

8:31 διδασκειν   present infinitive; διδασκω   "to be ..."
πολλὰ   adjective; NAPl; πολύς   "many things"
παθειν   aorist infinitive; πασχω   "to ..."
ἀποδοκιμασθηναι   aorist passive infinitive;
ἀποδοκιμαζω   "to be rejected"
ἀποκτανθηναι aorist passive infinitive; ἀποκτεινω
τρεῖς   numeral   "three"
ἀναστῆναι   aorist infinitive; ἀνίστημαι   "to rise"

8:32 ἐπιτιμᾶν   present infinitive; ἐπιτιμαω   "to be ..."
ὑπαγε   present imperative; 2S; ὑπάγω
(translate as progressive command)

8:34 τις   pronoun; MNS; τις   "anyone"
ἀπαρνησάσθω aorist imperative; ἀπαρνέομαι   "he must ..."
ἑαυτὸν   pronoun; MAS; ἑαυτοῦ   "himself"
ἀράτω   aorist imperative; αἴρω   "he must ..."
ἀκολουθείτω present imperative; ἀκολουθέω   "he must ..."

8:35	θέλη	aorist; 3S; θέλω (trans. as summary present)	

| 8:37 | δοῖ | aorist optative; 3S; δίδωμι | "might . . ." |

8:38	ἐπαισχυνθῇ	APS3S; ἐπαισχύνομαι	"is ashamed"
	μοιχαλίδι	adjective; FDS; μοιχαλιδος	adulterous
	ἔλθῃ	AAS3S; ἔρχομαι	"comes"

9:1	ἑστηκότων	PfAPtcMGP1; ἵστημι	"I am standing
	οὐ μὴ		"never (!)"
	γεύσωνται	ADS3P1; γεύομαι (trans. as simple future)	
	ἕως ἄν	subordordinate conjunction	"until"
	ἴδωσιν	AAS3P1; ὁράω (trans. as summary present)	

Translation Helps for 1 Thess 1:1-10
(For use with Chapters 24-25)

| 1:2 | πάντων | adjective; MGP1; πᾶς | "all" |

| 1:4 | εἰδότες | participle; οἶδα | |

| 1:5 | πολλῇ | adjective; FDS; πολύς | "much" |

| 1:6 | πολλῇ | adjective; FDS; πολύς | "much" |

| 1:7 | πᾶσιν | adjective; MDP1; πᾶς | "all" |

| 1:8 | παντὶ | adjective; MDS; πᾶς | "every" |

Beginning with Chapter 26, no translation helps other than Kubo's lexicon should be necessary to enable you to translate passages in 1 Thessalonians.

Appendix G: Glossary

Ablative – the case function within the genitive case form which indicates separation.

Absolute Use of Participle – an adverbial participle which defines the circumstances in which the action of the verb in the main clause occurs, but which has a subject different from that of the main clause.

Accusative Case – the case form which indicates limitation/extension.

Active Voice – the voice which indicates that the subject performs, produces, or experiences the action.

Adjective – a word which modifies a noun.

Adverb – a word which modifies a verb, an adjective, or another adverb.

Adverbial Clause — a clause which is introduced by a subordinate conjunction and modifies the action of a verb in the main clause.

Anarthrous – a noun which is not accompanied by a definite article.

Antecedent – the noun which a pronoun replaces and to which it refers.

Aorist Tense – the tense most frequently used to indicate summary action.

Apostrophe – a diacritical mark at the end of a word which marks the omission of a final vowel.

Appositive -- a noun which closely follows another noun and renames or further identifies it.

Articular – a noun which is accompanied by a definite article.

Attributive Use of Adjective – an adjective which follows a definite article and qualifies or limits a noun

Augment – the prefix Ɛ added to the stem of a verb in the indicative mood to indicate past time.

Breathing Mark – a diacritical mark placed over a vowel or diphthong which begins a Greek word.

Case – the property of a noun which indicates its function in a clause or sentence.

Clause – a group of words which has a subject and a verb and is used as part of a sentence.

Comparative Degree – the inflectional form of an adjective which compares two persons or things.

Complement – the part of the sentence which completes the idea of the subject and verb.

Completed-Stative Action Tenses – verb tenses which present the action as completed, but with continuing results (Perfect, Pluperfect).

Conjunction – a function word which connects words or word groups.

Consonant Contraction – the inflection which takes place when a tense sign is added to a verb with a stem ending with a consonant.

Contract Verb - a verb which has a stem ending with the vowel α, Ɛ, or ο.

Coordinate Conjunction - a conjunction which connects words, phrases, clauses, sentences, or paragraphs of equal value

Coronis – a diacritical mark in the middle of a word which marks the omission of one or more letters when two words are combined.

Crasis – the merger of two words into one.

Dative Case – the case form which indicates personal interest.

Declension – the regular pattern of change (inflection) which Greek nouns follow.

Definite Article – a word used with a noun to limit, individualize, or give definiteness/indefiniteness to the noun ("the").

Demonstrative Pronoun – a pronoun which points out a particular person or thing ("this, that, these, those").

Dental Verb – a verb which has a stem ending with δ, θ, or τ.

Dependent (Subordinate) Clause – a clause which does not express a complete thought and is attached to a main clause by a connector

Deponent Passive – a verb which has entirely lost both its aorist active and aorist middle forms so the aorist passive form is translated with an active sense.

Deponent Verb – a verb in which the active form has fallen out of use, and the middle form has taken its place.

Diaeresis – a diacritical mark which is placed over the second vowel of an apparent diphthong to indicate that the vowels are to be pronounced separately.

Diphthong – two vowels which are combined in one syllable to create a single sound.

Direct Object – the noun which receives the action of the verb.

Elision – the deletion of a vowel at the end of a word when the next word also begins with a vowel.

First (Weak) Aorist – the aorist form of a verb which retains the regular stem and adds a σ tense sign.

First Person – the inflectional form of a verb which indicates that the speaker acts ("I, we").

Future Tense – the tense used in the indicative mood to indicate summary action in future time.

Gender – the property of an noun which indicates whether it is masculine, feminine, or neuter.

Genitive Case – the case form which indicates description/possession.

Gutteral Verb – a verb which has a stem ending with γ, κ, or χ.

Imperative – the verbal mood by which the speaker presents the action as intended but dependent on the volitional response of the person addressed.

Imperfect Tense – the tense is used in the indicative mood to indicate progressive action in past time.

Indefinite Pronoun – a pronoun which generalizes ("someone, anyone").

Independent (Main) Clause – a clause which expresses a complete thought and could be a sentence by itself.

Indicative– the verbal mood by which the speaker presents the action as real or certain.

Indirect Object – the noun which tells to/for whom the action is done.

Infinitive – a verbal mode which combines the designative power of a noun with the action aspect of a verb.

Inflection – the change in form which Greek words exhibit as they change function.

Instrumental – the case function within the dative case form which indicates instrument/agency/means.

Intensive Pronoun – a pronoun which is placed in apposition to its antecedent for emphasis.

Interrogative Pronoun – a pronoun which asks a question.

Intransitive Verb – an active voice verb which has no direct object.

Labial Verb – a verb which has a stem ending β, π, or φ.

Lexical Form – the form of any Greek word which appears in a lexicon or dictionary entry.

Linking (Copulative) Verb – a verb which provides a link of identity or description between the subject and its complement (e.g., "to be").

Liquid Verb – a verb which has a stem ending with λ or ρ.

Locative – the case function within the dative case form which indicates position.

Middle Voice – the voice which indicates that the subject produces or experiences the action in such a way as to participate in the results.

Mood – the property of a verb which indicates the speaker's degree of certainty about an action.

Moveable nu – the letter ν added to a word ending in ε or ι, usually when the word is followed by any sort of punctuation.

Nasal Verb – a verb which has a stem ending with μ or ν.

Nominative Case – the case form which indicates designation.

Noun – a word which names a person, place, or thing.

Noun (Substantival) Clause – a clause which is introduced by a subordinate conjunction and functions as a noun (subject, object, complement, appositive) in relation to the main clause.

Number – the property of a noun or verb which indicates whether one or more than one person, place, or thing is involved.

Object of Preposition – a noun which is related to the rest of the sentence by a preposition.

Optative– the verbal mood by which the speaker presents the action as potential without reference to existing and known circumstances.

Participle – a verbal mode which combines the descriptive power of an adjective with the action aspect of a verb.

Passive Voice – the voice which indicates that the subject is acted upon by the action described.

Perfect Tense – the tense most frequently used to indicate completed-stative action.

Person – the property of a verb which expresses the speaker's relationship to the actor.

Personal Pronoun – a pronoun which designates one or more particular person or thing ("I, you, he, she, it, we, they").

Phrase – a group of words which functions as a unit within a sentence and does not contain a subject and finite verb.

Pluperfect Tense – the tense is used in the indicative mood to indicate completed-stative action in past time.

Postpositive Conjunction – a conjunction which cannot stand first in its clause or phrase.

Predicate Adjective - an adjective which follows a linking verb and modifies the subject of the sentence.

Predicate Nominative – a noun which follows a linking verb and refers to the same person, place, or thing as the subject.

Predicate Use of Adjective – an adjective which does not follow an article and makes a statement about a noun

Preposition – a connecting word which clarifies how a noun is related to the sentence containing it

Prepositional Phrase – word group which includes the preposition and its object.

Present Tense – the tense most frequently used to indicate progressive action.

Primary Tenses – verb tenses which present action in present or future time in the indicative (Present, Future, Perfect) .

Principal Parts – the six essential forms on which all other forms of a verb are built.

Progressive Action Tenses – verb tenses which present the action as in progress without regard to its beginning or end (Present, Imperfect).

Pronoun – a word which takes the place of a noun.

Reciprocal Pronoun – a pronoun which denotes the interchange of action among more than one subject ("one another").

Reduplication – the repetition of the first character of a verb to indicate completed-stative action.

Reflexive Pronoun – a pronoun which refers the action back to the subject ("–self").

Relative Clause – a clause which describes, explains, or restricts a noun in some way.

Relative Pronoun – a pronoun which relates the clause in which it occurs to a noun or pronoun in another clause ("who, whom, whose, which").

Second (Strong) Aorist – the aorist form of a verb which is characterized by a stem change.

Second Person – the inflectional form of a verb which indicates that the speaker addresses the actor ("you").

Secondary Tenses – verb tenses which present action in past time in the indicative (Imperfect, Aorist, Pluperfect).

Sentence – a group of words which expresses a complete thought.

Sibilant Verb – a verb which has a stem ending with ζ, ξ, σ, or ψ.

Subject – the word or combination of words naming the person, place, thing, or idea about which about which a statement is being made.

Subjunctive – the verbal mood by which the speaker presents the action as possible but contingent on existing and known circumstances.

Subordinate Conjunction – a conjunction which connect subordinate (dependent) clauses to main (independent) clauses.

Substantive – any part of speech which acts like a noun.

Summary Action Tenses – tenses which present the action as viewed as a whole without regard to its continuity or completion (Future, Aorist).

Superlative Degree – the inflectional form of an adjective which compares three or more persons or things.

Transitive Verb – an active voice verb which acts upon a direct object.

Tense – the property of a verb which expresses the kind (and time) of action.

Third Person – the inflection form of a verb which indicates that the speaker describes the actor ("he, she, it, they").

Verb – a word which expresses action or a state of being.

Vocative — the case function within the nominative case form which indicates address.

Voice – the property of a verb which expresses the subject's relationship to the action.

Vowel Contraction – the inflection which takes place when a noun or verb ending is added to a word with a stem ending with the vowel α, ε, or O.

Subject Index